# INDUSTRIAL LOCATION PROCESSES AND REGIONAL EMPLOYMENT GROWTH

To Lynette

# Industrial Location Processes and Regional Employment Growth

GRAHAM GUDGIN

SAXON HOUSE

British Library Cataloguing in Publication Data

Gudgin, Graham
  Industrial location processes and regional
  employment growth
  1. Labour supply — England — Midlands
  2. Labour supply — Great Britain 3. Industries,
  Location of — England — Midlands 4. Industries,
  Location of — Great Britain
  I. Title
  331.1'2        HD5766.M/

  ISBN  0-566-00144-6

Published by

Saxon House, Teakfield Limited,
Westmead, Farnborough, Hants., England

ISBN   0  566 01144 6

Manufactured in England by Short Run Publishing
Services

Printed and bound by Ilfadrove Limited, Barry,
Glamorgan, S. Wales

# Contents

TABLES

# Preface

When a mechanical system, a car for example, breaks
down a mechanic will attempt to identify the faulty
part and then mend or replace it. Because the inter-
relations in such systems are well understood, there
is no need to find out how the whole works before
correcting the part. Regional economies are also
complicated systems with interlocking parts, but they
are less well understood. Despite this it is common
to focus attention on the characteristics of the
problem areas, but our inability to know exactly what
to look for makes it more efficient to turn aside and
to examine regions which are performing well. Only
then will there be a reasonable set of standards
against which to compare the problem areas.

The study is an attempt to discover how and why
things go wrong with some regions when others
flourish. The centrepiece is an investigation of the
ways in which growth is achieved in one prosperous
region - the East Midlands. This is set in a wide
context which compares the experience of this region,
as far as is possible, with that in other areas. In
addition, a second theme running throughout is the
methodological one of how best to tackle the question
of regional differentials of employment growth in
manufacturing.

The East Midlands is a region with a long industrial
history, characterised through most of this century by
a tendency to perform better than the national average.
This has been true of the postwar period without the
aid of net in-movement of industry from other regions
or abroad. Most relevant is the fact that the East
Midlands began the postwar era with an economy which
in retrospect was overburdened with slowly growing or
declining industries, especially those in textiles and
clothing. Despite this unpromising legacy, growth has
been relatively rapid and this success invites us to

question why this has been possible when it has proved so conspicuously difficult to achieve in most regions with poor industrial endowments. In chapter one the context is set by examining the pattern of British postwar regional growth. After a brief discussion of the consequences of slow growth, an attempt is made to separate the indigenous performance from that which has been produced by the direct influence of regional policy.

The question of comparison between regions is more difficult than it looks, and a very basic difficulty is knowing where to direct attention. Traditionally, manufacturing was examined in terms of its component industries reflecting a belief that these were the most meaningful units in the overall system. There are many other ways to look at manufacturing and some of these may well provide clearer insights into the causes of differences in growth between regions. To be most effective, the divisions of a complex system should reflect the principal processes which operate to cause the problem in hand, and in this study the nature of these processes provides a starting point. A fundamental necessity is to decide whether spatial variations in the costs of production and distribution are the prime influences on location and growth, or alternatively whether other factors are more important. This distinction is a vital one since it determines the whole form of the subsequent investigation.

Part two takes up this issue, and in chapter two the importance of costs is examined, resulting in a conclusion that the variation is too small to have much influence on the location activities, but that it may have some long-term influence on the growth of companies. In the light of these conclusions chapter three suggests that the different processes involved in location and growth should form the basic categories on which attention is focused to compare the performance of regions. The set of categories, or 'components' derived in this chapter forms the basis around which the rest of the book is constructed. The components are based on the processes of locating new firms, of growth (and decline), of closure and of industrial movement. The final chapter in part two assesses the quantitive importance of each of these processes in the postwar employment growth of the East Midlands.

An understanding of the causes of differences in regional growth requires two further steps. Firstly, the nature of each process must become clear and secondly, this knowledge should be used to interpret and explain spatial variation in the rate of action of each process, i.e. in the entry-rates of new firms and in the rates of growth, closure and movement. The nature of the component processes forms the subject matter of part three. The least known of the processes is that concerned with the locating of new firms, and consequently most effort is given to this question including the characteristics of entrepreneurs and their new firms, the context within which locations are selected, and the factors which bear on the locational choice. The questions of growth and closure have been more extensively studied and less original work is needed. The industrial movement process has been extensively studied over the last fifteen years, and is well understood as a location process. Consequently, no further attempt is made in this book to review or to examine this facet of industrial behaviour.

The final section, part four, examines spatial variation in the rates of action. Once again most effort is spent on entry-rates and least on industrial movement. This concludes the overall explanatory strategy which can perhaps be best summarised with reference to new firms. Over the twenty year period used in this study new firms accounted for about two-thirds of the net increase of employment in the East Midlands. If it is the case that the contribution of new firms is less in some other regions, as seems likely, then it is important to explain why. Such an explanation is best sought via a thorough understanding of the process of establishing and locating new firms. Once this is achieved then it is possible to go on to examine and account for spatial variation in the rate of formation of new firms. The importance of a process, its nature, and its rate of action are seen as three elements in the path to explanation and each is dealt with in a separate part of the book. Much remains to be done but it is hoped that this study provides at least a start in the right direction.

The book is based on a PhD thesis begun in 1968 but not completed until 1974 mainly due to the large amounts of work involved in assembling the necessary data. Any project which extends over a period as long as this inevitably builds up an extensive debt to a large number of people. Initial interest in the subject was stimulated in lectures from E.M. Rawstron, at Queen Mary College. Since then a large number of people have contributed to the development of the research. Early ideas change slowly through reading and discussion, and few are in a position to claim that even a fraction of their final ideas are original. Authors have responsibility for sifting, and selecting from, the variety of suggestions put to them, but without these numerous and often individually small contributions most work would be infinitely the poorer. To this extent all research comes from a common pool. Often, however, much stimulation can come from people working in unrelated fields, and Peter Taylor has fulfilled this function in my case. His wide-ranging interests and his enthusiasm for scientific rigour has made research a very much more exciting activity than would otherwise have been the case.

Individual debts which should not go unacknowledged are due to several people spanning the years. The Health and Safety Executive, formerly the Factory Inspectorate, deserve special thanks since without their generous and repeated help it is absolutely certain that this study would never have materialised. Peter Mounfield is to be thanked for taking on the arduous task in reading through a mass of difficult manuscript and for his many helpful comments. Those with special skills are invaluable at times of crises and Chris Horn's generous and ever available advice on computing provided a lifeline in a sea of Fortran. Another skill is cartography, and gratitude is due to the cartographic staff at Newcastle University for drawing the diagrams. Although this work spans eight years and Steve Fothergill has been associated with it for only the last few months, his contribution and advice have been of great value. The fact may not be obvious from anything that follows, but a great deal has been learnt about presentation from being an Open University student, and in a number of ways this experience has proved stimulating and helpful.

Greatest thanks go to Lynette who has given so much support and encouragement. Not only has she put up with continued inroads into family time, but whenever necessary has taken on the roles of data processor and secretary. The depth of family support is most evident when difficulties arise and parents-in-law and grandmother-in-law have helped a great deal in many and varied ways. Thanks are also due to Pam for her cheerful assistance in the routine tasks on which research is built.

# PART  I

## INTRODUCTION

# 1 The regional problem

## 1.1 DEFINING THE FIELD OF INTEREST

It is a commonplace observation that rates of employment growth in manufacturing vary geographically. These variations have consequences, both social and economic, which make it important to discover the mechanisms which underlie growth differences. Although much work has been undertaken around this question, a basic contention of this study is that current knowledge does not add up to a satisfactory understanding. Satisfactory, in this context, is taken to mean a level of understanding which would permit predictions to be made of both direction and degree of change, or allow the design of policy measures with some quantified prediction of the consequences. This book is an attempt to construct and justify an approach to the question of employment change which it is hoped will prove more fruitful than the collection of methods in use at present.

The importance of employment growth as a research topic stems from the problems which arise when employment growth fails to match population increase. The direct consequences of unemployment, net migration loss and low participation rates are well known, and for the UK are also well documented. There are in addition a wide range of indirect problems. Housing shortages, for example, are very difficult to solve in labour deficit regions if a queue of latent migrants is always available from areas of higher unemployment. It is not the intention of this study to describe these problems nor to draw the links between them and employment growth, but it is important to bear in mind that the problems are serious ones which make the study of regional employment growth of much more than merely academic interest.

The field of interest is a broad one and an accurate

delimitation of what is to follow requires that the boundaries of the field be more precisely described. Spatial variation in employment change, as in anything else, occurs at a variety of scales. In this study interest centres on the inter-regional scale although the adjacent intra-regional scale will also figure predominantly. Only factors which are relevant to these scales will be considered, and it is largely because similar processes affect both that they can be considered together. As the geographical scale shifts, upwards to the international, or downwards to the intra-urban, the mechanisms relevant to understanding spatial variation become different, although even here there are overlaps and these will be made apparent where this is appropriate and feasible. Most of the material is drawn from the United Kingdom, and to a large extent from a single region - the East Midlands. The study is, however, an investigation of an approach and of processes of change which are of more general applicability. The East Midlands serves as a case study of the approach although it is fortunate that the region is one with a relatively good postwar performance within the UK context. This means that the region can serve as an example against which the depressed regions within the UK can be compared.

The question of scale arises for time as well as space. The focus of attention in this study is long-term change. Regional variations in growth over a short timescale of a year or so will be dominated by changes in demand, whereas long-term changes in productive capacity involve a wider range of influences of which demand for the initial products is only one. Any explanation of the actual rate of growth is a complex matter and the much less ambitious aim here is to investigate why the rates might differ between regions.

Two major and related influences on growth are industrial movement between regions and government regional policy. Both of these have been intensively studied within the UK context and will not be examined here. Both deal with the reallocation of employment

largely in response to existing differences in the
'indigenous' growth of regions. Without these
indigenous differences reallocation is largely unnec-
essary, and hence the question of the indigenous
growth is the major underlying one in the overall
growth of regions. It is indigenous rather than total
growth that we shall be concerned with in this study.


## 1.2  INDIGENOUS EMPLOYMENT GROWTH IN UK REGIONS

The considerable importance of regional policy and
industrial movement in the UK makes it difficult to
discern what the indigenous performance has been.
Although there are important problems, both practical
and conceptual, an attempt will be made in this section to describe indigenous employment change since
1953.(1) Indigenous change is defined as that which
would have occurred without net industrial movement
and without the effects of regional financial aid upon
non-mobile industry.

Taking out net industrial moves leaves that employment which can be considered to have been locally
generated. Any employment in moves originating outside a region is viewed as having been generated
elsewhere, while moves out of a region are viewed here
as containing employment which was generated within
that region but subsequently 'exported'. Only a small
amount of industrial movement is of the type which is
attracted by materials and markets not available
locally.(2)  Table 1.1 shows the figures for total
employment change in manufacturing. Until 1966 the
major contrast was between the Southern and Midland
regions (referred to below as the Non-Assisted
Regions). The one exception was Wales, where the
performance of manufacturing was well above average.
After 1966 two major changes occurred. Manufacturing
employment was by this time in national decline,
while the most rapidly declining regions included the
former centres of prosperity, the South East and the
West Midlands. The Northern Region, Wales, and until
1971 Northern Ireland, all performed better than

5

average although by the 1970s decline had become an almost universal condition.

Table 1.1
Manufacturing employment change 1953-75

|  | 1953-66 | 1966-71 | % change 1971-75 |
|---|---|---|---|
| South Eastern England | +19.3 | | |
| South East | | -8.0 | -12.0 |
| East Anglia | | +9.8 | + 4.2 |
| South West | +22.5 | +2.3 | - 2.7 |
| West Midlands | +15.9 | -7.8 | - 7.5 |
| East Midlands | +14.1 | -2.1 | - 5.0 |
| Yorks and Humberside | + 4.9 | -9.7 | - 5.7 |
| North West | - 2.9 | -9.6 | - 7.9 |
| North | +12.8 | 0.0 | - 1.5 |
| Wales | +18.1 | +2.2 | - 2.2 |
| Scotland | - 0.1 | -7.1 | - 4.8 |
| Northern Ireland | + 0.5 | -2.9 | - 9.4 |
| United Kingdom | +10.1 | -6.2 | - 7.0 |

Source of data: Dept of Employment

In terms of the growth which actually occurred there is a clear difference between the pre-1966 period and the post-1966 and this very approximately coincides with the stengthening of regional policy in the mid-1960s. Let us now turn to the question of indigenous change.

In the period up until 1966 regional policy and industrial movement had relatively little influence except in the last three years, and the removal of employment in net moves provides an adequate measure of indigenous change. One qualification is needed due to the great importance of regional policy in the period 1945-51 in which building licences combined with strong postwar demand conditions led to a very large volume of industrial movement. Since factories

build up their employment only gradually after
'moving' (3), there will always be a spillover of
employment growth into periods following the cessa-
tion of particular policy measures.(4)   In this
context the build-up of employment will have occurred
up until the mid-1950s.  Also, as demonstrated in
table 1.2, it is likely to have had significant
effects upon growth in two regions: in the North, and
more especially in Wales.

Table 1.2
Net industrial movement 1945-51

| Region | No. of moves per 100,000 in manu- facturing in 1952 | 1966 employment in moves as % of 1952 employment in manufacturing |
|---|---|---|
| South East ) | | |
| East Anglia) | -10 | - 4 |
| South West | - 6 | - 1 |
| West Midlands | - 5 | - 4 |
| East Midlands | - 4 | - 1 |
| Yorkshire and Humberside | - 2 | - 2 |
| North West | 0 | - 2 |
| North | +24 | +14 |
| Wales | +53 | +24 |
| Scotland | + 9 | + 6 |
| Northern Ireland | +20 | + 7 |

Sources of data:   Howard Report (1968)
                   Dept of Employment

Records do not exist to show just how significant
this build-up was, but its likely impact can be gauged
from the fact that in Wales, for instance, a quarter
of 1966 employment was in plants which had moved
between 1945 and 1951.  It is likely that a significant minority of these jobs appeared during the
build-up stage  after 1953.

The figures in column one of table 1.3 show

7

employment change omitting net industrial movement. The contrast between the Assisted and Non-Assisted Regions is sharper than formerly, and the dichotomy is probably complete if the remarks above about Wales and the North are borne in mind.

Table 1.3
Indigenous employment change in manufacturing

| Region | 1953-66 | 1966-71 |
|---|---|---|
| South Eastern England | +23.0 | |
| South East | | - 5.9 |
| East Anglia | | + 6.4 |
| South West | +13.0 | + 0.6 |
| West Midlands | +17.2 | - 6.3 |
| East Midlands | +11.6 | - 1.3 |
| Yorkshire and Humberside | + 4.8 | - 9.5 |
| North West | - 7.0 | -10.2 |
| North | + 6.1 | - 4.2 |
| Wales | +12.0 | - 3.5 |
| Scotland | - 6.3 | - 9.9 |
| Northern Ireland | -13.4 | -10.3 |
| United Kingdom | +10.0 | - 6.3 |

Sources of data:  Dept of Employment
                  Dept of Industry

The second column in table 1.3 shows employment change, without employment in net movement, for 1966 to 1971. No figures are as yet available for post-1971. In the period 1966 to 1971 all of the Non-Assisted regions emerge with performances equal to or better than the national average. Among the Assisted areas, Wales and the North perform well in relation to the national norm. If, however, allowance is made for a final aspect of regional policy then the tradional contrast between the Assisted and Non-Assisted areas is restored completely. The policy measures in question are the effects of differential investment incentives and the Regional Employment Premium on

8

non-moving firms. These effects have been estimated by Moore and Rhodes (1973, 1974, 1975), and if their figures are used then the following alterations need to be made to the second column of table 1.3 to produce growth rates which are due to indigenous performance unaided by government regional policy.

WALES      9.1%
NORTH      8.1%
SCOTLAND  11.1%

The pattern with these amended figures is clear. All of the Assisted Areas have employment performances significantly poorer than any of the Non-Assisted areas. It seems that beneath the umbrella of regional policy things were much as before.


1.3  AN APPROACH TO EXPLANATION

Indigenous employment growth varies considerably between UK regions, and in a highly consistent way which contrasts the core regions of the South and Midlands with the peripheral areas to the north and west. How is it possible to explain these differences? Two broad types of explanation have been the following:

(1)  Growth differences between regions are merely the spatial manifestation of general changes in output and productivity which affect industries differentially. This idea that poorly performing regions are merely those saddled with slow growth industries is often called the structural hypothesis.

(2)  Growth differences between regions are due to the relevant characteristics of the regions other than their industrial structure. Such characteristics might include cost disadvantages, management inefficiency, lack of investment, or a host of other factors. The peripheral position of the problem areas, provides a strong suggestion that costs of production or distribution may be a root cause.

9

It is important to distinguish between these two
possibilities because different policies follow
logically from each diagnosis. A weak industrial
structure implies either that the pattern of demand
be manipulated in favour of products produced in
lagging regions, or, if this is not feasible, that the
industrial structure is changed through attracting new
investment. Non-structural causes imply that the
sources of weaknesses be identified and appropriate
remedial action taken. Alternatively a general
subsidy can be applied to counter unidentified disadvantages.(5)

Attempts to quantify the importance of structural
and non-structural factors have not been conclusive,
probably because the importance varies over time and
between regions, but not least because changes in data
definitions hinder temporal analyses. It is not
difficult to show however that structural explanations
are far from the whole story. The East Midlands for
example entered the postwar period with a poor industrial structure, which on national levels of growth
would have led to employment growth well below that
for the UK as a whole through the 1950s and 1960s.(6)
The actual performance was characterised by growth at
a rate well above the national average. A second
example is drawn from the area within the UK which
probably has the poorest performance of all, namely
West Central Scotland. One analysis, conducted over
a period with no major changes in data definition,
showed that manufacturing employment declined by 5 per
cent in this area between 1959 and 1968.(7) After
allowance for industrial structure, the multiplier
effects of decline in shipbuilding, and the effects of
regional policy,(8) the decline increases to 10 per
cent or a shortfall of 43,000 jobs below what could be
expected on national rates of growth. Thus we have
two areas performing very differently even if their
similarly poor industrial structures are taken into
account.

The influence of the effects of industrial structure
upon growth is probably of considerable importance in

10

some regions. In this study however a choice has been made not to attempt to measure this effect region by region. Instead a single region is examined in which industrial structure accounts for none of its above average growth. This means that factors other than industrial structure are given prominence. As a by-product of the approach adopted it is however possible to examine in detail some of the mechanics of the link between industrial structure and growth.

Irrespective of whether industrial structure is or is not a dominant influence on regional differences, the problem still remains of how to go about examining the non-structural factors. Progress depends upon recognising a critical distinction within the category of potential causes. On the one hand cost of production and distribution may be dominant, in which case the body of classical location theory becomes relevant in explaining regional differences. On the other hand if cost variation is of little importance then the search for the real causes is probably best conducted through an investigation of the location and growth decisions made by entrepreneurs and managers.

The latter argument is elaborated upon in chapter three and is introduced here only to point up the need to know the importance of spatial cost constraints on freedom of action in both location and growth. This latter question is taken up in the following chapter, while chapter three develops a strategy of how to proceed in explaining employment change when cost-constraints are few. The strategy outlined in chapter three forms the basis for the substantive section of the study in chapters four to eleven.


NOTES

(1) The initial date is determined by the data, which contain inaccuracies for earlier dates.
(2) Cameron and Clark (1966) estimated that only 10 per cent of moves to Scotland were to serve the local

market rather than due to the attractions of government policy or labour.

(3)   Two studies of this phenomenon are the Howard Report and Moore and Rhodes (1976)

(4)   I am grateful to S. Fothergill for forcing me to take note of this effect.

(5)   The Regional Employment Premium operating in Britain between 1968 and 1977 is an example of this.

(6)   This point is elaborated upon in chapter four.

(7)   West Central Scotland Plan 1974 Part I, Section 2.

(8)   ibid.  Part I, Section 2, plus industrial movement estimates p.189, plus estimates of Moore and Rhodes (1974) for regional policy on indigenous industry.

# 2 Cost Constraints on locational freedom

The stated intention of chapter one was to attempt to account for differences between regions in long-term rates of employment change. Additionally it was asserted that an important first step towards achieving this aim is to determine whether regional variations in costs of production and distribution are a major influence on location and growth. If the answer is that cost variation is important then the subsequent explanations of location and growth will be very different from the case if cost variation is unimportant. The former implies an industry by industry analyses backed by (classical) location theory while the latter situation would lead into the comparatively new world of behavioural factors.

The purpose of this chapter is to determine what degree of constraint is imposed on locational choice (and indirectly on growth) by considerations of cost variation. In the absolute sense it is possible that spatial margins exist beyond which profitable production is not possible, even within a country as small as the UK. Cost variation in this case would be such that some places could not act as profitable locations in competition with least cost sites. In a more relative sense, profitable production may be feasible at all locations, but in some places profits might be reduced to such a degree that very few firms would want to be located there. This chapter will examine the question from both points of view, although of course the latter subsumes the former. The major problem is that of data, and because available statistics are in general not adequate to undertake a rigorous study it is necessary to proceed on the basis of a best guess.

Despite the inadequacy of data it is now the conventional wisdom that cost variation is not a major

13

factor at the UK scale (Brown, 1969). Even at the
larger scale of the United States or of Canada, Smith
(1971) has produced figures to show that cost variation was relatively slight in light industries. In
this study the intention is to probe a little deeper
than is usual in an attempt to assess the accuracy
and applicability of the conventional wisdom. The
empirical evidence outlined below will include a
review of spatial variation within the principal
categories of production costs, followed by brief
case studies of two industries.

Before proceeding to this evidence one theoretical
point needs to be made in connection with transport
costs. This concerns the different influences which
transport costs can have on location patterns. In
particular, costs of assembling materials and components may have effects different from the costs of
distribution. Transport costs on inward goods will
always contribute towards production cost differences
between locations, and will have some tendency towards
concentrating production in some areas at the expense
of others. In contrast, distribution costs may
reduce the area of profitable production if they are
low relative to variation in production, but not
necessarily otherwise. If production costs on some
items were lower in Japan than elsewhere for instance,
and distribution costs relatively unimportant, then
profitable production might be impossible in other
countries (leaving aside questions of tariff protec-
tion, subsidies, etc.). If distribution costs are
high in relation to spatial variation in production
costs however, then the distribution costs will tend
not to form margins, but instead to disperse production within the margin.(1) Brewing, brick production,
and manufacturing metal containers are all industries
with high distribution costs, which consequently tend
towards dispersed production patterns. The significance of this distinction between types of transport
cost is that the two should be investigated separately.

## 2.1 MATERIAL AND TRANSPORT COSTS

The costs of procuring raw materials and components are likely to vary over space in an irregular fashion, and it is thus difficult to generalise about their effect on industrial location. This difficulty can be circumvented, however, by noting that the magnitude of variation must be less than that of transport costs from the cheapest source. Material cost variation can then be subsumed within a discussion of transport costs alone, although it should be noted that in well developed countries there are frequently several dispersed sources of many materials. Within the United Kingdom the ports, coalfields, and industrial areas provide a choice of sources for materials and components although in some cases, of course, the alternatives are more limited.

In the case of the transport costs involved in assembling the materials for production, Chisholm (1966) and Cook (1967) assert that uniform delivered prices are normal within Britain except for a limited range of basic commodities. There are two points to be made about the effects of uniform pricing. Firstly, transport costs on assembled goods in such industries will not affect the decision of managers comparing alternative locations. Secondly, transport still has to be paid for and is in fact a hidden element of distribution costs. It is of value to know how large these hidden costs may be, although the very act of uniform pricing may suggest that they are small.

The cost of transport (2) in Britain is given in the Census of Production (1968) for each of the 110 Minimum List Heading industries, and this information is summarised in figure 2.1. Before commenting on the figures it is important to make several points about them. Firstly, the figures refer solely to transport costs incurred within the United Kingdom and exclude importing and exporting costs. However, in a consideration of costs within the United Kingdom this is unlikely to be an important factor, since for many

15

foreign material sources additional distances to different ports within Britain will be proportionately very small. The main exception may be in trade with the nearer European countries.

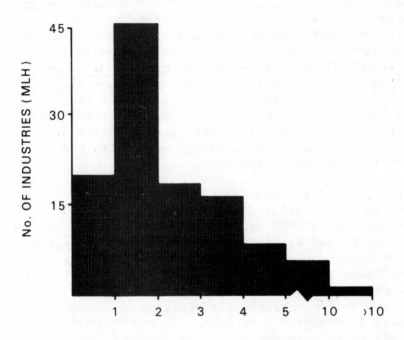

TRANSPORT COSTS AS % OF GROSS VALUE OF OUTPUT.

Figure 2.1   Transport costs as a percentage of total
costs UK Manufacturing Industry 1968
Source of data:   Census of Production 1968

A second point is that the figures are derived from the existing location patterns of manufacturing, whereas they are to be used in this discussion to compare all possible alternative locations. In widely dispersed industries there is little problem but in a few industries, particularly heavier ones, real transport costs are only low by virtue of the fact that the

16

actual locations are carefully chosen and close to the minimum cost points. Metal production, electricity generation, shipbuilding, oil refining and sugar beet processing are principal examples, but in most industries the figures are not likely to be greatly misleading. A final point is that the costs have been expressed as proportions of the gross, rather than net, value of output. This has been done to enable comparisons to be made below with profit figures expressed in the same way.

From figure 2.1 it can be seen that almost three-quarters of British industry incurs total transport costs at levels of less than 3 per cent of the value of gross output. In 95 per cent of industry, by value of production, the transport costs are less than 5 per cent of total costs. Since these figures include distribution costs as well as the concealed assembly costs, the latter must be smaller than the total transport costs and represent only a very small fraction of overall production costs in most industries. This conclusion relates only to the average transport costs incurred by a whole industry. This average may be composed of low costs in some locations and higher costs in others. Although there is clearly little possibility of large areas haveing costs very much higher than the average, given the smallness of the latter, it is nevertheless necessary to estimate the degree of variation around the average. One way of doing this is to discover how transport costs increase with distance and to calculate the difference between locations which are maximum distances apart.

Two sources of data are available to describe the relationship between cost and distance. Bayliss and Edwards (1970) calculated the costs of transporting a neutral good (3) by both road and rail, based on a detailed study of four widely defined industries. A second source is provided by the unpublished data of B.M. Deakin and T. Seward which was obtained and analysed by Chisholm (1971). The latter was based on a survey of road haulage firms covering thirty-four

17

commodity groups.  From the Bayliss and Edwards' calculations an equation can be constructed for the
cheapest mode of transport.(4)  This is:

$$C = 29.98\ D^{0.27}$$

Where C is the cost of transporting one hundredweight of a neutral good (in pence) and D is the
distance in miles.

This expression means that the costs of transport
involve a relatively high terminal cost, but increase
only slowly with distance.  If we use a short-haul of
twenty miles as an arbitrary base, then transport
costs double at 243 miles and treble at 1,089 miles.
Put another way, a journey eighty times as long as the
twenty mile short-haul costs only three times as much.

   Variations between different commodity groups can be
gauged from the Deakin and Seward data analysed by
Chisholm.  Relating to road transport only the mean
terminal cost was 78p per ton in 1968, and costs
increased linearly with distance with an average
slope coefficient of 0.197.  These values are of a
similar magnitude to those of Bayliss and Edwards.  On
average, a journey of 1,089 miles is three and a half
times more expensive than a twenty-mile journey,
agreeing fairly closely with the Bayliss and Edwards'
figures for road transport alone.  Chisholm analysed
twenty-three of the commodity values and reported a
range of terminal costs approximately 25p (roughly a
third) on either side of the mean, except for three
basic commodities (5) with very low terminal costs,
and machinery at nearly double the average costs.  The
slope coefficients were generally within 25 per cent
of the average.  In general the relationships for the
individual commodities were not far removed from that
of the all-commodity mean.  Only with basic commodities such as coal, crude minerals and building
materials, which have low terminal costs and relatively high movement costs, does the ratio between long-
haul (1,089 miles) and short-haul (20 miles) charges
vary significantly.  The extremes were 14:1 for crude
minerals and $2\frac{1}{4}$:1 for machinery.

What can be concluded from all of this?  To reach a
conclusion we would need to know the cost of assembling materials at the cheapest location and to compare
this with some extremely distant location.  For most
industries the real, although concealed, cost of
assembling materials averages out as a part of up to
3 per cent of total costs.  The assembly costs at the
cheapest location will be less than this, i.e. a part
of a part of 3 per cent or less.  If for the purposes
of argument we say that the average distance over
which materials are transported is only twenty miles,
then a location 250 miles away using the same material
sources will have to pay on average twice as much.
That is, twice some fraction of 3 per cent.  In this
illustrative example most of the figures are towards
the upper extreme of costs.  It would seem likely
then, as a best guess, that differences in real costs
of assembling materials vary by only 2 or 3 per cent
at the most (probably much less in most light industries) between best and worst location.  Given the
multiplicity of sources and possibilities for sub-
stitution between materials in many industries even
the above conclusion probably overstates the case.  In
the light of the low values of these figures, it is
perhaps not surprising that most firms prefer the ease
of uniform charging to the complexity of adding a
transport charge.  In the same vein, Cook (1967) found
that Midlands firms were often unaware of their own
level of costs.  One study which examines the effects
of variable material costs in a more detailed way than
has been possible here is Tornqvist's (1964) study of
transport costs in the Swedish light clothing industry.  In Sweden the raw material sources are highly
concentrated within the area near Güthenburg in the
South West.  Tornqvist calculates that the transport
costs on these materials delivered to various
locations amount to 0.2 per cent of total production
costs in the South West, and that this increases to
0.7 per cent for the Arctic North.  Transport costs
thus do little to increase costs at different
locations, and clothing cannot be considered a particularly unrepresentative industry in this respect.

This is not to say that transport (assembly) costs
are in all cases insignificant. Industries with bulky
raw materials and those to which relatively little
value is added are highly restricted in their locational choice, and other industries may be affected in
some way. In the 1973 Expenditure Committee investigation into regional policy incentives, five out of
the seventeen major companies questioned specifically
mentioned transport cost disadvantages in development
area locations. Three of these were large motor
manufacturers and one other concerned a steel tube
mill. In the motor industry cases an important aspect
was the need to ferry bodies, and engines between
plants, although the Chrysler company in Scotland also
mentioned higher transport costs involved in purchasing components. In this case the large size of the
customer may cause an exception to the common rule
that sellers absorb transport cost to customers. The
important point here is that regional policy had
caused the production process to be split between
locations thus raising transport costs (and inventory
costs) considerably. Significantly, there was no
suggestion in any of the motor industry cases that the
increased costs seriously impaired the commercial
success of the plants. Although important, these
motor industry cases appear to be isolated exceptions
to the general rule than inward transport costs are
not of great significance in production cost variability for most of manufacturing.


2.2  DISTRIBUTION COSTS

The evidence of figure 2.1 on transport costs is
likely to relate largely to distribution costs since
it is these rather than inward transport costs that
producers usually pay. The conclusion that three-
quarters of industry (by either employment or output)
have transport costs of less than 3 per cent of
output should thus be seen largely in the context of
distribution. In industries with costs higher than
this level production tends to be dispersed; while in

other industries the effects of cost differences depend on the type of market.

## 2.2.1 National markets

To illustrate the range of variation in costs of distribution to the national market, an exercise was conducted to calculate the costs of delivering a 'neutral' product to the British market. Great Britain was divided into fourteen regions; (6) and distribution costs calculated on the basis of distances from the largest city in each region to all other regions. This can be written as follows.

$$C_i = \sum_{j=1}^{14} P_j \cdot T_{ij}$$

where $C_i$ is the total cost of delivering a product from region i to all other regions j(= 1,14)

$P_j$ is the population in the $j^{th}$ region in 1967
$T_{ij}$ is the cost in pence of transporting one hundredweight of a neutral product from region i to region j

and    $T_{ij} = 29.98 \times D_{ij}^{0.27}$    (as before)
where   $D_{ij}$ is the distance in miles between regions i and j.(7)

The assumptions made in this exercise are that the cheapest mode of transport was used, and that per capita consumption is uniform between regions. The latter assumption is unrealistic to the extent that incomes, and thus purchasing power, vary between regions. The effect of this variation is very small, although it will have the effect of slightly under-estimating costs in peripheral regions relative to central regions. The assumption that the product is transported in uniform loads was arbitrary, and it should be noted that since most long distance consignments will be larger than short distance ones (and will be transported at lower rates per unit weight),

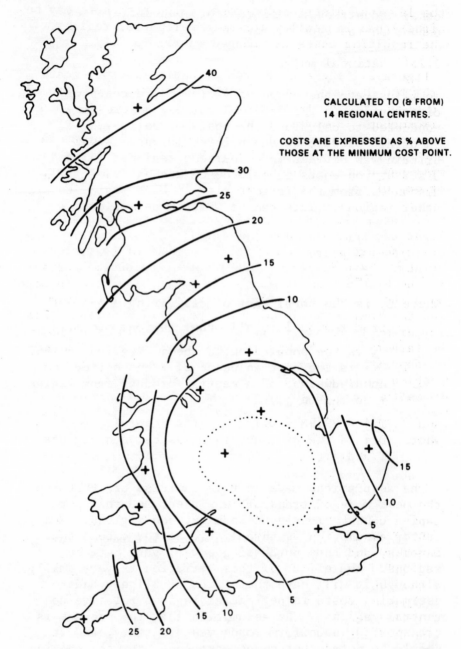

CALCULATED TO (& FROM)
14 REGIONAL CENTRES.

COSTS ARE EXPRESSED AS % ABOVE
THOSE AT THE MINIMUM COST POINT.

Figure 2.2    The cost of distributing a product to the national market

the level of distribution costs calculated here may be higher than in reality for more peripheral regions. The resulting costs are mapped in figure 2.2.

Figure 2.2 shows an increase in distribution costs from the Midlands outwards, with costs in the north of Scotland some 40 to 50 per cent higher than at Birmingham. However, since distribution costs were less than 3 per cent of the value of gross output in the majority of industries the highest cost areas will pay distribution costs amounting to 4 per cent, or so, of total costs.

G. Tornqvist (1964) in his study of the Swedish light clothing industry has undertaken a similar exercise but using a far larger number of control points. Tornqvist concluded that distribution costs to the Swedish market varied by a factor of two to one with the lowest cost point to the west of Stockholm and the maximum cost point in the extreme north. This larger scale of variation over similar distances can be largely explained by the very unequal distribution of population in Sweden. Within the more densely peopled southern half of Sweden that scale of variation is similar to that of Great Britain as a whole. For the light clothing industry total production costs, including distribution costs, are increased by only 0.5 per cent if the product is distributed from the extreme north as compared with the south central area.

2.2.2 Small area markets

Many markets for industrial products are not nation-wide but instead are restricted to small areas, or even to single factories. In these cases the existence of distribution costs automatically favours locations close to the market, ceteris paribus. If distribution costs are an important element of costs then distant locations will find it difficult to compete, and it is conceivable that margins to profitable production would exist even within an area as

23

small as the UK. One author who has briefly examined the effect of distribution costs on a British industry, ironfounding, is M. Taylor (1970). Taylor examined the cost of delivering foundry castings to the West Midlands conurbation market. Assuming that the cost structure of each firm conforms to the average cost structure of the industry and further assuming a ten per cent profit margin, Taylor finds that, using road transport, margins would appear 644 miles from the market. He concludes, 'These figures would suggest that the West Midlands market for ironcastings could be served at a profit from any location in the United Kingdom.' This conclusion is reached notwithstanding the fact that the iron foundry industry lies in the highest quartile of British industries (by value of output) with total transport costs comprising 3 per cent of gross output. The fact that this is not the only market for castings reinforces the conclusion that a variety of production locations may be possible. The multiplicity of industrial centres within Britain should also make this true for most other products. If Taylor's conclusion is correct then it would seem most unlikely that margins, caused by distribution costs to single markets, would exist in many industries within Britain.

2.2.3  The significance of distribution costs

In the three-quarters of British industry in which transport costs comprise a low proportion of gross output, differences between the cheapest and most expensive locations are unlikely to amount to more than one or two per cent of gross output. A similar conclusion is reached by Edwards (1975) using a different approach. Edwards calculated the regional variation in transport costs actually paid by firms in different regions in 1963. He concluded that the difference between the highest and lowest cost regions amounted to less than 1 per cent of sales value. Since the figures used in his exercise omit costs incurred by firms in operating their own fleets, the 1 per cent should be increased to perhaps 1.5 per cent.

The pattern of cost variation observed by Edwards is similar to that depicted in figure 2.2. The least cost locations include the two Midland regions and the South East. The highest cost regions are Northern, Scotland and East Anglia. The omission of Wales and the South West from Edward's list reflects the fact that production is concentrated in the more accessible parts of these regions.

## 2.3  LABOUR COSTS AND PRODUCTIVITY VARIATIONS

Spatial variations in labour costs are likely to have a large impact on total costs for the simple reason that labour costs form a relatively high proportion of the cost of production and distribution. In 1968, labour costs in most industries accounted for a quarter of the value of turnover (although the figure was lower in food and chemicals). Since our concern here is with cost variation there will be no direct discussion of labour availability although this is naturally related to the question of cost. Also, since the concern is with the real cost of labour or 'wage efficiency', it is necessary to consider wages together with productivity.

The most obvious characteristic of either wage or productivity variation is the fact that variations between industries or sizes of plant are as great or greater than differences between regions. In any one region factories will be paying a variety of wage rates, and this internal variation is often greater than the differences in regional average. This much is evident from official statistics on wages or output, and the persistence of this situation over time is indicated by single industry studies undertaken in the early 1950s (Knowles and Verry, 1954; Knowles and Hill, 1954, 1956).

Average wage levels tend to vary between regions by five to ten per cent on either side of the national mean (New Earnings Survey, 1972), and the present pattern of high and low wage areas has remained fairly stable for most of the postwar period (Coates and Rawstron, 1971).

Table 2.1
Average earnings in UK regions full time male manual workers. All manufacturing industries 1967.

Regional average as a percentage of UK average

| Region | Actual weekly earnings 1 | Weekly earnings assuming national employment structure 2 |
|---|---|---|
| London and South East | 104.9 | 104.0 |
| Eastern and Southern | 103.8 | 101.8 |
| South Western | 96.8 | 95.9 |
| Midlands | 102.2 | 100.5 |
| Yorkshire and Humberside | 93.9 | 94.2 |
| North Western | 96.6 | 98.0 |
| Northern | 99.1 | 97.8 |
| Wales | 102.9 | 95.9 |
| Scotland | 96.4 | 96.5 |
| Northern Ireland | 86.7 | 89.5 |
| United Kingdom | 100.0 | 99.2 |

Source: Department of Employment and Productivity Gazette, March 1969, p. 233

Average wage levels may be strongly influenced by the industrial or sex composition of employment. For present purposes we are interested in regional variations in the cost of similar types of labour and must make allowances for variations in composition. One study which did this is reported in table 2.1. This shows that male manual wage levels tend to be highest in the South East and Midlands, and also that differences of industrial structure do not affect the

pattern much except in the case of Wales. In the
latter case the importance of the steel industry
increases wages. Much the same pattern is described
by Brown (1972) (8) even though his figures are not
restricted to manufacturing. He also shows a considerable degree of stability existing through the
1960s except for increases relative to the national
average in the second half of the decade in Scotland
and Northern Ireland.

The existence of stable differences in regional
average earnings is clearly shown by the above
evidence, but it is less easy to measure the degree to
which these differences reflect variations in
productivity. Regional differences in net output per
head do exist, with high levels in the South East
(Census of Production 1971), and once again the
differences appear to have been characteristic of the
UK for almost half a century (see Singer and Leser,
1948; and Leser, 1950).

Brown (1972) examined regional productivity variations and found that regional variations did exist
even after allowance for industrial structure, but
that these differences were smaller than those between
industries. Using figures for 1954 Brown (1972) (9)
concluded that: 'It is clear that there is a strong
positive correlation between our regional dummies
(indicating general productivity differences in value
terms) and earnings differences...' The 'productivity
dummy variable' for London and the South East...
indicated a general average for Scotland, Wales, the
North, North West, South West and Yorkshire. London
and the South East's advantage over them in average
male manual earnings when statistics started a few
years later was of the same order of magnitude.'
The more recent figures table 2.2 shows wage and
productivity figures for 1971. No allowance is made
for industrial structure since the same structure
underlies both sets of figures. In some regions the
two figures are close to one another but the table
does suggest that wage efficiency may be high in the

27

Southern regions and Scotland and low in the Midlands
(especially the West Midlands) and the Northern
region.

Table 2.2
Regional wage and productivity levels 1971

| Region | (UK = 100) Average weekly earnings adult male manual workers | (UK = 100) Net output per head |
|---|---|---|
| North | 101 | 94 |
| Yorkshire and Humberside | 92 | 89 |
| East Midlands | 94 | 88 |
| East Anglia | 92 | 101 |
| South East | 105 | 117 |
| South West | 96 | 99 |
| West Midlands | 103 | 92 |
| North West | 98 | 100 |
| Wales | 103 | 102 |
| Scotland | 97 | 103 |
| Northern Ireland | 92 | 89 |

Sources of data: Regional Abstract of Statistics
1974 table 57 (net output)
table 82 (wages)

The evidence is only suggestive since the wage data
excludes females and non-manual workers while the
productivity figures include all employees. In
addition a major potential complication is the lack of
evidence on capital stock. It is possible for
instance that differences in capital intensity account
for some or all of the variations in wage efficiency.
If this were the case then the apparent labour cost
variations would imply little for new firms. To
counter this possibility it may be appropriate to
introduce evidence on recently located establishments.

One large-scale survey of newly opened plants was
undertaken by the Department of Trade and Industry

(Expenditure Committee 1973). This study asked firms to compare unit labour costs between the new plant and the previous or parent plant. Leaving the Regional Employment Premium out of consideration equal numbers of firms reported higher costs, lower costs and similar costs. Rather more firms locating in development areas (especially Merseyside) complained of higher costs. Locations within the South and Midlands had a greater tendency to report lower unit costs. The difference was not however dramatic, and neither is the interpretation entirely clear. All of the new plants had been set up within the previous six years, and must certainly have been experiencing higher costs specifically due to initial settling in. Plants in development areas are usually larger than average, and further removed from parent factories. It is possible therefore, that development area factories incur higher levels of initial settling in costs. Not all development areas showed the higher costs however, and in particular the northern region was reported on as favourably as anywhere else.

Other evidence is more fragmentary and subjective. In the verbal evidence given to the House of Commons committee on regional policy incentives two of the seventeen firms complained of high unit costs in the North East, but in neither case was it suggested that these significantly affected performance. Several firms singled out Merseyside as a problem area on labour costs.

The authors of the West-Central Scotland plan considered that in 1963 most industries on Clydeside were operating with high unit labour costs relative to the rest of the country, (West-Central Scotland Plan 1974). This evidence does not necessarily conflict with the evidence of table 2.2 that Scotland has low unit labour costs. Beside the difference in dates, there appear to be strong contrasts in many aspects of industrial performance between East and West Scotland. This point taken with the last may indicate that sub-regional variation is more pronounced than that at the regional level.

Evidence of low unit labour costs in Wales is available from Unilever (Expenditure Committee, 1973) and from Radio and Allied Ltd in 1960. In the latter case the company managed by Arnold Wienstock was paying female semi-skilled workers at two-thirds of rate paid by GEC Ltd in Coventry. He considered the major radio manufacturers to be over conservative in response to (female) cost differentials (Jones and Marriot 1970). It is perhaps a comment on his judgement that he subsequently became managing director of GEC and went on to control a large section of the British Electrical Industry. In the case of Northern Ireland a study by Law (1964) showed that over half of the branch plants in that region operated with lower unit labour costs than branch plants elsewhere, and indeed that some of them had gone there for that reason.

It is difficult to summarise these disparate strands of evidence except to say that wages and productivity undoubtedly vary between regions and that regional wage efficiency differences also appear to exist. It is not easy to go on from this evidence to conclude that genuine labour cost savings can be made by locating in some regions rather than others.

The great variability within regions and lack of knowledge on capital stock make it unclear that systematic regional differences exist, and the evidence from individual firms is mixed. Certainly there is little evidence to suggest that managements recognise or act upon the existence of wage efficiency differentials. Although the evidence is dated now, Luttrell (1962 p.116) in perhaps the most detailed empirical study conducted on plant location found that: 'the expectation of paying lower wages was rarely a factor persuading firms to move ... nor does it seem to have played a part in the decision of where to go once the firm had decided to move.' Luttrell also found considerable variation in wage-

levels between plants of the same companies but concluded that these usually reflected skill differentials. Luttrell's evidence, although suggestive, is
drawn from a period after the last war in which
labour was in short supply and his sample contained
relatively few cases of location in the most
peripheral areas.

General considerations might lead to the expectation that real wage costs were lowest in areas of
highest unemployment. Within the UK such areas have
usually been in peripheral regions. On top of this
pattern there is also the factor of local wage
expectations conditioned by the local industrial
structure (especially where steel and coal are
important local industries) and pressed by strong
unions. Also there are areas in which the labour
force is less willing to submit to the industrial
disciplines of routine assembly work or shift work.
The development areas in general, and Merseyside in
particular, have a reputation for labour difficulties
shown in such things as high rates of absenteeism
(e.g. Dunlop Co. 1974). The effects of both industrial structure and local attitudes to industrial
work are probably localised, appearing at the sub-
regional rather than the regional scale. If this is
the case then companies will be able to move
production between regions while avoiding localised
high cost areas. Male manual wages may be high in
parts of Wales for instance, but female wages or
manual wages in other parts may be relatively low.

The conclusion of this section is that wage and
productivity variation is a complicated issue.
Regional differences do not appear to be an important
location factor, although it seems likely that lower
real costs may be obtainable in some areas. This
section has been couched in terms of location, but it
should be noted that real labour cost differences
might have a greater effect on the growth of firms in
areas affected.

31

## 2.4 OTHER PRODUCTION COSTS

It is unlikely that regional variation in the cost of
land and buildings, fuel and power or capital would be
significant influences on location or growth in as
small and homogenous area as the UK. The reasons
are, that cost variation tends to be slight at the
regional scale, while the significance of these items
within the total cost of production is small in most
industries.

Land costs vary markedly between city centres,
suburbs and rural areas but there is much less variation in cost between regions for comparable types of
location. There are few figures for industrial land
as such, but land for residential construction
provides a rough proxy. The National Building Agency
(1968) and Stone (1970) (10) both show that minimum
and average land costs vary little between regions
with the exception of areas close to London. In
addition, the 1968 Census of Production showed that
net acquisitions of land and buildings by manufacturing industry comprised less than 1 per cent of the
value of output. Building costs are unlikely to vary
significantly, while land costs by analogy with
housing is unlikely to constitute more than one third
of the cost of the completed building. The small
degree of regional variation, together with the
overall insignificance of land and buildings within
the totality of production costs, leads to agreement
with Webers' conclusion of over half a century ago:
'for the choice of location it (land costs) does not
greatly matter as it influences the price in much too
small a degree'.(11)

Expenditure on fuel and power in 1968 amounted to
2.5 per cent of the value of turnover.(12) Nearly
half of this total was for gas and electricity in
which price variation is slight. Coal and coke vary
in price to a larger degree (13) but almost three-
quarters is absorbed by three heavy industries.(14)
Finally, liquid fuels form 18 per cent of expenditure

and exhibit some price variability. In overall terms, however, the small amount of price variation coupled with the low significance of these costs means that fuel and power are not a significant location factor except for a small number of heavy industries which require large amounts of power.

Capital costs are also unlikely to lead to significant cost differences between locations. Although there is a little evidence of geographical variation in interest rates this is not likely to be large.(15) In one of the research reports appended to the Bolton Report the question of regional variations in the availability and cost of finance was examined but few differences were discovered (Economic Advisory Group, 1972). Also important is the fact that firms have traditionally financed most of their expansion out of retained profits, and this is particularly true of small and unquoted firms (Bolton 1972). Larger firms have performance records and reputations with which to counteract any local disadvantage in interest rates, and quoted firms have access to the equity market. The problem is unlikely to arise for large multi-regional firms locating new branch plants, while for completely new enterprises bank borrowing is unusual in any case. Although there may be some cases in which costs are increased through higher interest charges, these seem unlikely to be a location factor of general importance.


2.5  COST VARIATION:  A SYNTHESIS

There are a number of industries for which geographical cost variation is still a potent influence. These are the heavy industries including metal manufacture, sugar refining, oil refining; industries with special locational requirements as in ship-building or frozen foods, and industries with high distribution costs. The remainder of manufacturing, roughly the 75 per cent with transport costs (on census definitions) at less than 3 per cent of the value of gross output, is not so tightly constrained. The evidence presented above suggests that only labour costs and transport cost of distribution are likely to have a significant influence on either location or growth at the regional scale. Savings in average labour costs may amount to one or two per cent of the value of output in low wage areas i.e. in Wales, Scotland and Northern Ireland or in Yorkshire, the East Midlands and East Anglia. The existence of real savings is critically dependent on productivity levels, and it is possible that low productivity would cancel the effects of low wages. The evidence is, however, that although some firms at least have realised lower unit costs by moving into the peripheral regions, there is probably no systematic tendency one way or the other.

Distribution costs depend on the nature and location of markets. Peripheral locations distributing to national markets may incur costs up to one or two per cent greater than the Midlands, and if so these would tend to reduce the advantage of any saving in labour costs. The overall conclusion appears to be that although there is a great deal of cost variation between factories, or even small areas, and although some locations may be inappropriate for specific markets, there is probably only slight variation across regions in average costs of production and distribution. This conclusion is tested below in two case studies, one for widespread markets and the other for a specific market.

2.5.1 Widespread markets: the hosiery industry

The first example is of an industry producing knitted goods for national (and international) consumer markets. Most production is concentrated in the East Midlands and this region will be used as a basis of comparison for other regions. Only distribution and labour costs will be considered, as the others can be safely left aside.

Transport costs constitute 0.9 per cent of the value of gross output (16) and this figure is likely to be comprised wholly of distribution costs. Since production is heavily concentrated in the East Midlands it can reasonably be assumed that distribution costs from the East Midlands are approximately 0.9 per cent (they should certainly be no greater than this). Using this value, together with the distribution cost values from figure 2.2, we can compare the size of distribution costs for different regions. A West Midlands location would be marginally cheaper, while Central Scotland and West Cornwall would be 25 per cent more expensive and North West Scotland up to 50 per cent dearer. This means that Central Scotland and West Cornwall would incur additional costs of some 0.2 per cent of turnover above the level of the East Midlands, while the figure for North West Scotland would be 0.46 per cent.

Labour costs, in the hosiery industry, amount to 22 per cent of the value of gross output.(17) Comparisons with hypothetical costs in other regions are difficult due to the complexities involved in assessing differences in productivity, although it is possible to make some progress. If we compare regions in their levels of hourly earnings for manual textile workers then we have some measure of the underlying wage differentials. Hosiery is a largely female employing industry, but in the figures used here, a more regionally extensive series is available for male workers. The pattern for female earnings appears to be rather similar. These figures include some element of the influence of industrial structure since, for instance, cotton and woollen industry earnings are on average below those of hosiery and thus deflate the figures for the North-West Region and Yorkshire. However, a hosiery firm locating in these areas could hope to pay wages reflecting earnings in local textile trades and this factor has been ignored, except to remove Wales from the analysis due to its predominant employment in artificial fibres which in some ways is more a chemical than a textile industry.

Although overall male earnings in the East Midlands are a little below average, those in textiles are somewhat above the textile average probably due to the factor of industrial structure. Earnings in textiles in other regions range from 10 per cent lower in Scotland and the North-West Region to 6 per cent higher in the West Midlands. Separate figures are not available for Northern Ireland, but it is likely that these would be lowest of all. The question of savings on labour costs turns more importantly on the point of productivity differentials. In the following analysis various assumptions can be made. If no differences in productivity existed then the North West or possibly Northern Ireland would be the lowest cost region with production costs at 2 per cent below the East Midlands, while the West Midlands would be the highest cost region at 1.3 per cent above the East Midlands. In round terms the difference between the lowest and highest cost regions might be of the order of 4 per cent of turnover.

If productivity differentials were equal to labour cost differences then unit labour costs would be regionally uniform. In this case only distribution cost would be of relevance, and variation on total costs would be very slight but would favour the Midlands. As a final assumption we can consider the case in which low wage regions have even lower productivity levels. If unit labour costs were to be as much as 10 per cent above the East Midlands in peripheral areas then these areas would have higher total costs of up to 2.5 per cent of average gross output.

How do these suggested cost differences compare with the range of profitability between firms? Figure 2.3 presents figures on the profit (as a proportion of sales value) made by a sample of 116 hosiery firms in the East Midlands.(18) It can be seen that profit levels are approximately normally distributed with a wide spread of values presumably reflecting differences between firms in such things as management efficiency.

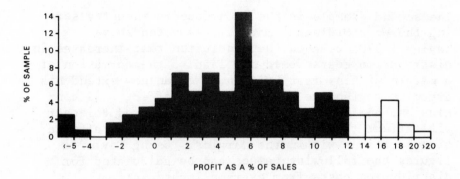

Figure 2.3   Distribution of profit as a percentage of
             sales between a sample of 116 hosiery
             firms 1968-69
Source of data:   National Economic Development Office,
                  A Study of Profitability in the
                  Hosiery and Knitwear Industry,
                  HMSO 1971

These figures are a cross-section for one year and may
not represent the long-term distribution of profitability.  However, on the one year alone an increase in
costs of one or two per cent incurred by these firms
if they relocated in higher cost locations would make
only a marginal difference to the viability of the
firms.  The great majority would still make a profit.
This argument is a hypothetical one and not meant to
suggest that actual moves, with their attendant
disruption and additional influences, would give the
predicted results.  On this hypothetical argument
however, it is clear that no absolute margin of
profitability exists for hosiery production at the
British scale.  Indeed, there, is little to suggest
that differences exist which would be perceptible to
most entrepreneurs or managers given the great

37

uncertainties involved in comparing such things as
earnings, and labour productivity.

2.5.2 A specific market:  the iron foundry industry

The second example is the iron foundry industry serving the West Midlands' market.  As noted above
Taylor (1970) reached the conclusion that increases in
distribution costs would not lead to the formation of
a margin within Great Britain.  We can now extend his
argument to inquire how other costs affect this conclusion, and how all the factors considered together
will affect the comparative profitability of alternative locations within the margins.  Using Taylor's
figures the following values can be calculated for
distribution costs from extreme locations:
    Distribution costs as a percentage of sales value
    Dover       3.7
    Penzance    5.1
    Inverness   7.9

In the iron foundry industry labour costs on
average comprise 32 per cent of the value of gross
output.  In metal manufacture the evidence suggests
that there is a 10 per cent difference in actual
earnings between high and low earnings regions
excluding Northern Ireland.  Making no allowance for
productivity variation, this implies a difference in
labour costs equal to 4 per cent of gross output
between the South East on the one hand and the North
of England plus Scotland, on the other.  With the
exception of Northern Ireland the regions with
possibilities of lower labour costs are not necessarily those with high distribution costs.  Comparing
the three locations given above for instance we get:
    Labour costs as a proportion of gross output
    compared with the South East
    Dover       same    (assuming SE average)
    Penzance    -2.5    (assuming SW average)
    Inverness   -2.0    (assuming Scotland average)
Clearly in this case the labour cost savings (assuming
that there are any, and that productivity does not

vary) are not large enough to outweigh higher distribution costs. Peripheral locations in England and Wales, it seems, will be able to service the Birmingham market but with costs of 2 to 3 per cent above West Midlands foundries. In Scotland the figure will be 4 to 5 per cent, and at a guess, Northern Ireland will be similar. If in contrast it is assumed that productivity differences are equal to wage differences, then distribution costs remain the sole source of variation and the differences are wider.

It has not been possible to construct a frequency distribution of profitability in the foundry industry, and instead a distribution is presented for the mechanical engineering trades, in figure 2.4. It is not known whether this is representative of iron founding, all that can be claimed is that both are examples of metal using trades with not dissimilar size and organisational structures. The data drawn from 271 firms show a distribution rather similar to that of hosiery but with larger mean and spread.(19) The spread of values is not due to regional differences in profitability in any large measure since the regional means are not statistically different at the 5 per cent significance level, nor is the single year cross-section particularly unrepresentative, since five-year averages drawn from the period 1966-71 did little to reduce the dispersion in the frequency distribution.

2.6   CONCLUSION

Although the data used in the above sections is not strictly suitable for the use to which it was put, it is nevertheless possible to reaffirm the main conclusions with reasonable confidence. These are that for some three-quarters of manufacturing industry, by employment or by output, spatial margins to profitable production are most unlikely to exist within the UK (to serve markets within the UK). Moreover, for much of industry the cost differences are likely to be

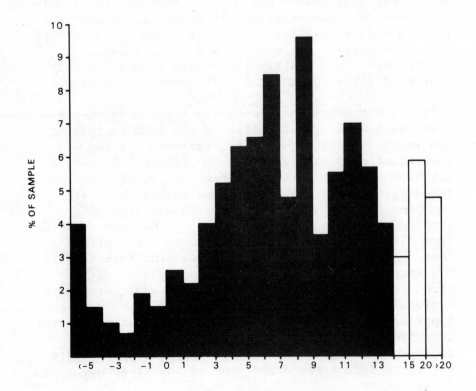

Figure 2.4   Distribution of profit as a percentage of
             sales between a sample of 271 mechanical
             engineering firms 1970-71
Source of data:   NEDO May 1972 (Mech. Eng.) Co,
                  Financial Results 1966-67 - 1970-71

40

sufficiently slight as to be either imperceptable for most location decisions, or else are well within the scope of management to overcome by cutting costs or increasing efficiency.(20)  In addition, a large variety of non-cost factors such as planning restrictions and labour availability, as well as a host of minor factors, will influence any individual case of location.  The discussion above is couched in terms of broad averages whereas in real life averages have a habit of not providing accurate descriptions of individual cases.

It is likely that cost differences may have a long-term and subtle influence on growth, even if they are too small to greatly affect decisions.  Higher costs, including labour costs, can be absorbed by lower profits or higher prices.  In the latter case it is likely that competitiveness will suffer even though prices are not the only relevant factor in competition.  It is this loss of competitiveness which will in the long-term reduce rates of growth.  If high costs are absorbed by lower profits, and there is a little evidence (presented below) that this may be the case, then in the long-term sources of finance for growth may be more expensive leading ultimately to slower growth.  The increased capital costs would result from firstly, the need to borrow higher propotions of any given investment, and secondly, from the increased difficulty of borrowing with a relatively poor profit record.


NOTES

(1)  This conclusion only holds for markets which can be viewed as continuous (e.g. consumer goods markets).  If a market is located at a small number of points then high distribution costs will tend to draw production towards those markets.
(2)  Not including indirect costs of transport such as insurance, nor costs of holding large inventories in remote locations.

(3)   Defined as a commodity requiring no special container or service.
(4)   Road for journeys up to 125, and rail for longer hauls. The expression has been calculated from two curves on p.88 of Bayliss and Edwards (1970).
(5)   Coal and coke, building materials, and crude minerals other than ore.
(6)   The ten standard regions, with the North, Wales, Scotland and the South West subdivided into two divisions in each case.
(7)   Distances within regions (internal distances) were arbitrarily set at thirty miles in England and Wales and at fifty miles in Scotland.
(8)   Brown (1972) p.235
(9)   Brown (1972) p.58
(10)  Stone (1970) p.152
(11)  A. Weber (1929) p.31
(12)  Census of production 1968, p.156, table 6
(13)  In 1968 the price of household coal varied by about one-third between regions according to Manners (1971) p.165
(14)  Metal manufacture, chemicals, bricks, pottery etc.
(15)  Times (1972) quoted in Keeble (1976) p.71. Regional variation in interest rates may increase in times of serious recession. One of the few previous references to the problem claimed that it was difficult to finance enterprises within the depressed areas in the 1930s, PEP, (1939).
(16)  Census of production 1968, p.156, table 8
(17)  ibid. table 1
(18)  These are figures from NEDO (1971). They are of pre-tax, pre-interest profits. Some of the firms have some of their production outside the East Midlands.
(19)  These figures on the same basis as those for the hosiery industry are from National Economic Development Office (1972). Locational information was added from trade directories.
(20)  The Meriden motor-cycle factory is said to have increased its productivity by 30 per cent since becoming a worker' co-operative. If increases of this

magnitude are possible then most of the regional differences discussed in this chapter are relatively insignificant by comparison. The special circumstances make this an unusual case but nevertheless large productivity increases are probably feasible in a large number of factories.

# PART II

# THE COMPONENTS OF CHANGE

# 3 The Components of Change approach

Since aggregate employment change represents the
composite result of individual acts of location and
growth (1) and since it was argued that variation in
production costs do not have a significant influence
on location decisions, and only a very weak influence
on growth, we must ask what does influence these
activities in the absence of strong cost constraints.
Some immediate factors spring to mind including such
things as the availability of labour, but it is the
purpose of this chapter to take a wider view and to
evolve a general approach to the problem of firstly
explaining decisions and then using these essentially
micro-level explanations to understand aggregate
employment changes.

## 3.1 UNDERLYING PRINCIPLES

If cost constraints are slight then firms can be said
to be operating in an economic environment which is
locationally permissive.  Under a permissive economic
regime decision makers have a wide latitude of choice
in making location decisions.  Also the influences on
growth and closure will not necessarily differ from
place to place.  This is not to say however, that
decision makers have a free choice in these matters.
In practice, a variety of factors will influence the
choice of location and the performance of firms, and
it is the purpose of this study to attempt to discover
what these factors are and how they operate.  Many of
these influences will still be loosely economic in
nature, but it is nevertheless important to
distinguish between these and the cost factors
discussed in the last chapter.

In explaining almost any decision two fundamental
considerations are the type of decision and the

47

context in which it is made. The main distinction in
this case is between location decisions and growth
decisions. The location decisions sub-divide further
into, firstly, those cases where an enterprise is
starting up for the first time (i.e. 'new' firms),
secondly, relocations, and thirdly the establishment
of branch plants, each of these being made in a
significantly different context. The 'growth'
decisions include both decline and closure as well as
growth itself. In addition to the type of decision,
the other important variable determining the context
in which decisions are made is ownership. Independent
firms make decisions within a different context from
that of subsidiary firms. Also firms with production
concentrated in a single area have a different
perspective from multi-regional or multi-national
firms.

An objection to the categories outlined above might
be that all of the decisions are investment decisions
and as such they should be viewed together and not
separated. While this view must certainly be the
correct one for understanding the actions of individual firms, the difficulty comes in generalising from
the specific cases. The view here is that all enterprises are affected by general influences external to
the organisation and that these will usually have a
powerful influence on whether investment takes the
form of new locations, closures or in situ change.
As long as these influences are in aggregate more
important than the vagaries of companies' status and
internal position and organisation then the categories
here can be justified. Explaining spatial variations
in any category then becomes a matter of identifying
the general factors, and viewing the rest as random
influences without a significant geographical
dimension.


3.2  AN ACCOUNTING FRAMEWORK

In order to bridge the gap between the micro-level

48

decisions and aggregate employment, an accounting
framework is used which incorporates the categories
outlined above. These categories can be then termed
components of change. This involves the construction
of employment accounts for each sub-region within a
defined area, with subsequent work to explain the
spatial variation in each component. The principles
are essentially the same as those underlying the
construction of the National Income accounts and
their role in Keynsian macro-economics despite the
fact that in the regional context there is not the
strong body of theory which underpins the Keynsian
case. These principles are:

1 Aggregate changes have a variety of causes
   and total change can only be understood through
   a disaggregation into components.
2 The components are selected for their useful-
   ness in explanation. To achieve this they
   should reflect coherent types of decisions or
   decision-makers. In the National Income
   accounts consumers and government are two such
   groups.
3 Explanation of total change is achieved by
   explaining firstly the variation of individual
   components, and secondly the interactions
   between components.

The Keynsian problem of explaining short-term
temporal fluctuation in the level of activity has
much in common with the present task of dealing with
long-term spatial differences in employment change
as a problem. The choice of components, the
individual explanations and almost all other aspects
will of course be dissimilar.


3.3  THE RESEARCH STRATEGY

The components of change approach can be described as
working backwards from the effects to the causes. At
each stage the employment totals can be broken down
until components are reached for which simple

49

explanations can be deduced. The explanatory variables thus appear at the end of the process rather
than at the beginning as with formal hypothesis
testing in what might be termed the 'classical'
scientific method. The advantages of the disaggregation method over hypothesis testing are threefold.
Firstly, the factors are quantified at every stage,
and measurement in this sense precedes a precise
specification of the variables. This is an important
advantage because it allows effort to be concentrated
on quantitively important effects. The existence
of large unexplained components will act as a spur to
further research, and hence provide more likelihood
of long-term progress towards understanding.

The second advantage is flexibility. As long as
data are available for individual factories, components can be formed or disaggregated in a variety of
ways. The disaggregation process allows a sort of
convergence to occur on to the causal factors. This
does not imply that the final explanantion takes the
form of a large number of small, almost unique,
factors. It is quite likely that the same factors
will influence several components, perhaps in different ways, and if so the action of important factors
may be clarified. The final advantage is that of
completeness. This is an important consideration
because the need to identify all components means
that important unexpected factors may come to light.
In this study the principal example is the surprising
importance of new independent firms. The major draw-
back with the method is of course the large amount of
data required. This is not usually available from
official sources and requires prodigious amounts of
work to turn basic information into useful data. The
difficulties involved necessarily impose some constraints on the degree to which the research strategy
can be carried through. The list of components (down
to two stages of disaggregation) which would ideally
be used are the following:

1  New establishments
   (a)  independent new firms

    (b)    new subsidiary companies
    (c)    new branch plants of locally based companies

2   Local changes in 'permanent' plants

    (a)    single region organisations
           (i)    independent companies
          (ii)    subsidiary companies or divisions
    (b)    multi-region organisations
           (i)    plants of locally based organisations
                  (independent companies, subsidiaries or
                  divisions)
          (ii)    plants of non-locally based companies or
                  divisions

3   Closures

    (a)    independent companies
    (b)    subsidiary companies
    (c)    branch plants

4   Industrial movement (from other areas)

    (a)    company transfers
    (b)    new branch plants

The first-order components have already been justified except to say that in dealing with changes in
'permanent' plants (i.e. those in existence throughout
the period in question) it is the locally retained
growth which affects the local employment performance.
This involves explaining variations in both rates of
growth and in the degree to which jobs are 'exported'
to other regions in the form of industrial movement.
The second level of disaggregation involves a
distinction between independent companies, subsidiary
companies (or divisions) and branch plants, and is
based on the belief that each type of organisation has
different degrees of decision-making autonomy.  The
independent companies in this context will be
primarily small companies which do not have their own
hierarchies of subsidiaries and divisions.  It appears
that in Britain, unlike America, large companies de-
volve most of their operational decisions to the level
of the subsidiary company.  Although the final

authority for investment decisions lies with the corporate or (ultimate) management, and although it is common for all expenditure above low ceilings to be referred up to headquarters, the principal motivating forces behind decisions on the nature and location of investment (or disinvestment) appear to reside in the headquarters of subsidiary organisations. The role of the corporate headquarters is often akin to that of the merchant bank rewarding good performance with access to funds for future expansion.

The components used in future chapters are broadly those described above at the first level of dis-aggregation. It has not been possible to complete the second level of disaggregations, although in some cases this is feasible in part. The second-level components which proved easiest to identify are those within the 'new establishments' category.

## 3.4   COMPARISON WITH AN ALTERNATIVE APPROACH

The choice of approach does not in itself do much to guarantee a successful explanation, the quality of analysis for the individual components will do that, but the importance of at least starting out in the correct direction cannot be over-emphasised. This point can perhaps be illustrated by comparing the components of change approach with one based on regression analysis, the important characteristic of the latter being its use of aggregate data rather than its reliance on the particular statistical technique. A regression approach attempts to explain or predict aggregate change directly from background variables. These may be briefly categorised for present purposes as either reflecting structural factors or environ-mental factors. Structural variables might include measures of the effects of industrial structure or size of plants, while environmental influences would include such things as labour supply, planning regulations or distance from major markets.

If the existence of different types of decision is explicitly recognised and conceptually interposed between the independent and dependent variables of the regression then the situation would look something like the following:

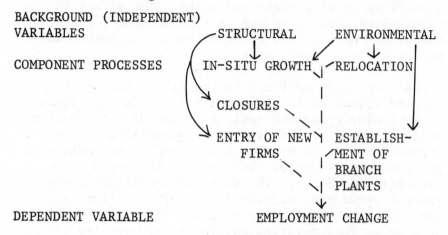

BACKGROUND (INDEPENDENT) VARIABLES

COMPONENT PROCESSES

STRUCTURAL   ENVIRONMENTAL

IN-SITU GROWTH   RELOCATION

CLOSURES

ENTRY OF NEW FIRMS   ESTABLISHMENT OF BRANCH PLANTS

DEPENDENT VARIABLE   EMPLOYMENT CHANGE

The arrows refer to the major relationships which appear to be present. Other relationships than those above will no doubt exist but are probably less important, with the exception of the obvious 'feedback' link from employment change to the structural and environmental variables. Structural influences act largely on industry which is already located in the area and have little direct influence on industrial movement. The effects of industrial structure act on in situ growth and on closures. Although industrial structure also affects entry of new firms, as will be demonstrated in subsequent chapters, this influence is quite different from the influence on growth and closure since in this case ease of entry is the vital characteristic and not changes in demand or productivity. Environmental influences may act on both indigenous and incoming industry but elements such as labour supply probably have little effect on entry of new firms (given their small initial size) or on closures.

Attempts to work directly from the background variables to employment change will mix these various influences together, and in some cases may miss important influences where these act in opposite directions on different components. The effect is rather like viewing an object through opaque glass, the broad outlines may be discernible but much information never filters through.

The components approach is capable of identifying the individual influences, and has the further advantage of clarifying the residual terms of a regression analysis which by definition are unexplained. The approach does this by focusing attention on individual processes which can be clearly seen to have a probabilistic basis. The entry of new firms is one example since the decision to establish a firm is surrounded by a multitude of small influences which show up as random variation almost irrespective of the number of factors for which it is possible to control. The growth of companies is another example.

3.5   PLAN OF THE REMAINING CHAPTERS

For each of the component processes there are three facets of interest. These can be summarised in the following table:

|  | Importance of the process | Nature of the process | Rate of action of the process |
|---|---|---|---|
| Location of new firms |  |  |  |
| Change in permanent plants |  |  |  |
| Closures |  |  |  |
| Industrial movement |  |  |  |

With four first-order components and three dimensions of interest there are twelve cells to be completed, and each subsequent chapter deals with one or more of these. Chapter four deals with the importance of each of the processes, with importance being taken to mean the proportion of employment change accounted for by each component. Chapters five to seven describe the nature of the processes of initial location, growth, and closure. Most of the original work relates to the initial location of new firms, and industrial movement is left aside since this is a topic which is intensively and satisfactorily covered within the UK context by other studies. The rate of action of the processes refers to geographical variations in rates of entry, closure, growth and movement. These are analysed in chapters eight to ten with a distinction maintained between the various spatial scales of interest.


NOTES

(1)  As in previous chapters 'growth' really means 'change' and includes both growth and decline. The word 'change' is avoided because of its wider connotations.

# 4  Employment accounts for the East Midlands

This chapter describes the quantitive importance of
the component processes for a single English region
over the period 1948-67. The region in question, the
East Midlands, was selected for reasons of convenience
rather than for more positive motives, but as
indicated earlier the choice has been a fortuitous
one. The region has maintained a better than average
growth performance throughout the postwar period.
This has been achieved in spite of a persistently poor
industrial structure through most of the period, a
characteristic which sets it apart from most of the
other regions which performed well over the same
period.

If the industries of the East Midlands (at the start
of the period) had performed no better and no worse
than the national averages for those industries over
the period, then the region's employment would have
grown at only 75 per cent of the national rate.(1)
In reality the rate of growth proved to be 40 per cent
greater than the national average. This indicates
that the region performed very much better than might
have been expected given the unpropitious fact that
the dominant local industries were the declining or
stagnating textile, clothing and footwear trades. It
is valuable to study location and growth processes in
the context of a regional success story, and doubly
valuable to do so when the success was achieved
'against the odds'.

For those unfamiliar with the system of standard
regions, the East Midlands is the area (2) included
in figure 4.1. Although the region is still second
only to Yorkshire and Humberside as a producer of
textiles and clothing the more important industries
are now in engineering. The industrial structure is
more variable than formerly, but contains little heavy

industry other than the steelworks of Corby and Derbyshire.

## 4.1 DATA AND METHODS

The methods used in compiling the employment accounts are described in detail in appendices I, II and IV, but because some of the sets rely on estimation procedures it is necessary to say something at this point. The basic data units consist of a record giving name, address, product, and employment for every industrial establishment in the region in the late 1960s. The employment figures are staggered over a four year period centred on 1967, although the great majority are for 1967 or immediately adjacent years. This lack of a single year cross-section would be a serious handicap over short periods, but for a twenty year time-span the data is adequate for the conclusions to be drawn. In addition, the employment totals from the establishments compare well with official employment statistics for 1967.

In the case of Leicestershire (3) similar records were also available for 1947, and for a period centred on 1957. This means that through a process of cross-checking between dates, and extensive use of trade directories and street directories augmented by direct survey work, the establishments can be assigned to the various components used in this and subsequent chapters. The most difficult element to identify proved to be industrial movement, but in this case it was fortunately possible to use official statistics on industrial movement collected in connection with the Howard Report (1968) for the overlapping, but not identical, period 1945-66.

Accounts for the remaining counties of the region, which include two-thirds of the total employment, relied on estimation techniques. These techniques, although less reliable than direct counting, could be assessed against the more accurate figures in the case of Leicestershire; and this test indicated the methods to be broadly sound. Once again the figures most difficult to estimate were those for industrial movement. Since the Howard figures on movement were again used in place of individual estimates the areal basis also had to correspond to that on which the movement data was collected. The areas in question correspond broadly to administrative counties. The figures for aggregate employment at the beginning and end of the period were also derived from official sources. The proportions of new and 'permanent' establishments in the 1967 population, and the employment within them, were estimated from a large-scale postal survey (described in appendix II). Distinctions between independent firms and branch plants were also estimated using the same source.

The weakest element of the estimation procedure concerns the employment lost in those establishments which were in production in 1948 but which closed before 1967. Since no direct information was available, the growth of permanent plants (estimated from the questionnaire returns) was projected backwards, and subtracted from the (known) initial employment totals in 1948. This procedure results in an estimate of the 1948 employment lost in subsequent closures, but its accuracy depends on the correct identification of growth in permanent plants.

4.2  EMPLOYMENT ACCOUNTS FOR THE REGION

Employment in the East Midlands expanded by 96,200 jobs, or just over 20 per cent, between 1948 and 1967.(4)  In 1967 total employment in manufacturing amounted to 576,800 jobs in 6,860 individual establishments. Table 4.1 shows how these totals are distributed between the components used in this analysis.

In employment terms the predominance of establishments which were in existence throughout the period (i.e. 'permanent') is not surprising, but less expected is the number of new firms, and even more so the large number of jobs in those firms.

Table 4.1

The composition of East Midlands employment in 1967

| | Establishments | | Employment | |
|---|---|---|---|---|
| | Nos. | % | Nos. | % |
| Permanent establishments | 3,505 | 51 | 453,300 | 79 |
| New firms | 2,929 | 43 | 65,600 | 11 |
| New branch plants of local firms | 306 | 4 | 24,300 | 4 |
| In-moving establishments | 120 | 2 | 33,600 | 6 |
| Total | 6,860 | 100 | 576,800 | 100 |

The employment created by these new firms, although constituting only 11 per cent of employment in 1967, amounts to two-thirds of the net employment increase over the period. This is a very significant proportion and clearly establishes the importance of new firms as a determinant of regional employment change, despite the very small size of individual firms.

The nature of the new firms will be discussed at length in chapter five, but at this point it is appropriate to attempt to distinguish between new independent companies and those companies which were established originally as subsidiary companies of some other organisation. It was not possible to make this distinction comprehensively, but a questionnaire survey was undertaken of fifty-five new companies in Leicestershire which were subsidiaries at the end of the period. This revealed that almost 90 per cent had been bought by their present owners. Although this does not necessarily indicate that the companies were begun as independent concerns, this is very likely to have been the case. The main class of companies begun

as subsidiaries are those under foreign ownership.
Foreign firms must necessarily set up their British
operations as registered companies, and at the same
time they have a high propensity to set up their own
factories rather than to buy up existing British
companies. In the figures used in this study, however, such enterprises originating outside the region
will normally be included within the official figures
for industrial movement. The remaining subsidiary
companies are those established by locally based
firms. There appear to be only a very small number of
these, although they can be expected to have larger
employment than new independent companies. The great
majority of the new companies are independent firms,
and as will be shown below most of these are founded
by local entrepreneurs.

In addition, the distinction between new independent
and new subsidiary companies may be a somewhat fine
one. Most new subsidiaries are set up to produce some
new product outside the range of the parent company's
normal activities. Several cases were encountered,
however, in which the subsidiary was established under
the control of the son of the head of the parent firm,
and the existence of the subsidiary may have owed as
much to a desire to set up the son in business as to
anything else.

Four per cent of both establishments and employment
in 1967 were in new branch plants of companies based
within the same county. Again there is little direct
evidence that all of these were originally established
as branch plants. Evidence from the questionnaire
survey, however, suggests that this was the case for
80 per cent of branches. The other 20 per cent were
presumably bought as independent companies and subsequently absorbed into the parent organisation as a
branch plant rather than subsidiary company, or were
bought as branches from another company.

In-moving establishments include those moving into
the East Midlands from other regions, and also moves

60

between counties within the region. If the latter are excluded then the figures in table 4.1 reduce to ninety establishments and 25,600 jobs.(5) As can be seen, three-quarters of the moves thus originated outside the region. Only a very small number of plants were involved in movement, and this is to be expected in a region which had only small pockets of surplus labour in this period. The employment in these establishments is less insignificant and in fact accounts for a third of the region's net employment growth. If the intra-regional moves are excluded however this proportion falls to a quarter. Since this is so, it can be considered that 75 per cent of the net growth was self-generated in the sense that it originated largely from local firms or from individual entrepreneurs based within the region.

This conclusion understates the region's potential for generating new employment in that a large number of jobs were exported to other parts of the UK in the form of branch plants or transfers. In fact the region was a net exporter of jobs over the period, and 128 establishments and 31,500 jobs in other regions originated from East Midlands parent companies. If these jobs are considered together with those retained within the region then local companies can be said to have generated more than the total net increase in this region's employment. Shortages of labour combined with regional policy measures (especially the refusal of IDC certificates) are the major probable reasons behind the fact that so many jobs were 'exported' to other regions.

The employment in 1948 within those establishments which closed before 1967 is estimated at 135,000 or 26.7 per cent of total employment in 1948. As explained in appendix IV this estimate is based on assumptions about growth-rates and is unlikely to be precise, but as an approximate order of magnitude it is probably satisfactory. It has not been possible to subdivide this figure further, according to the ownership of closed establishments, but for part of the

region this can be achieved and is done below in
section 4.4.

This figure for closures is the final one needed to
produce a set of accounts for employment change, and
these are presented in table 4.2.  In this table the
net increase in employment is added to the employment
in closures to arrive at a total of 'new' jobs.

Table 4.2

Employment accounts for the East Midlands

| | | |
|---|---|---:|
| 1 | Employment in closures 1948-67 | 134,800 |
| 2 | Net increase in employment 1948-67 | 96,200 |
| 3 | New jobs (row 1 + row 2) | 231,000 |
| 4 | Employment as % of row 3 | |
| | New firms | 28% |
| | Permanent establishments | 46% |
| | New branches of local firms | 11% |
| | In-moving establishments | 15% |

This definition of 'new' employment is a partial one
ignoring as it does some new jobs created within
permanent establishments.  These are combined with
jobs lost in declining permanent establishments and
appear as a (concealed) part of the net employment
increase.  This measure of 'new' jobs is preferable to
net increase as a basis for evaluating the importance
of each component, since it avoids the necessity for
percentages which sum to totals greater than 100 per
cent.

Almost half of the new employment is seen to be in
permanent establishments and if the branches of local
firms are added to this, then local permanent firms
account for over half of the total.(6)  New firms
account for just over a quarter and in-moving establishments about one-seventh of the new jobs.  This
method of presenting the figures brings out the
importance of the permanent firms, but should not be

allowed to disguise the fact that without the new firms and the in-moving establishments there would have been no net increase in employment at all. Indeed, even a relatively small decrease in the employment provided by new firms would have reduced the region's aggregate growth to below the national average rate.

Table 4.2 demonstrates two things quite clearly. The first is that the gross changes are larger than the net change. The net change in this region, and presumably in others also, represents a balance between much larger numbers of job losses and gains. The second point is to emphasise the fact that new jobs are largely generated locally with less than one in eight coming from outside the region. In a growing region like the East Midlands (during the period in question) it may come as no surprise that almost all growth is internally generated. It is important to learn that nearly 30 per cent of new jobs, on the definition above, were in the form of companies which were not in existence at the beginning of the period and which were formed largely due to the enterprise of local individuals. The day of the small entrepreneur it seems is not yet over, or at least if it is, then the end has come since 1967.

## 4.3 SUB-REGIONAL ACCOUNTS

The next question of interest is whether the importance of the various components proves to be variable within the region. In this section the sub-regional scale will be investigated, followed by a view of the more detailed local scale in the next. The sub-regions used in this study are those listed in table 4.3. These correspond with the sub-regions used by the Department of Industry for industrial movement purposes except that it is possible in some cases to divide the Nottinghamshire/Derbyshire sub-region into its constituent counties. In most tables a joint figure for Nottinghamshire/Derbyshire will be given alongside the individual figures. Table 4.3 shows that differences between the counties in their rates of postwar growth are not large, and in particular that the performances of Leicestershire, Nottingham- shire and Derbyshire were very similar.

Table 4.3

Employment growth between 1948 and 1947 for the manuf- acturing industry in the counties of the East Midlands

|  | 1948 | 1967 | Increase | % Increase |
|---|---|---|---|---|
| Leicester-shire | 148,800 | 178,700 | 29,900 | 20.1 |
| Nottingham-shire(a) | 134,800 | 162,700 | 27,900 | 20.7 |
| Derbyshire(b) | 87,200 | 105,000 | 17,800 | 20.4 |
| Northampton-shire(c) | 66,500 | 77,700 | 11,100 | 16.7 |
| Lincoln-shire(d) | 42,500 | 51,900 | 9,400 | 22.1 |

Source:   Department of Employment
Notes
    (a)   Excluding the Newark and Retford Employment Exchange Areas
    (b)   Excluding the Employment Exchange Areas of Chesterfield, Stavely, Eckington and Clay Cross (des- cribed as Greater Chesterfield on Figure 4.1)
    (c)   Excluding the employment in the steelworks at Corby.  This employed well over ten thousand people by 1967 and dominated employment growth over the period. Its influence will therefore be dealt with separately as a special case.
    (d)   Including the Newark and Retford Employment Exchange Areas

The case of Northamptonshire is a somewhat complicated one.  The total growth, including that in steel, was 26 per cent and the highest among the East Midlands counties.  Without the steelworks expansion at Corby the rate of employment growth was the slowest in the region, and if Corby New Town is excluded altogether the rate of growth is less than half of the East Midlands average. Northamptonshire, in fact, consists of three contrasting parts. The footwear area comprising the bulk of the county grew very slowly while Corby in the north, and the Daventry and Towcester areas in the south, both grew rapidly from low initial employment totals. Employment in Lincolnshire (including East Nottinghamshire) grew slightly more rapidly than the rest of the region as a whole, with the Holland division of Lincolnshire growing rapidly while the Newark and Sleaford areas had very low growth-rates.

The next stage in the analysis is to disaggregate total employment change, into components corresponding to the various location processes. The estimates for both numbers of establishments and employment in 1967 are given in table 4.4. These estimates are expressed as percentages of the total numbers of establishments and total employment respectively, in tables 4.5 and 4.6. The principal points to emerge are the following. Firstly, the proportion of permanent establishments is identically 47 per cent in Leicestershire and Rutland, Nottinghamshire and Northamptonshire. In the other two counties the figure is higher, but overall the balance between new and permanent establishments appears not to deviate from the average by very much. The composition of the populations of new firms is more variable. Three counties have close to 40 per cent of establishments in the form of new firms. In Nottinghamshire the figure is a little higher and in Lincolnshire it is much lower. Only a small proportion of new establishments are branch plants of local firms, and the differences between counties may be due to sampling fluctuations. The proportion of in-moving establishments is very small elsewhere, but over double the average in Northamptonshire and below half of the average in Leicestershire.

In terms of employment, the permanent establishments are much more important, comprising about 80 per cent of jobs in manufacturing in all of the counties

## Table 4.4

### The composition of employment in 1967 by sub-region

| | Permanent establishments | | New firms | | New branch plants of local firms | | New in-moving establishments | |
|---|---|---|---|---|---|---|---|---|
| | No. | Employment | No. | Employment | No. | Employment | No. | Employment |
| Leicestershire | 1,109 | 137,300 | 952 | 21,300 | 145 | 9,900 | 25 | 11,000 |
| Nottinghamshire(a) | 912 | 130,100 | 951 | 18,700 | 25 | 5,800 | (71)(f) | (8,200)(f) |
| Derbyshire(b) | 594 | 85,700 | 416 | 11,500 | 43 | 3,400 | (71)(f) | (4,400)(f) |
| Nottinghamshire and Derbyshire | 1,506 | 219,000 | 1,367 | 30,200 | 68 | 9,200 | 41(e) | 8,600(e) |
| Northamptonshire(c) | 554 | 52,300 | 480 | 10,200 | 76 | 4,200 | 44 | 11,000 |
| Lincolnshire(d) | 336 | 44,700 | 130 | 3,900 | 17 | 1,000 | 10 | 3,000 |

Sources of data: Questionnaire survey. Establishment records. Howard Report.

Notes

(a)-(d)  See table 4.3

(e)  These figures are derived from the Howard Report but with allowance made for the omission of Chesterfield using information from Steel (1972)

(f)  Unlike the other figures in this column these are estimates from questionnaire and are not from the Howard Report

Table 4.5

Numbers of establishments in component categories: sub-regions 1967

| | Total No. of establishments | Permanent establishments % | New firms % | New branches of local firms % | New in-moving establishments % |
|---|---|---|---|---|---|
| Leicester-shire | 2,340 | 47 | 41 | 6 | 1 |
| Nottingham-shire(a) | 1,959 | 47 | 49 | 1 | 4 |
| Derbyshire(b) | 1,063 | 56 | 39 | 7 | 7 |
| Nottingham-shire and Derbyshire | 3,022 | 50 | 45 | 2 | 2 |
| Northampton-shire(c) | 1,187 | 47 | 40 | 6 | 4 |
| Lincolnshire | 539 | 63 | 24 | 3 | 2 |

Sources of data: Establishment records. Questionnaire survey. Howard Report.

Notes

(a)-(d)  See table 4.3

Row percentages do not sum to 100% since independent estimates do not necessarily sum to (known) total number of establishments

Table 4.6

Employment in component categories: sub-regions 1967

| | Total employment | Permanent establishments % | New firms % | New branches of local firms % | New in-moving establishments % |
|---|---|---|---|---|---|
| Leicester-shire | 178,700 | 77 | 12 | 5.5 | 6 |
| Nottingham-shire(a) | 162,700 | 80 | 11.5 | 3.5 | (5)(e) |
| Derbyshire(b) | 105,000 | 82 | 11 | 3.0 | (4)(e) |
| Nottingham-shire and Derbyshire | 267,700 | 81 | 11 | 3.5 | 3.5 |
| Northampton-shire(c) | 77,700 | 67.5 | 13 | 5.5 | 14 |
| Lincolnshire | 51,900 | 84.5 | 7.5 | 2.0 | 6 |

Sources of data: Dept of Employment. Establishment records. Questionnaire survey

Notes

(a)-(d)   See table 4.3
(e)       These figures are based on questionnaire estimates and are not from the
          Howard Report unlike the remaining figures in this column

except Northamptonshire. Some 12 per cent of employment is in new firms, and a little less is in branch
plants in all counties except for Lincolnshire with
fewer jobs in new firms, and Northamptonshire which
has a very high proportion of its employment either in
the branch plants of non-local firms or in firms which
transferred from other regions.

A final addition to these employment accounts is an
estimate of the number of jobs lost due to the
closure of establishments which were in production in
1948. This estimate is contained in table 4.7 and
shows similar rates of loss in all counties except
Northamptonshire in which the figure is almost 40 per
cent of employment in 1948.

Table 4.7

Estimated employment in establishments which were in
production in 1948 but closed by 1967

| | Employment in 1948 | Employment as a % of total employment in manufacturing in 1948 |
|---|---|---|
| Leicestershire | 38,800 | 26 |
| Nottingham-shire and Derbyshire(a)(b) | 60,100 | 27 |
| Northampton-shire(c) | 25,600 | 38 |
| Lincolnshire(d) | 10,300 | 24 |

Source of estimates:  (see text)
Notes
    See table 4.3

Armed with the estimates for employment in closures
it is again possible to move from cross sections in
time to a consideration of employment change. The
figures in table 4.8 show the gross changes, as
before, to be much larger than the net changes. New
firms contribute over a quarter of 'new' employment in

69

all areas except Lincolnshire. Although it does not
follow from this that the entry-rate of new firms is
necessarily low in Linclonshire, it will be shown in
chapter eight that this is in fact the case, and
moreover that it is also true of Derbyshire. The
proportion of new jobs contributed by the net expansion of permanent establishments is the largest single
item in each sub-region, although in Northamptonshire
the margin over other components is slight.

In the case of Northamptonshire the low employment
proportion provided by permanent plants partly reflects the relative importance of in-moving establishments, a characteristic which itself reflects the
proximity of this county to the South East region,
the major source of mobile industry in Britain. It is
probably also the result of decline in the footwear
industry. In addition, the considerable shortage of
labour in the footwear areas must have hampered
expansion. This shortage combined with greater
availability of labour in the Corby and Daventry areas
has led to a greater amount of expansion taking the
form of a local branch rather than occurring in situ
at the existing plants.(7)

In Leicestershire the poor industrial structure may
have lowered the performance of permanent firms, but
once again the shortage of labour, coupled with the
effects of regional policy were probably the major
factors. The high proportion of employment in new
branch plants of local firms also indicates that
shortage of labour has been an influence as does the
fact shown in table 4.9 that Leicestershire 'exported'
proportionately more employment to other areas than
any other sub-region. The curious fact that in-
moving establishments form an above average proportion
of new employment in Leicestershire can be ascribed to
special cases described in 4.4.

The employment growth within permanent establishments is more substantial in Nottinghamshire, Derbyshire and Lincolnshire, all areas with a less

Table 4.8

Employment accounts for sub-regions within the East Midlands

| | Employment in closures 1948-67 | Net increase 1948-67 | Col 1 + Col 2 | Employment as a % of col 3 | | | |
| | | | | New firms | Permanent establishments | New branches of local firms | New inmoving establishments |
| | 1 | 2 | 3 | 4 | 5 | 6 | 7 |
|---|---|---|---|---|---|---|---|
| Leicestershire | 38,800 | 32,000 | 70,800 | 30 | 39 | 14 | 16 |
| Nottinghamshire and Derbyshire(a)(b) | 60,100 | 45,700 | 105,800 | 29 | 54 | 9 | 9 |
| Northamptonshire(c) | 25,600 | 11,100 | 36,700 | 28 | 31 | 11 | 30 |
| Lincolnshire(d) | 10,300 | 9,400 | 19,700 | 20 | 55 | 5 | 20 |
| Total/average | 134,800 | 98,200 | 233,000 | 28 | 46 | 11 | 15 |

Source of data: (see text)

Notes

See table 4.3

pressing shortage of labour.(8)   In each area there
was a consequential low proportion of expansion in the
form of local branch plants.   The availability of
labour in Lincolnshire is also a part cause of the low
level of out-movement shown in table 4.9, and of the
high level of in-movement indicated in table 4.8.   In
the latter case the availability of agricultural raw
materials in a period of expansion in food processing
was also of importance.

The fact that aggregate growth-rates were relatively
uniform across regions, while the importance of
individual components differed considerably, indicates
the presence of some equilibriating mechanism.   This
mechanism as indicated above is almost certainly the
action of variation in the availability of labour.   In
general, the established firms and new entrepreneurs
of the sub-regions performed so well as to outstrip
the growth of labour supply.   The attainment of the
full employment threshold meant that much employment
was exported, although the refusal of Industrial
Development Certificates was also a factor.   In cases
where employment was growing less rapidly, due to
structural causes in Northamptonshire for example, or
where a rundown in agriculture or mining led, the
labour supply to grow faster than employment, then
industrial in-movement was available to plug the gaps.

Some of this mobile employment took the form of
branch plants of parent companies based within the
region, but many plants came from elsewhere.   In this
respect the position of the East Midlands adjacent to
the major sources of industrial movement was fortunate,
especially the coincidence that the main potential
problem area, in Central Northamptonshire, was the
closest part of the region to London.   Without the net
gain of employment from industrial movement the growth-
rate in Northamptonshire (omitting the steelworks)
would have been only half the national average.   To
keep the matter in perspective however, it should be
noted that at half the national average the rate of
indigenous growth would have still been considerably

Table 4.9

Establishments moving out of East Midlands counties (branches and transfers) between 1945 and 1965

| | Number of establishments | Aggregate employment 1966 | Employment as a % of total employment in manufacturing in 1967 |
|---|---|---|---|
| Leicestershire | 81 | 17,000 | 9.5 |
| Nottinghamshire and Derbyshire(a)(b) | 46 | 14,000 | 8.5 |
| Northamptonshire(c) | 19 | 4,600(e) | 6.0 |
| Lincolnshire | 13 | 3,200(e) | 6.0 |

Source of data: Howard Report 50 x 50 matrix

Notes

(a)-(d)  See table 4.3
(e)  These figures have been estimated by assuming that establishments were on average the same size as the mean for Leicestershire, Nottinghamshire and Derbyshire

73

better than several of the development areas further north despite an industrial structure which was probably as poor as any.

## 4.4   EMPLOYMENT ACCOUNTS AT THE LOCAL SCALE

The importance of the component processes of employment change were found to vary to an extent, although not markedly, at the sub-regional scale.   In this section the final set of accounts is constructed; these are for small areas each consisting of a single employment exchange area.   The employment exchange areas are each centred on a separate town and in approximate terms correspond to labour market areas for those towns.   The availability of data restricts this analysis to Leicestershire alone, but in this case no estimation has been required in deriving the figures.   The location of the areas is described in figure 4.1.   The growth of both aggregate employment and of the individual components in Leicestershire as a whole have already been described in tables 4.3 and 4.8.   The overall rate of growth during the period was 20 per cent, but as table 4.10 shows there were marked contrasts within the county partly reflecting the great diversity in the amount of industry present in the areas.   Oakham, for instance, had only 300 people working in manufacturing in 1948, and in this situation the arrival of a single branch plant can easily launch the growth-rate into three figures. Two areas performed notably poorly mainly for structural reasons, these being Hinckley and Market Harborough, but elsewhere the fastest growth occurred in the smaller towns and not in Leicester itself.

The initial accounts are described in tables 4.11 and 4.12.   The figures refer to operatives alone since data on office employment was not available in 1947, but this factor should have little effect on the conclusions except to slightly increase the apparent importance of new firms over permanent plants.(9)   The figures in columns one and two of

74

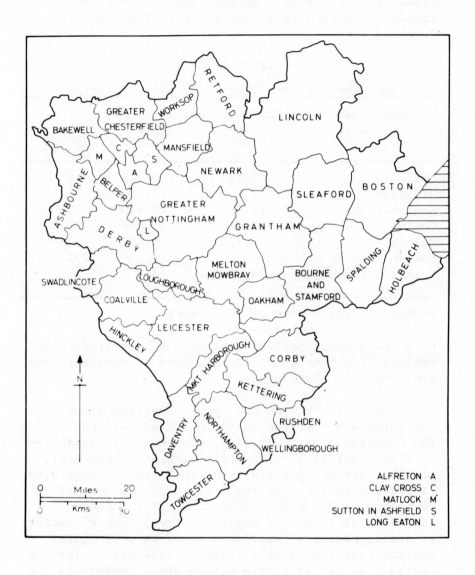

Figure 4.1　Employment exchange areas in the East
Midlands 1967

table 4.13 show the same pattern of change for operatives as that for all employment except for the declines recorded in the Market Harborough and Hinckley areas.

Table 4.10

Employment growth 1947-67 in Leicestershire

| Employment exchange area | Employment in 1948 | Employment in 1967 | % change |
|---|---|---|---|
| Leicester | 101,190 | 117,270 | 16 |
| Hinckley | 15,440 | 16,100 | 4 |
| Loughborough | 19,550 | 25,330 | 30 |
| Coalville | 6,000 | 11,000 | 83 |
| Melton | 3,970 | 4,470 | 50 |
| Oakham | 310 | 1,040 | 231 |
| Market Harborough | 3,410 | 3,450 | 1 |

Source of data:   Dept of Employment

Only the general postwar expansion of non-production employment prevented an overall loss of manufacturing employment in these areas.

The contrast between the more industrial areas and the rural areas is continued in tables 4.11 and 4.12. The importance of the various components is relatively stable across the industrial areas of Leicester, Loughborough and Hinckley, but much greater diversity is present in the more rural areas of Melton, Market Harborough and Oakham. Coalville, as the name suggests, is largely a coalfield area, with a scatter of small industrial settlements and is in an intermediate position in this respect. The reason for the contrast is partly that outlined above concerning the potential impact of individual establishments in small areas. Also important, however, is the probabilistic nature of the processes of growth, entry and closure. As will be shown in subsequent chapters a 'law of large numbers' effect tends to average out random

76

Table 4.11

The composition of employment within Leicestershire 1967

| Employment exchange area | Permanent establishments | | New branches of Leics. firms | | New firms | | New in-moving establishments | | Total |
|---|---|---|---|---|---|---|---|---|---|
| | No. | % | No. | % | No. | % | No. | % | |
| Leicester | 65,946 | 77 | 6,040 | 7 | 11,196 | 13 | 2,653 | 3 | 85,835 |
| Hinckley | 11,091 | 78 | 951 | 7 | 1,960 | 14 | 167 | 1 | 14,169 |
| Loughborough | 6,000 | 86 | 1,057 | 6 | 1,166 | 6 | 330 | 2 | 18,653 |
| Coalville | 6,630 | 81 | 305 | 4 | 584 | 7 | 662 | 8 | 8,181 |
| Melton | 1,751 | 52 | 319 | 10 | 235 | 7 | 1,005 | 31 | 3,310 |
| Oakham | 76 | 9 | 517 | 58 | 202 | 22 | 100 | 11 | 895 |
| Market Harborough | 1,944 | 83 | 32 | 1 | 332 | 14 | 45 | 2 | 2,353 |

Source of data: Establishment records

fluctuations in areas with sufficiently large numbers of plants, but elsewhere the random fluctuations can dominate employment change. The randomness is derived largely from the unpredictable variations in the distribution of entrepreneurs and in the ability or success of managements within individual firms.

Permanent establishments account for close to 80 per cent of employment in most of the areas (table 4.11). If the local branches formed since 1947 are added to the permanent plants then we have a measure of the expansion undertaken locally by permanent firms. The employment contributed in these ways by permanent firms is close to 85 per cent in the major areas except for Loughborough where the proportion is higher. The greater proportionate importance of permanent firms in Loughborough is largely due to the relatively small amount of employment contributed by new firms. This will be shown later to be the result of a sig-nificantly low entry-rate, and will form an important piece of evidence in the attempt to explain why entry-rates differ widely between areas. In two rural areas the importance of locally generated expansion is much less, mainly because of incoming branch plants and subsidiary firms using local surplus labour. In Melton the decline of an old established ironworks, which has subsequently closed, was also partly responsible.

The new branches of local firms were virtually all formed by companies which were already in existence within the area by 1947. In addition, the branches in the industrial areas are mostly derived from parent companies within the same area. They are thus very local forms of expansion, often little more than departments which happen not to be contiguous to the main factory. In the rural areas the opposite is generally true since branches have been formed, mainly by Leicester companies, to tap pockets of labour in surrounding areas. Only a very small number of branches are involved however, and most of the employ-ment in branch plants formed by local firms has occurred in more distant areas, often in development areas.

Establishments set up since 1947 by companies based outside the county are of most importance in areas where declines in either agriculture or mining led to the availability of labour. In the Melton and Oakham areas close to half of the employment in 1967 was in factories which had been established by companies based outside the immediate area, either in Leicester-shire or beyond. In Coalville the proportion was 10 per cent but elsewhere it was of little importance.

The same set of evidence, but in terms of numbers of establishments rather than of employment, is contained in table 4.12. The permanent establishments comprise a remarkably stable proportion of the total in all areas except the most rural which is Oakham. It is the case that the number of establishments has been remarkably stable over time as well as between areas. Since the proportion of permanent plants is close to half this means that about half of the establishments in 1947 have subsequently closed and been replaced by a very similar number of new plants. Most of the closures and the new plants consist of independent firms, the majority of which are small. The overall picture is one of a consistent number of plants being maintained while an active turnover of firms and establishments is occurring, but occurring in such a way as to balance numbers of openings and closures. This turnover is more active than most people would imagine, presumably because the overall balance con-ceals the underlying change.

In the two most rural areas (Melton and Oakham) changes were more obvious, not only because in-move-ment was occurring but also because the closure-rates were mainly those of very small concerns, such as blacksmiths or bakeries, representing the last of the formerly widespread rural industries to suffer from the trend towards centralisation. It is interesting to note that in some countries, of which Germany is a

79

Table 4.12

Numbers of establishments in component categories Leicestershire 1967

| Employment exchange area | Permanent establishments | | New branches of Leics. firms | | New firms | | New in-moving establishments | | Total |
|---|---|---|---|---|---|---|---|---|---|
| | No. | % | No. | % | No. | % | No. | % | |
| Leicester | 761 | 47 | 138 | 8 | 685 | 42 | 40 | 3 | 1,624 |
| Hinckley | 102 | 48 | 22 | 10 | 83 | 39 | 5 | 3 | 212 |
| Loughborough | 106 | 51 | 24 | 12 | 73 | 35 | 4 | 2 | 207 |
| Coalville | 62 | 50 | 13 | 10 | 37 | 30 | 12 | 10 | 124 |
| Melton | 23 | 49 | 4 | 9 | 18 | 38 | 3 | 4 | 48 |
| Oakham | 6 | 33 | 5 | 28 | 7 | 39 | * | - | 18 |
| Market Harborough | 30 | 53 | 4 | 7 | 23 | 40 | * | - | 57 |

Source of data: Establishment records

Notes

* These numbers have been amalgamated with those of branches of Leicestershire firms for reasons of confidentiality

80

notable example, the craft industries have not suffered such mortal declines, partly because they have a stronger institutional framework in the Handwerk system (Bannock, 1976).

Table 4.12 also shows that in virtually all areas 40 per cent of the establishments were owned by firms founded since 1947. The vast majority of these establishments were in fact small single plant companies founded by local entrepreneurs. Only on the coalfield was the proportion significantly below 40 per cent, in this case mainly because of the relative importance of new branch plants. Branch plants and transfers from beyond Leicestershire were numerically insignificant in all areas except Coalville, but in the rural areas the few which did arrive tended to have a large impact on local employment.

The construction of employment accounts for employment change requires figures for employment in closures and these are provided in column one of table 4.13. Although half of the establishments in production in 1947 closed by 1967 these were on average smaller than the survivors, and as a result the employment in the closures was only 26 per cent of total employment in 1947. This is taken as the measure of employment lost in closures, although it does not of course measure the employment which would notionally have existed if the establishments had remained open. The latter is a hypothetical concept open to many influences and no attempt has been made to measure it.

The proportion of 1947 employment lost is close to the county average in most areas, with the notable exception of a very low rate in Market Harborough. The coincidental fact that the permanent plant employment declined drastically in that area points towards the possibility that closure-rates may be linked to the performance of surviving or new establishments in the same area. The justification for expecting a relationship of this type would come via a general shortage of labour. If pressure is exerted

Table 4.13

Employment accounts for Leicestershire 1947-67

| Employment exchange area | Jobs lost in closures (1947 employment) | | Net change (employment) | | New jobs (col. 1 + col. 3) | Net change in permanent plants | Employment as % of col. 5 No. of operatives | | In-movement since 1947 |
|---|---|---|---|---|---|---|---|---|---|
| | | | | | | | New branches of Leics. firms | New firms | |
| | No. | % | No. | % | | | | | |
| | 1 | 2 | 3 | 4 | 5 | 6 | 7 | 8 | 9 |
| Leicester | 22,534 | 27 | 3,124 | 4 | 25,658 | 22 | 24 | 44 | 10 |
| Hinckley | 4,929 | 32 | -1,041 | -7 | 3,888 | 20 | 25 | 50 | 5 |
| Loughborough | 2,919 | 17 | 1,587 | 9 | 4,506 | 44 | 23 | 26 | 7 |
| Coalville | 1,383 | 24 | 2,488 | 44 | 3,871 | 60 | 8 | 15 | 17 |
| Melton | 545 | 22 | 800 | 32 | 1,345 | (-16) | 24 | 17 | 75 |
| Oakham | 79 | 37 | 734 | 456 | 813 | (-1) | 64 | 25 | 12 |
| Market Harborough | 131 | 5 | -404 | -15 | -273 | (-250) | 12 | 122 | 16 |
| Total | 32,520 | 26 | 7,288 | 6 | 39,808 | 25 | 23 | 39 | 13 |

Source of data: Establishment records

on weak firms through competition for labour then greater numbers may be forced to close. They might either be unable to obtain labour or alternatively be forced to pay higher wages, but in either case the outcome could eventually be closure. The same pressures might also lead firms to areas where labour was more plentiful, but with the data used in this study it is not possible to separate the two processes.(10) The other side of the process would be if high closure-rates occurred for some autonomous reason, structural or otherwise. High closure-rates would release labour and place less pressure on growing firms to 'export' their growth.

The evidence for this theory, obtained by examining the relationship between closure and growth within other areas of Leicestershire, is weak but in the right direction. The main problem is that there are other systematic influences on the spatial incidence of closures, especially those of industrial structure and size structure, and allowance should be made for these. A rigorous test would require a larger number of base areas. Further research is called for, but the evidence at this point is at least suggestive.

The differences of employment in closures among the more industrial areas show clear signs of the influence of industrial structure. The major industries with high rates of closure were footwear and clothing and the areas with most employment in these industries especially Hinckley, had the highest rates of closure.

The employment accounts in table 4.13 are set out in the same way as in previous sections with new employment defined as the sum of employment lost in closures plus net change. This table demonstrates the variety of experience which occurred in the seven areas, even when a similar end result was achieved. The end result can be measured in a slightly different way by expressing the new employment (as defined above) as a percentage of total employment in 1947. This forms a measure of jobs created after making allowance for the

level of closures. It is thus an indication of the
success of each area in generating, and retaining new
employment given its level of closures. On this
measure Leicester emerges with 30 per cent compared
with 25 per cent in Hinckley and Loughborough. The
remaining areas, other than Market Harborough, all
have a score of over 50 per cent reflecting the influx
of new employment from sources outside their boundaries. Both Hinckley and Loughborough were relatively
poor generators of new employment. In the former case
a poor industrial structure retarded growth, and in
the latter, a low entry-rate meant low employment in
new firms. Both areas, nevertheless, had persistent
shortages of labour and attracted little immigrant
employment.

The performance of Leicester was formed in a very
similar way to that of Hinckley with local permanent
firms contributing slightly under half of the new
employment in net in situ expansion or in local branch
plants, and new firms about half also. The higher in-
movement figure for Leicester was largely due to the
special case of a large branch of the English Electric
company being formed on the site of a former government gas turbine research station. In the Loughborough area the low entry-rate of new firms meant
that permanent firms were proportionately more important. Although the industrial structure was rather
more favourable than in Hinckley the rate of creation
of new employment was no higher, and this suggests
that the low entry-rate of new firms did lower the
rate of aggregate growth in employment rather than
merely releasing labour for further expansion in other
components.

In the more rural areas the importance of new firms
is relatively low, again largely because their impact
is overshadowed by incoming branch plants or subsidiary firms. The dominance of individual large
plants shows itself in the erratic contribution made
by permanent establishments. In the Coalville area
the permanent plants dominated new employment, but in

the other rural areas their effect was negative. The
great importance of in-movement in Melton can be
traced to a single firm, Petfoods Ltd. This moved
from the Slough headquarters of its parent company
(Mars) in 1952 with under a hundred employees. It has
since expanded many times over, and now employs over
2,000 people.


4.5   CONCLUSION

The sections above have necessarily been detailed
accounts of change within a single region, but what
general conclusion can be drawn? New firms provided
over half of the net employment increase in the East
Midlands. The importance of this component in other
regions will depend on both the birth-rate of new
firms and their subsequent growth. The former aspect
is dealt with in chapter eight. The importance of new
firms was variable at the sub-regional scale within
the East Midlands, and even more so at the local scale.
The greater erraticness at the local scale is likely
to be a general feature, caused not by variation in
birth-rates but rather by the more variable performance of other components, especially industrial movement. The evidence from the East Midlands outlined in
subsequent chapters suggests also that variability at
the sub-regional scale is likely to be a feature of
the new firms component in most regions.

   Most new employment was generated by permanent
firms. The evidence on the net expansion of employment in permanent firms pointed towards two factors of
general relevance. Firstly, industrial structure is
important, and areas dominated by nationally declining
industries had somewhat slower employment growth in
this component (but not actual decline in most cases).
Secondly, and more important was the labour factor.
Areas with labour shortages tended to divert high
proportions of their expansion in permanent firms into
branch plants. Some of these were set up near to the
parent plants, but many went to destinations outside

the region. These factors were evident at all scales, although at the very local scale the erratic perform-ance of individual plants made a considerable impact on total employment especially in the more rural areas.

The proportion of employment lost in closures again appeared to reflect industrial structure, although a large number of jobs were involved in all areas. The fact that net change represents a balance between a large loss of employment in closures and a large number of new jobs is probably true of virtually all areas. Again, random variability is of increased importance at very local scales in rural areas, but at larger scales this is damped down to reveal only the more general factor of industrial structure.

Locally generated employment accounted for virtually all net change in the East Midlands, but this is one aspect which is not true of all regions. The pattern of industrial movement within the UK means that indus-trial movement accounts for a large amount of new employment in the Assisted Areas but is of negligible importance in the major source regions. Only a small minority of new jobs in the East Midlands came in with moving establishments, but at the sub-regional and local scales this component was of great importance in some areas.

The principal finding of this chapter has been the importance of new firms. Although individually small these had a critical impact on the rate of employment growth. Without them the region would have grown at only half the national average. With them it achieved a rate considerably in excess of the average. New firms are important not mainly because of their size or rate of growth, although these can be considerable; the more important feature is the sheer volume of new firms. With almost 3,000 of them in the East Midlands they contribute a large number of jobs in aggregate, despite their individually small size.

NOTES

(1)   The actual rate of growth in the East Midlands
was 21 per cent compared with a UK figure of 15 per
cent.   The expected rate of growth, given the initial
composition of industry was 11.4 per cent.   These
calculations use figures from the Department of Employment (ER II) returns, and make allowance for the
changes in the Standard Industrial Classification
which occurred in 1958.   The expected figure was
calculated at a level of industrial disaggregation
corresponding to Minimum List Headings but with some
amalgamations necessitated by the 1958 changes.
(2)   Figure 4.1 has amalgamated a number of small
areas to form 'Greater Nottingham' and 'Greater
Chesterfield' respectively.
(3)   Throughout this study Leicestershire refers to
the present administrative county, and thus includes
the former county of Rutland.   On figure 4.1 Leicestershire includes the employment exchange areas of
Leicester, Hinckley, Coalville, Loughborough, Melton
Mowbray, Oakham and Market Harborough.
(4)   Figures were compiled using Department of Employment figures, excluding the Chesterfield area (described as Greater Chesterfield on figure 4.1) and
also the steelworks at Corby.   In the case of Chesterfield the data for subsequent analyses is unavailable
and thus this area is omitted.   The steelworks
dominate employment change in Northamptonshire and
should be treated separately as a special case.
(5)   These figures are derived from the 50 x 50
origin/destination matrix supplied by the Department
of Industry in connection with the Howard Report.   In
some cases of inter-county moves numbers of establishments are given without employment.   In these cases it
has been assumed that the moving establishments were
of average size for the region as a whole.
(6)   Virtually all of the local branch plants originated from permanent firms rather than from new firms.
(7)   Labour was in extremely short supply in Central
Northamptonshire and in Leicestershire.   In both areas
the unemployment rates were the region's lowest,

averaging 0.7 per cent through the period. Female
activity rates were the region's highest at almost 40
per cent in both cases. In other parts of Northamptonshire (especially Corby) unemployment was much
higher, and in Corby the female participation rate was
the lowest of any area in the region, at only half the
level experienced in Central Northamptonshire.
(8) The highest average unemployment levels in the
region over the period were in South Lincolnshire 2
per cent - 3 per cent and on the Nottinghamshire coalfield 1.3 per cent. Female activity rates were low in
all coalfield areas (i.e. Nottinghamshire and Derbyshire) at 25 per cent, and average in Lincolnshire at
30 per cent.
(9) This slight distortion results from the fact that
new firms are generally smaller than permanent plants
and also because small plants generally have lower
proportions of white-collar and other non-production
staff.
(10) From the Howard Report data on industrial movement it can be deduced that only a small proportion of
the closures can have opened up outside the country.
It seems probable that very few did so. See note (1)
in chapter seven.

# PART III

# THE NATURE OF THE PROCESSES OF CHANGE

# 5 The initial location of new firms

In the understanding of the processes underlying
spatial variations in industrial change, and those
underlying the development of the geographical distribution of industry, the location of new firms (1)
forms a keystone.  Studies of other aspects of location behaviour such as relocation, or the location of
branch plants point to the fact that such behaviour
strongly reflects the original location of the firm.
In view of this strategic position in the chain of
understanding it is something of a paradox that among
the wealth of research on industrial location there is
little on the initial location of new firms.  This
omission has probably been conditioned in some cases
by a belief that similar factors affect all types of
locational activity, and in perhaps all cases, by a
belief in the insignificance of new firms in employment terms.  Some studies have been aimed at a wide
spectrum of types of firm but have biased their
samples towards branch plants with a high cut-off
point for plant-size.  In other cases the traditional
factors assumed to affect location have appeared to
affect all types of firm alike.  This has sometimes
occurred because questions in surveys have prejudged
the issue in favour of such factors by asking respondents to select important factors from a given list
of possibilities.  The instructions are rarely
specific enough to ensure that the factors indicated
were actually relevant to the actual origins of the
individual firm, rather than merely being of importance to industry in general. (2)

In order to construct a picture of the location
behaviour of new firms, the obvious starting point is
an enquiry into the circumstances in which such firms
are started.  This is undertaken in the next section
and leads to a hypothesis on location behaviour which
is subsequently tested.  The evidence on which this

is based is mostly drawn from the postwar East Midlands, but using studies in other countries it is
possible to reach the view that the process discovered
in the East Midlands is typical of a variety of
industrial countries, and other time periods.


## 5.1 ENTREPRENEURS AND THE FOUNDING OF FIRMS

### 5.1.1 The initial size of firms

One of the most characteristic and pervading features
of new firms is their very small initial size. For
Leicestershire in the period between 1947 and 1955 it
has been possible to obtain a complete list of all the
firms founded. The evidence of the questionnaire
survey (appendix II), and of records of surviving new
firms in the following decade in Leicestershire,
suggest that these firms are typical of both the
region as a whole, and the full period from 1947-67.

The distribution of initial sizes of the independent
firms is presented in figure 5.1. Like all industrial
size distributions it is very highly skewed to the
right, indicating a small number of very large firms
and an extremely large number of very small ones.
This distribution which is approximately lognormal in
form is difficult to portray on normal graph paper,
but can be displayed on log-probability paper. The
latter, which is used in figure 5.1 and in subsequent
graphs, has a logarithmic horizontal axis and a vertical axis with uneven spacing. Together these have
the effect of portraying lognormal distributions as
straight lines. This form of graph, which becomes
easy to use with a little practice, has a number of
useful qualities. The first is that the geometric
mean (approximating to both the median and mode of
the distribution) can be read immediately by tracing
across from the 50 per cent point on the vertical
axis, to the line on the graph, and then down to the
horizontal axis. The geometric mean of the Leicestershire distribution on figure 5.1 is, for instance,

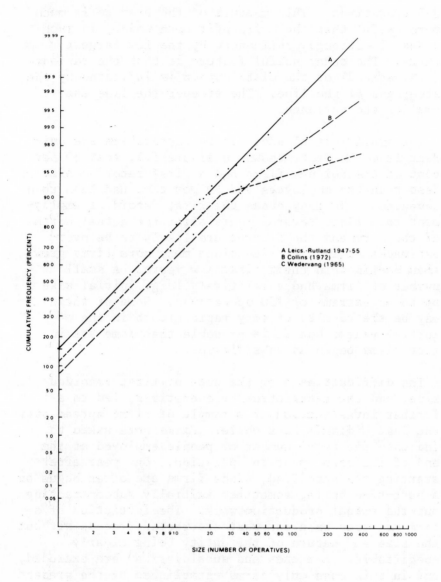

Figure 5.1   Initial size distribution of new firms set
            up in Leicestershire 1947-67 compared with
            two other studies
Source of data:  Establishment records

3.5 operatives. This measure of the average is much more useful that the arithmetic mean which, in such cases, is strongly influenced by the few largest firms. The other useful feature is that the variance (i.e. spread) of the distribution is indicated by the steepness of the line. The steeper the line the smaller the variance.

The small initial sizes in Leicestershire are evident from the fact, shown in figure 5.1, that 80 per cent of the 681 new firms had a first recorded size of less than ten employees and 90 per cent had less than seventeen. In many cases the first record of employment took place several years after the actual birth of the firm and the figures are likely to be over-estimates of initial size since many more firms grew than declined in their first few years. A small number of firms had a relatively large initial size up to an extreme of 150 operatives. Some of these may be the results of very rapid growth in the initial years, but it is probable that some are in fact firms begun as subsidiaries.

The difficulties over the date of first recorded size, and the restriction to operatives, led to a further investigation of a sample of firms spread over the East Midlands as a whole. Firms were asked to indicate the total number of people employed at the end of the first year in operation. One year after starting was specified, since firms are often begun on a part-time basis, sometimes initially subcontracting out the actual production work. The initiation of a firm may thus be a somewhat protracted process without the size and nature of the entity being clearly specifiable. Branches and subsidiaries were excluded, and in this case only firms established by the present owners were included to avoid the possibility of respondents stating the size on takeover rather than the original foundation size. The size distribution figure 5.2 is approximately lognormal with a mean of five employees and 90 per cent of the cases starting with less than twenty-five employees. The sizes are

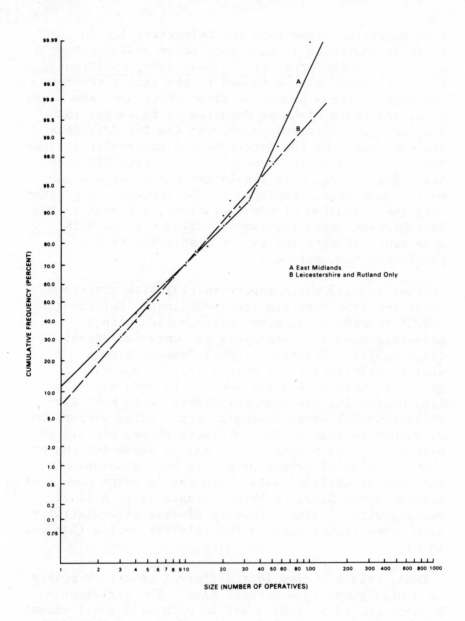

Figure 5.2　Initial size distributions of new firms
　　　　　　East Midlands and Leicestershire 1947-67

Source of data:　Questionnaire survey

thus a little larger than for Leicestershire in
1947-55, and there is also a relative deficiency of
new firms in the upper tail (above forty employees).
This deficiency may be caused by the exclusion from
the East Midlands sample of firms which had been taken
over, and these might be expected to be larger than
average.  The differences between the two data sets
are not caused by the more extended geographical frame
since Leicestershire firms within the East Midlands
are, if anything, a little larger again, with a geometric mean of 5.5 employees.  The reasons are presumably the inclusion of non-operatives, although in the
East Midlands case the sample includes firms with a
wide range of ages and is not restricted to any
particular time period.

Other studies which report initial size distributions describe very similar conditions.  Collins
(1972) records a lognormal distribution with a
geometric mean of 6 employees for Ontario 1961-65
(figure 5.1).  Wedervang (1965) demonstrates a
similar disribution for Norway 1930-37 but with a
geometric mean of 4.4 employees.  In both cases
'employees' include non-operatives.  Also both distributions, although having a very similar dispersion
of values to that of East Midlands firms, contain an
excess of large plants.  This can be accounted for by
the inclusion of branch plants in both studies.  In
the case of Collins' data there are 'a large number of
foreign owned American branch plants'.(3)  A final
example with an almost exactly similar size-distribu-
tion comes from Sweden in the interwar period (Dahmen,
1970)

Thus, evidence from four different countries points
to a highly consistent conclusion.  The differences
between the sets of data are in each case small enough
to be easily explained in terms of composition of the
data sets, including industrial structure.  The
average new firm appears to start business with about
five employees, while the vast majority begin with ten
or less.  In addition, a number of studies for the
United States in the interwar period indicate a

similarly small starting size, although the data is not directly comparable being in terms of value rather than employment.(4)

Returning to the early postwar evidence from Leicestershire, it can be seen in figure 5.3 that the small initial size of new firms holds in a wide variety of industries. The geometric mean varies from two or three employees in the case of wood products, printing and engineering industries, up to nine or ten in clothing and footwear. These are the main industries with enough observations to construct complete size distributions. This also means that it is these industries in which there are large numbers of small new firms, but it is not the case that Leicestershire has an industrial structure which is particularly biased towards small firms. From official statistics on the size of establishments (Business Monitor PA1003, 1971) it can be seen that most industries are dominated by small plants, and that in only a very few tightly defined industries does the proportion of very small establishments fall below less than half the national average.(5)

5.1.2   The entrepreneurs (6)

The aggregate information on size describes only one facet of the initiation of firms and a more rounded impression can be gleaned from a number of studies of entrepreneurs, small firms and industrial organisations. The most penetrating of these is a study by N.R. Smith of fifty-two Michigan firms founded since the last war.

Smith conducted a series of 'in depth' interviews with entrepreneurs and concluded that there were two characteristic types of entrepreneur, the craftsman and the opportunist. The former, comprising 65 per cent of his sample, tended to have skilled working class backgrounds and a technical education not usually extending beyond school. Success at work was characteristic, although always in the mechanical

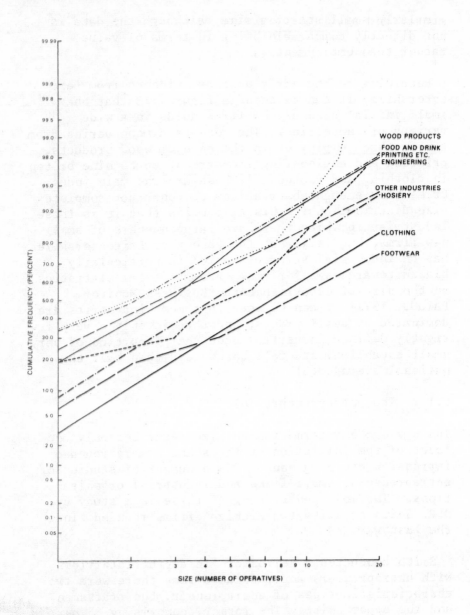

Figure 5.3  Initial size distribution of new firms by
major industrial categories
Leicestershire 1947-55
Source of data:  Establishment records

sense, and such entrepreneurs never rose to management levels, nor identified with management. Craftsmen-entrepreneurs usually had no long-term ambition to start their own business, but instead founded it at a time in their lives when few alternative ways of further developing their talents were available. Even so, some catalytic event was necessary to induce them to take the plunge into business. Their firms were often started on a part-time basis, using only their own capital or that of close friends. Loans from banks or finance houses were avoided at all costs. Customers were obtained by personal contact, and often customers needed to have placed orders before the decision to start the business would be taken. In short, such entrepreneurs had little business experience and little confidence or capital. Firms were frequently started along with a few close friends. Following its foundation the firm continued to be run within limited horizons and constrained ambitions. Growth was slow and almost all business was done by personal contact with known and trusted individuals.

The opportunistic entrepreneur provides a contrast to the craftsman in almost every sense. The background was usually middle class, often a family owning a small business. A much more rounded education was characteristic, commonly extended to college, and if not, then to nightschool where the entrepreneur was often a social and sporting success, as well as an academic success. Work experience was similarly more varied, usually at management level, and involving knowledge of marketing and administration. The ambition to found a company was a long-held one, and was taken at some time when career prospects were slowed down or temporarily blocked. No catalytic event was needed and the decision was made on a once and for all basis. The actual initiation of the firm was marked by flexibility. Capital was raised in any way possible, and the firm could be started in unfamiliar trades or locations if the entrepreneur considered it expedient. The subsequent development of the firm was also flexible and open minded with an active

99

policy to search for new products and markets. Most
dramatically Smith observed that within his small
sample firms run by opportunistic-entrepreneurs grew
twelve times as fast as those run by craftsmen-entrepreneurs.

Many of Smith's observations have been corroborated
by other studies, and his descriptions particularly of
the craftsmen-entrepreneur fit the entrepreneurs
interviewed for the East Midlands study (described
below) surprisingly well. One study which gives
independent support to the notion that this description of entrepreneurs is a general one applicable to
many countries is that of Dahmen (1970) for Sweden.
In a subset of large new firms in Sweden 55 per cent
were founded by ex-manual workers. Among all new
firms the proportion must have been significantly
larger than this.

An indication that the craftsman-type of entrepreneur may be proportionately more common in Britain
than in Smith's sample, is provided by a recent study
showing the educational background of the director
managers of 133 small firms (Merret Cymax Associates,
1972). Seventy per cent of these had no post-school
qualifications, and only 10 per cent had a degree.
This was the case even though many of those in the
sample were not founders, but were second or subsequent generation owners. It is perhaps reasonable to
expect that the children of entrepreneurs would tend
to have more extended educations than their parents,
and thus that the founders of firms had very little
post-school experience. Somewhat unexpectedly this
study also found that out of a small sample of
eighteen founders of firms only eleven (60 per cent)
had had previous direct experience in the same
trade.(7)

Further evidence on the occupational background of
entrepreneurs in the prewar USA is presented by
A.R. Oxenfeldt (1943). In a study of the owners of
362 US footwear manufacturers it was found that 62

per cent had previously worked in footwear manufacturing firms. If those owning firms as a first gainful occupation are excluded (these will presumably be the children of existing owners in the main), the figure increases to 77 per cent. Oxenfeldt also cites a study by J.E. Wood, which showed that 96 per cent of silk firms in Paterson NY founded between 1926 and 1936, were begun by men previously engaged in the same industry. G.E. Oxenfeldt investigated the backgrounds of the founders of thirty-nine of the seventy-four largest new corporations founded in the USA from 1933 to 1939. The entrepreneurs were found to have previously been presidents, directors or upper management in twenty-nine of the cases. The other ten were described as 'engineers'.(8) Additionally, the majority manufactured the same or a similar product, while 13 per cent started firms in completely unrelated fields. Finally, Oxenfeldt states that 'the automobile industry furnishes many familiar illustrations of executives in established concerns setting up businesses in the same industry as their own', and gives Walter Chrysler as one example. These examples fit Smith's description of the opportunistic-entrepreneur, having a management background and both the willingness and the ability to raise capital. If Smith's descriptions have general applicability then the larger new firms will presumably be founded by this type of entrepreneur.

One interesting aspect of new firms (although not of direct relevance to the current discussion) is that of innovation. It is sometimes suggested that the major benefit derived from new firms comes in this respect. This judgement is probably misplaced in several senses, although it is true that many important innovations during this century have originated from individual inventor-entrepreneurs (Little, 1977). The vast majority of new firms appear not to be innovative. Dahmen (1970 p.204) is emphatic on this point. In the UK context Little (1977) has attempted to trace all of the firms founded since 1950 on the basis of some 'new technology-based innovation. He managed to find only

105 cases, employing in aggregate some 16,000 people
in 1974. If it assumed that the East Midlands is more
or less representative of the UK then there are
probably about 36,000 new firms currently in existence
which have been established since 1950, employing
700,000 in all. This means that technologically
innovating firms may only account for about 2 per cent
of all employment in new firms. New technology-based
innovations are not the only innovations, but when the
net is cast wide definitions become problematic. A
more marketable pair of pliers or a new dress design
are both examples of innovations in the widest sense.
The East Midlands study (reported below) led to the
impression that most new firms began life without any
innovation, although the more successful ones later
evolved their own proprietory products which would
often have some element of originality. All new
firms, innovators and otherwise, are of value to
regional and even national economies, as long as they
are competitive. In the regional context, if an area
contains non-innovating firms which are competitive
and replace other firms located elsewhere, then a net
transfer of production and employment will accrue to
that region. The same argument can of course be
transferred to the national level.

5.1.3 Location decisions: case studies from published
sources

Case studies of the development of new firms in the
published literature usually describe entrepreneurs
who fit Smith's 'opportunist' category. This is to be
expected since the firms concerned are typically the
large and fast growing ones which have attracted
attention as notable successes. They are by their
nature, therefore, unrepresentative of new firms as a
whole.

A number of examples are described in Edwards and
Townsend (1964). One such example is the Dowty
Group Ltd founded in 1931 by Sir George Dowty who was
then working as a design draughtsman for the Gloster

Aircraft Co. The business began with £300 and three employees in a Cheltenham garage, making 'a new and unconventional undercarriage system'. He (Sir George Dowty) states 'since I did not have the money to move elsewhere, I started my business where I was'. In many respects, a variety of jobs, flexibility in products (e.g. making metal garden plates when demand was slack), and active sales promotion, as well as borrowing commercially most of his starting capital, Dowty exemplifies many of the qualities found by Smith among the Michigan 'opportunist' entrepreneurs.

A second example is that of the Modern Equipment Company of Taunton founded by N.D. Svenson and his wife (Edwards and Townsend 1964). The company making indoor clothes drying cabinets was founded in 1956. Production was initially subcontracted out, but in 1957 a company was founded with £1,000 (£400 of which was borrowed). Assembly was begun part-time in the garden shed, with the products being sold through commission agents. By 1961 turnover was £300,000 p.a. Again, in terms of a background with previous management and business experience, long-term ambition, and starting in an unfamiliar trade the Svensons fit the category of the opportunist entrepreneur. Certainly the very rapid growth of the firm is characteristic.

Some of the United Kingdom's largest firms were begun on a small scale by entrepreneurs with experience in the same trade. Hawker Siddely (now part of Rolls Royce 1970 Ltd), or rather its antecedent aircraft companies, were mostly founded on a small scale by engineers who were also flying enthusiasts. The General Electric Company (now part of the GEC-AEI-English Electric empire) began in 1885 as an electrical warehouse in East London. Similarly, this process has been described with reference to science based industries in which highly qualified staff leave established firms to found new ventures (Branton, 1966). They do so because the limitations of capital and management within the original firm preclude the development at an early date of a promising new

103

opportunity. This last example would provide support
for the existence of a third type of entrepreneur outlined (but not developed further) by Smith, the
'inventor entrepreneur' mainly interested in developing ideas rather than in business or profit.

Most of these cases began business on a small scale
despite being characteristic of Smith's opportunistic
entrepreneur. However, the GEC example (for which
the initial size is not given) illustrates a way in
which relatively large new firms can be initiated.
Firms in wholesaling or other sectors of the economy
with interests close to manufacturing may start new
firms in manufacturing using their own accumulated
profits and borrowed capital which is easier to raise
when businesses are already running successfully.
Many confectionery firms appear to have begun manufacturing in this way, and the firms which now form
the British Sugar Corporation were similarly begun
with resources drawn from existing businesses (Watts
1971). Such firms may be properly regarded as
subsidiaries, and certainly the line between subsidiaries and independent new firms is difficult to draw.

It is difficult to say whether or not the formation
of large firms from small beginnings is still occurring at its former rate, since it takes at least two
decades for the fact to become apparent. Gloomy
prognostications about the effects of high marginal
tax rates on enterprise are probably a perennial
feature of life, and fail to take account of the
desire for independence as a spur to founding a firm,
or the tiny amounts of personal capital which often
suffice. That some firms founded by the 'opportunist-
type' of entrepreneur are still being set up is not
open to doubt, and examples of these appear in the
press from time to time. Two such cases are the Extra
Manufacturing Co. of Doncaster employing thirty, and
Darburn Ltd a small electrical company in London, both
of which were founded within the last seven years
(Guardian, June 6 1975). Both of these were located
very close to the founder's homes, in trades with

which they were familiar. Despite the fact that both
founders had backgrounds which could be broadly described as middle class, neither had wished to raise
any capital from the banks, unlike Smith's opportunists.

Even more certain is the fact that several substantial companies, within the top thousand in the UK
have been started since the last war. International
Caravans Ltd, M.Y. Dart Ltd and Condor International
Ltd are three examples.(9)  It is likely that other
similar cases exist, and that many more successes have
been bought up by major companies and now exist as
subsidiaries within larger groups. In the more
specialised case of new technology-based firms the
evidence, from Britain, Germany and the USA is that,
if anything, the rate of formation has increased in
the last decade (Little, 1977).

The most notable locational feature in these case
studies is the tendency for the firms to be established in the founder's home area. For the craftsman-
entrepreneur Smith suggested implicitly that local
locations would be chosen. These examples suggest
that this may be characteristic of the firms of
opportunist-entrepreneurs also. This discussion on
entrepreneurs and the ways in which firms are founded
has necessarily been somewhat diffuse. However, it
has been possible to construct a picture of entrepreneurial behaviour from which a location hypothesis
can be constructed.


## 5.2  A LOCATION HYPOTHESIS FOR NEW FIRMS

It is hypothesised that the founders of new firms will
rarely make active location decisions. Instead, new
firms are located within the entrepreneur's home area.
Also, the industry in which the firm operates will
normally be the one in which the entrepreneur previously worked. The decision which is made is whether
or not to go into business; the location and form of

production are to a large extent predetermined. The reasoning underlying this hypothesis is as follows.

1    Firms are usually begun with very little capital (hence their small initial size), and the entrepreneur will not normally want to dissipate any of his own capital by moving house.(10)    It is not easy to raise capital commercially to finance new small firms.  Hence, even the apparent minority of entrepreneurs willing to borrow commercially will usually have to begin with very limited capital resources.

2    Firms are tied to the home area of the entrepreneur because his principal initial asset in trading is a knowledge of local markets and a measure of goodwill.  The knowledge of the market appears to be crucial in the decision to begin production, entrepreneurs often not starting fully until after initial orders are secured.  Such market knowledge is usually gained through personal contacts which will normally be local.

3    The necessity of minimising the risks involved in starting production will similarly be expected to induce an entrepreneur to capitalise on his accumulated knowledge and skills.  This will lead him to produce in a familiar trade, but will also lead him to stay in the area where his knowledge of labour conditions, and in particular, reliable individuals, premises and suppliers is greatest.

4    The business may be begun on a part-time basis to decrease the risks involved.  If so, then its location is necessarily local while the entrepreneur maintains his (or her) existing job.  During this formative period many local ties will be forged which will increasingly make a later move unlikely.  The reason for initiating a new firm so cautiously is presumably the knowledge of the high probability of failure among small and young firms.

5    The entrepreneur has no reliable basis for seeking a cheaper or more profitable location as location theory suggests he should, since the size of

future output, the location of future markets, and
even in some cases the exact nature of the product are
all to some degree uncertain when the firm is first
started. One example may serve to illustrate this
uncertainty. A furniture firm, located just outside
Leicester and founded in the 1950s, developed a
specialism in the production of fairly high quality
specification furniture for schools which was purchas-
ed centrally by local authorities. The credit squeeze
in 1968 led to a fall in public investment in education, demand declined severely and new outlets were
sought. A large order for mass produced gas-fire
cabinets was obtained, to be supplied to a single
manufacturer twenty miles away. Thus, within a short
period of time most of the resources of the firm had
been switched to a different product, mass produced
rather than individually specified, and produced for a
market with a very different geography.

6 Lastly, the small initial size will usually
make a local location feasible. Skilled labour will
normally be available as the area will have other
firms in the same industry, since this is how the
trade of the new firm was determined. Even when
skilled labour of the right type is in locally short
supply it may be possible to persuade a few skilled
people to join the new firm. There is evidence to
suggest that job satisfaction is higher in small firms
even though wages are usually lower. (Revans 1956,
Cleland 1955). Providing the firm grows fairly slowly, other skilled workers can be trained within the
firm. Other requirements, such as premises, will also
be on such a small and undemanding scale that the new
firm finds it possible to squeeze into crevices in the
economy even in areas with apparent shortages. Also,
the small initial output may not require a geographically extensive sales area.

This hypothesis refers specifically to small new
firms, which form the majority of all new firms. In
addition to these, there exists a minority of firms
which have a larger initial size. These are cases
where the entrepreneur has, or can obtain, larger

amounts of capital. In the terms described by
N.R. Smith such entrepreneurs will be 'opportunists',
and thus willing to locate their firms in unfamiliar
areas if it is considered expedient. They may have
good reasons to remain in their home areas, similar to
those outlined above, but it is to be expected that
they would choose alternative locations if access to
raw materials or skilled labour availability or
similar clearly identifiable factors were seen to be
better somewhere else. However, although some entrepreneurs may plan ahead more sytematically than others
it will still not be easy to forecast future levels of
output and consequent market areas.

Taking the range of possibilities together, it is
expected that the great majority of locations will be
in the entrepreneur's home area, while the trade will
reflect his previous experience.

## 5.3 TESTING THE HYPOTHESIS ON A SAMPLE OF EAST
MIDLAND FIRMS

The constraints of the postal questionnaire method
meant that answers from a large number of respondents
could only be obtained on a small number of questions.
It was decided to test only the salient points of the
hypothesis by questionnaire and to subsequently elicit
a number of more detailed case studies by writing a
second time to a subsample of the respondents. Even
then, not all aspects could be tested.

### 5.3.1 The location

The most important point to ascertain was whether or
not the locations of most new firms were close to the
home of their founder (at the time of foundation).
The relevant question was directed solely to single
plant firms or to the main plant of a multi-plant
firm, and was in the following form:
    'Did the person(s) who founded this firm have any
strong association with this area which may have

influenced the decision to start the firm in this area and not elsewhere?'

It was not felt possible to specify further in the question either the nature of the association or the scale of area. The follow-up survey, it was hoped, would discover what the typical associations and areal ranges were. The question was applicable to 394 of the 731 respondents. The pattern of answers was:

| | | |
|---|---|---|
| Yes | 285 | |
| (i.e. local associations) | (81% of those able to answer) | |
| No | 67 | |
| (no local associations) | (19% of those able to answer) | |
| Don't know | 42 | |
| | 394 | |

In addition, a further eighty-one respondents answered the question since they regarded themselves as a separate firm rather than as a branch plant even though they were part of a larger group. In each case the firm had been bought by the latter and the foundation of the firm was as an independent unit. The answers in this case were:

| | | |
|---|---|---|
| Yes | 55 | (80% of those able to answer) |
| No | 14 | (20% of those able to answer) |
| Don't know | 12 | |
| | 81 | |

Pooling the two groups gives a total of 575 respondents. Of the 421 who could answer the question 81 per cent said 'Yes' and 19 per cent said 'No'. Given this result from a sample there is a 95 per cent probability that the true proportion for all firms in the region lies between 78 per cent and 84 per cent. The wider generality of this proportion is indicated by Dahmen (1970) who found that 80 per cent of Swedish firms had been located in this way.

There were no significant variations on this pattern of answers between geographical areas industries or initial sizes. The pattern of affirmative responses for counties was as indicated in table 5.1. The variations between counties are well within the limits

109

expected in random binomial fluctuations around the
mean of 81 per cent (0.05 probability level).

Table 5.1

Entrepreneurs with local associations by county

| County | Percentage with local associations |
|---|---|
| Derbyshire | 79 |
| Leicestershire | 82 |
| Lincolnshire | 89 |
| Northamptonshire | 81 |
| Nottinghamshire | 78 |
| East Midlands | 81 |

Source of data: Questionnaire survey

Similarly within industries the variations are no more
than expected; (table 5.2).

Table 5.2

Entrepreneurs with local associations by industry

| Industry | SIC Order No. (1958) | Percentage with local associations |
|---|---|---|
| Food, drink, tobacco | 3 | 94 |
| Chemicals | 4 | 81 |
| Engineering | 5-9 | 79 |
| Textiles | 10 | 83 |
| Clothing | 11,12 | 74 |
| Building materials | 13 | 73 |
| Wood products | 14 | 69 |
| Paper and printing | 15 | 88 |
| Miscellaneous | 16 | 85 |
| Total | 3-16 | 81 |

Source of data: Questionnaire survey

The value for wood products is just outside the 95 per

110

cent confidence limits. However, with nine categories the probability of having at least one 'significant' result is approximately one in three and hence
not particularly unexpected. Lastly, and somewhat
unexpectedly, firms with larger initial sizes did not
report consistently lower proportions of 'yes'
answers. The figures broken down by initial size are
given in table 5.3.

Table 5.3

Entrepreneurs with local associations by initial size
of firm

| Initial size (No. of employees) | Percentage with local association |
|---|---|
| 1-5 | 79 |
| 6-10 | 85 |
| 11-15 | 89 |
| 16-20 | 88 |
| 21-25 | 83 |
| 26-30 | 100 |
| 31-50 | 66 |
| 50+ | 75 |
| All sizes | 81 |

Source of data:   Questionnaire survey

Although the lowest proportions occurred in the two
categories with an initial size of over thirty employees, in neither case was the magnitude of difference
large enough for it to be concluded that random causes
were not responsible. It can thus be concluded that
the hypothesis of location due to 'local associations'
is strongly supported by the evidence of answers to
this one question.

5.3.2  The examination of alternative locations

It is of additional importance at this stage to know
the extent to which the entrepreneurs examined alternative locations in making the initial location

111

decision. If a location was chosen in an area with which the entrepreneurs had associations, and without consideration of alternatives, then a passive decision is indicated. Conversely, if alternatives were considered then a more active location decision is indicated, resulting in this case in the judgement that the 'local' location held some advantages. Firms were thus asked the additional questions:

'Were any areas more than 30 miles away from this factory strongly considered as alternative locations when the decision to situate this business in this area was taken?'

In this case the geographical scale was specified in order to rule out very local alternatives, and the adverb 'strongly' was introduced to attempt to distinguish between casual consideration and active examination of the possibility of alternative locations. Three hundred and twenty-four respondents had knowledge of the answers to both this question and to the previous one. Only 6 per cent had strongly considered an alternative location, and the proportion who did so was higher when the founder had no local associations.

|  |  | Local associations? | | |
|  |  | Yes | No | Total |
|---|---|---|---|---|
| Alternative | Yes | 13 (5%) | 8 (14%) | 21 (6%) |
| Locations | No | 253 (95%) | 50 (86%) | 303 (94%) |
| Considered? |  |  |  |  |
|  | Total | 266 (83%) | 58 (17%) | 324 (100%) |

A chi-squared test on this contingency table showed the frequencies significantly different from expectation at the 0.10 but not at the 0.05 level. Thus, although the proportion of respondents considering alternative locations was very low ,anyway, the proportion of those locating 'locally' who considered alternative locations is probably 'significantly' lower. The evidence strongly suggests that most entrepreneurs make passive rather than active location decisions when establishing new firms.

## 5.3.3 The industry

The question framed to examine the connection between the entrepreneur's previous experience and the industry in which the firm is engaged, was as follows:
    'Did the founder(s) of this firm have any experience of the type of production presently engaged in by this firm, which may have influenced the decision to set up a firm in this trade rather than in any other?'
In all, 344 respondents from independent firms were able to answer the question, and 88 per cent of these answered in the affirmative. In addition, sixty-eight firms now forming part of larger groupings, answered in respect to the initial (independent) founding of the firm. Pooling both sets of replies produced an overall 85 per cent answering affirmatively. The pattern of variation between counties was as shown in table 5.4.

Table 5.4

Founders with previous experience in the same trade by county

| County | Percentage with previous experience in same trade |
| --- | --- |
| Derbyshire | 73 |
| Leicestershire | 85 |
| Lincolnshire | 82 |
| Northamptonshire | 92 |
| Nottinghamshire | 89 |

Source of data:  Questionnaire survey

The (binomial) probability of getting 73 per cent as the case of Derbyshire is only 0.02. However, with five counties there is a one in ten chance of observing a result at this level of significance, and perhaps Derbyshire should not be viewed as different from the other areas without further supporting evidence. The county level of aggregation may, however, disguise underlying heterogeneity. If the East Midlands is

113

divided into nineteen 'districts' then greater spatial
variation is revealed. The results, omitting
'districts' with less than five cases, are displayed
in table 5.5.

Table 5.5

Founders with previous experience in the same trade by
district

| District | Percentage with previous experience in same trade |
|---|---|
| Nottingham | 90 |
| Mansfield-Worksop | 76 |
| Newark-Retford | 47* |
| Derby | 75 |
| Erewash Valley | 50* |
| Leicester | 86 |
| Hinckley | 78 |
| Leics.-Derbys. Coalfield | 58* |
| Market Harborough | 89 |
| Kesteven | 73 |
| Holland | 91 |
| Lincoln | 83 |
| Northampton | 87 |
| Kettering | 84 |
| Wellingborough | 96* |
| Daventry-Brackley | 71 |
| East Midlands | 85 |

Source of data: Questionnaire survey
Note
    * indicates a significant difference from the
regional average at the 0.02 significance level. The
districts are mapped in a different context in figure
9.1

This range of variation is most unlikely to have
occurred by chance, and it must be concluded that
there are geographical differences at this scale. The
pattern which suggests itself is a low percentage of
affirmative answers in coalfield areas plus Newark,

114

and higher than average percentages in the footwear
and clothing towns of Leicestershire and Northamptonshire.

As might be expected, variations exist between
industries in this respect, and the most likely
explanation for the geographical differences is that
of industrial structure. The industry breakdown of
answers to the same question is shown in table 5.6.

Table 5.6

Founders with previous experience in the same trade by
industry

| Industry | SIC Order No. (1958) | Percentage with experience in same trade |
|---|---|---|
| Food, drink, tobacco | 3 | 82 |
| Chemicals | 4 | 54* |
| Engineering | 5-9 | 86 |
| Textiles | 10 | 89* |
| Clothing | 11-12 | 94* |
| Building materials | 13 | 71* |
| Wood products | 14 | 83 |
| Paper, printing | 15 | 90 |
| Miscellaneous | 16 | 71 |
| All industries | 3-16 | 85 |

Source of data: Questionnaire survey
Note
      * indicates a significant difference from the all-
industry average at the 0.10 level.

Again this degree of diversity is most unlikely to
have occurred by chance. Areas with large numbers of
firms in hosiery, clothing and printing could thus
expect to have a high proportion of entrepreneurs with
previous experience in the trade. It can be tentatively inferred that areas with other industrial
structures will tend to have lower proportions. It
seems that entrepreneurs without previous experience

in their firm's industrial category are more likely to
establish firms on coalfields and in some rural areas
than in well established manufacturing centres. To
shed more light on this situation an analysis of the
three-way crosstabulations was undertaken. This showed that entrepreneurs without previous trade experience usually do have local associations with the area
in which their firm is situated. This suggests the
further inference that 'local' entrepreneurs in areas
without strong manufacturing traditions may still
establish manufacturing firms, although necessarily
in a trade in which they have little experience.
There is a hint in this finding, therefore, that
potential entrepreneurs may exist to a small degree
independently of already established manufacturing
firms, which in other areas act as 'breeding grounds'
for entrepreneurs. This may, however, reflect the
fact that people working in mining and some service
trades have the technical knowledge necessary to found
a particular type of firm, but by definition have no
experience of the manufacturing industry concerned and
thus answer 'no' to the question.

5.3.4  Location and trade considered jointly

Before progressing to examine other aspects of the
location hypothesis, the combinations of 'local
associations' and 'trade experience' can be examined.
In all, 386 respondents could provide information on
both aspects; and the various combinations were as
follows:

|                        | Trade experience | No trade experience | Total |
|------------------------|----------------|-----------------|-----------|
| Local associations     | 216 (69%)      | 46 (12%)        | 312 (81%) |
| No local associations  | 62 (16%)       | 12 ( 3%)        | 74 (19%)  |
| Total                  | 328 (85%)      | 58 (15%)        | 386 (100%)|

These proportions are exactly what would be expected
by the laws of multiplication of probabilities. There
is thus no tendency for 'local association' to be

combined with 'trade experience' above and beyond what is to be expected from their individual proportions. In other words the two characteristics are independent of one another. They are usually found together but only because each is very common in its own right.

This finding of independence also holds for the relationship between 'trade experience' and the consideration of alternative locations. The contingency table below again has exactly the entries expected by the multiplication of the individual probabilities.

|  | Considered alternative locations | Did not consider alternative locations | Total |
|---|---|---|---|
| Trade experience | 16 (5%) | 253 (82%) | 269 (87%) |
| No trade experience | 3 (1%) | 38 (12%) | 41 (13%) |
| Total | 19 (6%) | 291 (94%) | 310 |

Lastly, there was no apparent connection between trade experience and initial size, and this was not investigated further.

5.3.5 Market and supply areas

From the questionnaire it was possible to directly test only one other aspect of the hypothesis. This is the suggestion that entrepreneurs with local associations will tend to do more business with local suppliers and customers than will other (i.e. non-local) entrepreneurs. The questionnaire asked firms to say:
  (a) whether most of the firms' materials were procured from local suppliers i.e. those within thirty miles.
  (b) whether most sales were to local customers
  (c) whether most of the products were designed to customers' specifications, or to the firms' own designs or both.

In terms of procurement of materials and components,

117

firms founded with local associations did a little
more of their business locally. However, a chi-
squared test indicated no significant difference between the two types of firm at the 0.05 probability
level.

|  | Local associations | No local associations |
|---|---|---|
| Materials mostly bought locally | 23% | 20% |
| Materials not mainly bought locally | 55% | 60% |
| Varies from time to time | 23% | 20% |

There are two reasons however for expecting that
differences between types of entrepreneur would be
less muted in selling than with buying. Firstly, it
is to be expected that selling would be more influenced by personal contact than buying, except in
circumstances of shortages in supply. Secondly, in
many cases the number of possible individual markets
will often be greater than the number of suppliers.
In industries in which this is the case there is
greater scope for differences to emerge between entrepreneurial types. The contingency table for sales is
as follows:

|  | Local associations | No local associations |
|---|---|---|
| Most sales local | 23% | 16% |
| Most sales not local | 58% | 70% |
| Sales vary | 19% | 14% |

The differences in this case were stronger, and in the
expected direction but still not statistically significant at the 0.05 level. Since both results point in
the expected direction it is reasonable to lower the
levels of stringency in significance testing. Even so
the differences in the above table are only significant at the 0.20 level, giving a one in five chance

of being wrong.

One final strand of evidence does however, lend more weight to the suggestion that some difference exists between the two types of entrepreneur. Firms founded by entrepreneurs with local associations undertook, in almost half of the cases, work in which designs were specified by the buyers. Firms founded by non-local men in contrast undertook 'mainly specification' work in less than a third of the cases.

|  | Local associations | No local associations |
|---|---|---|
| Mainly 'own design' products | 43% | 49% |
| Mainly specification work | 47% | 31% |
| Both | 11% | 20% |

In this case the differences were significant at the 0.02 level. The relevance of this evidence lies in the fact that 'specification' work is largely sub-contracted out from other manufacturers and the links in this case between subcontractor and subcontractee are usually local ones. The last assertion was shown to be the case when all 731 respondents to the questionnaire were asked to specify if work which they subcontracted out was done locally: 353 replies said that the factory in question did 'put out' work, and of these 70 per cent said that the work was done locally. Thus, it seems likely that firms undertaking a majority of specification of work will do so for local firms. These differences again accord with Smith's findings for Michigan.

As a further test of this aspect of the location hypothesis it is possible to cross-tabulate the "sales area', 'supply area' and 'product type' variables against the age of firm. In order to support the hypothesis, the evidence ought to suggest initial differences between entrepreneurial types which diminish with age; however this is not shown to be the case. There were no marked differences in product type among firms founded within the last two decades. Among older firms, however, those founded by non-local entrepreneurs showed a greater tendency to do more 'own-design' work. Although this evidence is cross-sectional and does not describe changes over time within individual firms, it seems reasonable to draw the inference that young firms are more likely to rely on subcontracted work; but as experience is gained the more adventurous entrepreneurs (and thus those less likely to have chosen local locations), will increasingly develop their own products.

Since younger firms showed little variation in product type there is less reason to expect differences in sales area either. The crosstabulation of 'sales area' against age of firm suggested that only in firms over fifty years old did differences emerge, although among these older firms those originally founded by non-local entrepreneurs had a much higher proportion of non-local sales. In the case of procurement there was little pattern related to age. The evidence, when examined more closely, thus fails to support the expectation that local entrepreneurs will initially do more of their business locally. However, it should be noted that it was not possible to focus on the critical first few years in detail, and even for firms less than twenty years old the sample sizes were small. Moreover, since non-local firms are a relatively uncommon phenomenon the numbers of these in any sample will be relatively small. It has been shown, though, that young firms do undertake their business predominantly locally, and usually on a sub-contract basis. It can be expected that such a situation greatly favours those entrepreneurs who possess local knowledge, even if it cannot be shown that entrepreneurs without such knowledge are unable to succeed.

5.3.6  Summary

To summarise thus far, most new firms have very small

beginnings and tend overwhelmingly to be founded in an area with which the entrepreneur had personal associations. Most entrepreneurs also had previous experience of the trade of the firm. There would appear to be strong forces acting on entrepreneurs preventing them from locating in unfamiliar areas, and indeed the great majority reported that no other location had been strongly considered. It is probable that local entrepreneurs subsequently do more of their business with local contacts than do other firms. However, the questions on this aspect were not sufficiently sharply focused on the critical early years of a firm's existence to test the location hypothesis rigorously. In the next section a small sample of the respondents is examined in more detail, mainly to ascertain the nature of 'local associations', but also to shed more light on the general circumstances in which the firm was founded.


## 5.4   CASE STUDIES OF NEW FIRMS IN THE EAST MIDLANDS

The postal questionnaire method of investigation is ineffectual in several respects. It is not usually certain that the respondent has the necessary knowledge to reply accurately, and the lack of facility for the respondents to ask for clarification means that critical terms may be misinterpreted or at least interpreted differently by different people. In this case, the nature of local associations and the way in which the term 'local' in 'local associations' was interpreted were important points. To test and clarify the questionnaire responses a more detailed follow-up was planned. Fifty of the original respondents were re-contacted and asked for more details on these points. Half of these agreed, some suggesting an interview, others replying by letter. Another six case studies were added from detailed company histories or press reports, making thirty-one in all. Space permits that only seven of these be repeated here, but the full account given is in Gudgin (1974).

The requests were designed to obtain information from both those reporting local associations in their initial reply and those reporting no such association. In the event eighteen of the first type were received and thirteen of the second. The non-local entrepreneur proved something of a mirage however, since eight of the thirteen had interpreted the word local in a very restricted sense, confining it to a single village, or to the suburbs rather than city centre. Although the term will not be defined rigorously here, it can be taken to refer to a single town plus its immediate environs. Using this definition twenty-six of the thirty-one cases were in the 'local association' category. This category is divided below into four sub-categories. In the 'non-local' cases there are five sub-categories in all, and the seven studies here have been selected in such a way as to represent all five types.

## 5.4.1 Entrepreneurs with local associations

The case studies in this group can be usually divided into four categories. The first describes straightforward cases of entrepreneurs locally born, bred and trained, who set up a business in the same area. The second describes local associations other than those of being locally born and bred. A third section deals separately with somewhat longer distance relationships between the area of association and the location of the factory. Finally, firms set up by companies rather than by individuals are treated separately.

(a)  Entrepreneurs born and bred locally
(i)  Cousins Engineering, Earls Barton, Northampton-shire. This small company employing eight people making components for food handling machinery, was founded in 1965 by Mr R. Cousins. The founder had lived for most of his life in Earls Barton, and had, before starting his firm, worked as a lathe turner for a Northampton firm. The latter in a similar industry, had itself grown from very small beginnings in the early postwar period. Although he had long enter-

tained the idea of his own firm, not until his mid-
forties did he pluck up the courage to actually do so.
Two events can be considered to have triggered this
action. Firstly, the 1966 wages freeze gave him the
feeling of being externally controlled in his standard
of living, a situation to which he objected. Secondly
he had immediately previously spent some Saturday
afternoons working part-time for another recently-
established local firm, giving him his first detailed
insights into the establishment of a firm from
infancy.

The firm was begun on a spare-time basis after buying a second-hand lathe and installing it in his
garden shed. An initial order worth £36 was secured
with a local firm through a friend. Not until six
months later did he give up his full-time job. A cow-
shed, a warehouse amd finally a purpose-built rented
unit on a nearby industrial estate served as premises
as the firm gradually expanded from its beginnings
(with a capital of £200 plus hire-purchase), to its
1970 position with six lathes worth £1,000 each. The
firm has always done only subcontract work, almost all
for firms within 40 miles radius, orders usually being
obtained through personal friends. By 1970 firms
tended to approach him, although he did no advertis-
ing. In retrospect, Mr Cousins said he had no real
plans when he first started, 'things just happened,
and I had never consciously planned to expand.'

A slight variant on the straightforward 'born and
bred' type of entrepreneur-location relationship
occurs when a break occurs in the entrepreneur's
local experience. Although breaks like national
service have been discounted, other moves could lead
to the firm being set up in a different location.
However, in a number of cases the entrepreneurs
returned to their home areas before founding firms.
Their experience elsewhere often influenced the
product of the firm but does not seem to have affected
the location. The following is one such case.

(ii) <u>Maun Industries Limited, Mansfield</u>. This company began in 1942 on a very small scale but grew during the war to twelve employees by 1943 and eighty by 1947. It now employs 160 engaged in the manufacture of pliers and wire cutters and claims to be the largest manufacturer of these specialised tools in Europe. The two founders are both local people. Although the present engineering director started his career with a Mansfield engineering firm, both he and the commercial director gained most of their experience in Southern England, in the former case with large motor vehicle and aircraft companies. The firm was established by the engineering director as a subcontracting engineering concern, and was subsequently bought into by the other director (who was thus not strictly a founder). It was at this point that it was decided to select a proprietory article to manufacture. Although no other locations were originally considered Mansfield was felt to have positive advantages in that premises and labour were available.

(b) <u>Other types of local association</u>. In some cases an entrepreneur founds a firm in the area in which he is currently working although this is not the 'home' area. In some cases refugees from Germany founded firms in Britain and not surprisingly did not return to Germany, but in other cases the reasons are less dramatic, sometimes involving marriage. The following case is rather different in that there is a double association with the chosen location.

<u>Forvac Limited, Thurmaston, Leicestershire</u>. This firm employs three people in the manufacture of decorative plastic panels. It represents one of a population of some seventy plastics firms which have appeared in Leicester since the war. Although plastic heels in the footwear industry was one introduction of plastics technology into the town, another was the existence of a single large plastics firm from prewar days, Cascelloid Ltd. Forvac was founded in 1964 by two men. The senior partner had previously worked for Herbert-Ingersoll Ltd (machine tools) in Coventry in

the subcontract department. In this capacity he came
into contact with plastic forming machinery. Through
a contact in Leicester (an employee of Cascelloid), he
learned that Cascelloid wished to sell a small section
of their business which no longer interested them.
The other partner was a Leicester man who worked for
a local engineering firm. The business was bought,
and production was begun with three employees.
Thurmaston, a suburb of Leicester, was chosen because
land was available to build a small factory. No other
locations were considered nor were any advantages
cited other than land availability.

(c) <u>Wider separations between home or work and factory
location</u>. This subsection includes firms which were
located at a distance of ten miles or more from the
founder's previous workplace, and in a different town
or rural area. Such locations demonstrate ways in
which industrial growth generated in one area can leak
out to other neighbouring areas at a local scale. Two
case studies are included because they both illustrate
a number of interesting additional features.

(i) <u>Torquemeters Limited, Ravensthorpe, Northampton</u>.
Torquemeters, employing twelve people, manufactures
a high precision and highly specialised scientific
instrument sold to many of the world's largest electrical and atomic engineering companies. The founder
R.D. Van Millingen is a Scot 'by birth and education'
who married a Leicester girl, a fact he describes as
'a strong geographical·influence'. His experience was
gained with Power Jets Ltd of Lutterworth, (formed to
develop the jet engine in the period 1940-47) and with
English Electric near Leicester. The torquemeter was
developed in 1950 while he was at English Electric, to
solve a particular problem. In 1951 Van Millingen
left to fulfil a long-standing ambition to become
self-employed. Torquemeters Ltd was founded in 1951
in some out-buildings in the grounds of the family
home near Northampton. Manufacture was subcontracted
out until 1956. The first order was from English
Electric, although most of the early orders were for

Rolls Royce in Derby 'through contacts from Power Jet days'. The design help supplied by Rolls Royce is recognised as having been of great value to the infant company. Besides the ties to the East Midlands in the foregoing account, the Northampton location is considered central within Britain and close to Coventry for important specialist processes such as gear cutting, grinding and heat treatment. The fact that Scotland is considered to have 'little sophisticated engineering', was a further factor preventing a return, and no alternative locations were seriously considered. The reason for the 'leakage' of this industrial growth away from South-West Leicestershire is presumably the fact that Mr Van Millingen commuted a relatively long distance to work, something which is more common among professional level employees than among the manual workers who form the bulk of the entrepreneurs in the previous case studies. As a spin off from Torque-meters Ltd, a successful subcontracting business was set up in 1965 by the previous foreman and another employee. By 1971 this was employing twenty people.

(ii) GTC Engineering Company, Loughborough, Limited, Loughborough, Leicester. GTC with thirty employees is again a highly specialist precision engineering firm having had contacts with a major East Midlands engineering firm. The firm was founded in 1957 to manufacture test specimens for companies involved in high precision engineering. The founders all worked in the experimental department of Rolls Royce Ltd in Derby. They were unable to find premises in Derby, but managed to rent the top storey of a building in a North Leicestershire village for five months. They later heard about a vacant needle factory in nearby Loughborough, and this was leased and subsequently bought. The firm began with a contract which Rolls Royce did not want to undertake, the work being done on a lathe in the present managing director's garden shed. Markets, mainly large aircraft companies and Sheffield steel firms, have developed 'by word of mouth' although centrality is felt to be a necessity. As the firm grew, labour was attracted mainly from two

large Loughborough engineering firms (Brush Ltd and
Morris Cranes Ltd) although some retraining was
always necessary. The firm has maintained a single
line of work, but this has occurred other than by
design. A fabricating side of the firm split away and
later went out of business, while an attempt to diver-
sify into electronics 'didn't work out'. This firm
which was spawned by Rolls Royce thus managed to
become located in Loughborough, some fifteen miles
away, largely due to the availability of premises.
Even this distance was achieved in two stages via an
intermediate location.

(d) Subsidiaries of existing companies. Three of the
firms in the 'local entrepreneur' category illustrate
a rather different type of company formation. In each
case there was a pre-existing firm, usually owned by
the same family, the new firm being formed to develop
some new, although related, line of business. In such
cases the capital resources are greater than those
available to most employees. Nevertheless, the same
type of very local location was selected. All three
cases are in textile and footwear industries, a group
notably under represented in the other subcategories.
This sample is much too small to do anything other
than very tentatively suggest that a difference in
this respect may exist between industrial sectors.
Such an observation is, however, consistent with the
fact that the initial sizes of new firms established
in Leicestershire 1947-57 were above average in
hosiery, clothing and footwear (median 5-10 employees), and smaller than average in engineering and
printing (median 2-3 employees). Technical differences between industries will influence minimum
feasible firm sizes, and thus affect the type of
entrepreneurial behaviour involved in establishing the
firms. Only one of the three is described here,
although this takes the form of a double case.

Harold Chell Limited, Oadby, Leicestershire; Brian
Chell Limited, Spalding Street, Leicester. This case
study consists of two firms, owned by the members of
one family. The parent firm was formed in 1919 by

H. Chell and a partner to manufacture hosiery. Both
were local men. H. Chell had returned to Leicester
after the war and worked for a year in a local hosiery
firm (G. Rowley Ltd, now part of Courtaulds). Low
wages, few prospects and a desire for independence led
to the formation of the firm on a very modest scale.
After two years the partner withdrew and the firm
continued to grow in a gradual way. In the late 1920s
the firm changed to reconditioning hosiery machines,
after buying some fire damaged machines, and having to
sell them when the depression prevented them from
being usefully employed within the firm. Customers
asked for further orders and this line of business
soon became more profitable than hosiery which was
abandoned. Wartime work led to further diversification into general engineering. By 1959 the business
employed over 250 people, mainly working on a hosiery
machine developed within the firm. In 1959 it was
felt that future development could only occur with
massive capital investment. The family was unwilling
to take this step, and instead, this side of the
business was sold to a large Leicester manufacturer.
The small remnant company concentrated on general
engineering.

In 1964 the wheel turned full circle and the firm
once more took up hosiery manufacture, when an export
order of thirty hosiery machines was cancelled. They
decided to use the machines themselves and Brian Chell
Ltd was formed under the direction of the founder's
son to develop this side of the business. Harold
Chell Ltd now employs forty people, and Brian Chell
Ltd sixty people, after starting with seventeen in
1964. No locations outside Leicester were considered
for Brian Chell Ltd, skilled labour was felt to be a
particular advantage, although the managing director
had 'toyed with the idea' of moving to the Lake
District.

Local entrepreneurs: a summary and commentary.
Although the quality of information varied between
case studies, an overall impression clearly emerged

with few contradictions. Entrepreneurs in this category, and thus the great majority of all East Midlands' entrepreneurs on the questionnaire evidence, tend to establish firms close to their former place of employment and in the same trade. Sometimes they are locally born and bred, in other cases a variety of circumstances have brought them to the area and kept them there. In the latter category more mobile managerial level entrepreneurs are better represented than in the former. Once the decision to begin a business is made (the importance of a catalytic event was mentioned several times), a web of interrelated factors do seem to militate against establishing the firm other than near to the founder's home. The process in this respect was very clear.

Lack of capital, local knowledge of market opportunities, reliable workers and premises, and the need to begin on a part-time basis all tie production to the home area, while great uncertainty removes any solid reason for going elsewhere. The exact role of the various factors cited as advantages of the local area on the other hand needs more careful consideration. Several factors of this type were mentioned, but some were obviously ex post facto rationalisation. Centrality to customers comes within this category since the location decision is made before all but a few initial customers are known. Even general centrality is probably a personal rather than truly economic factor, especially when many markets are overseas. Premises and labour availability were by far the most commonly mentioned location factors. These appear to play a permissive rather than active locational role. There was never any suggestion that conditions were compared with those anywhere else. The critical question becomes 'what would happen if these factors were unavailable?'. Three comments can be made. Firstly, examples are given above of entrepreneurs being forced into neighbouring rural areas when premises could not be found in the town. Secondly, since movement to other areas is so rare among the questionnaire respondents as a whole, it seems more likely that unavailability of factors of production would deter or delay the decision to establish a business rather than change the location. Shortage of factors should thus influence local entry-rates, rather than determine locations among alternatives under consideration. Thirdly, shortages may be rare in the absolute sense, since the firms in the sample were mostly small enough to occupy 'crevices' in the local economy.

Labour shortages were particularly acute in Leicestershire, for instance, in the two decades after the war, and most other parts of the East Midlands (away from the coalfield) had very low unemployment levels. In spite of this, new firms were still established. Localised skilled labour is one influence, but most of the case study firms were in engineering in which the skills are more general and very widespread in Britain. The place of skilled labour in locational causation is itself probably contributary rather than a primary causal factor. In industries which are geographically concentrated, the entrepreneurs will be similarly located in the same concentrations, and by definition so will the skilled labour. If the entrepreneurs lived elsewhere (i.e. some other process selected entrepreneurs) then it is not at all clear that they would necessarily migrate to sources of skilled labour. The latter are somewhat nebulous in existence anyway, since industrial concentrations commonly exhibit shortages in the skills of the dominant trade. In Leicestershire where new firms were being established at a rate of some eighty per year, established firms were expanding by setting up branches elsewhere due to labour shortage. Labour availability and labour shortage can be ascribed to the same place and time to account for opposites in locational behaviour. The solution to the paradox lies in the greatly differing scale of needs at one time of large firms compared with tiny new firms.

One constraint due to availability deserves more attention however. The importance of the availability

of local markets was directly suggested by a few case
studies and underlies most of the others. The importance of initial subcontract work is paramount,
especially in engineering. In two cases 'lack of
local competition', presumably in an identifiable
market, was directly mentioned. One of these cases
was in printing, in which local demand can be expected
to be a severe constraint on growth as in other semi-
service activities of this type. Again there is no
suggestion that entrepreneurs actively evaluate
alternative locations in respect to market availability. Instead, the fact appears to act as a potent
influence on the entry-rate. The finding of Beesley
(1955) that contrasting entry-rates existed in adjacent parts of the West Midlands conurbation according
to the type of industrial production (assembly,
component manufacture etc.) may reflect differences in
the amount of subcontract work available to potential
entrepreneurs and their firms.

5.4.2   Entrepreneurs without local associations

The five cases in this category illustrated a variety
of individual circumstances that defy generalisation,
except that in each case the new firm had capital
backing sufficient to give it a large initial size and
thus independence from many of the constraints which
led to local locations in the above examples. Once
again constraints of space permit that only one of the
cases is reproduced here. This is the only case among
the five in which the firm was begun from an independent base rather than as a subsidiary of an existing
company.

Textured Jersey Limited, Anstey, Leicestershire.
Textured Jersey was founded in 1963 by Henry Knobil,
at the age of thirty, with a capital £40,000.(11)
Knobil was born in Austria and came as a child in 1939
to Nottingham, where his father established a dry
cleaning business. A career oriented very much
towards entrepreneurship was mapped out, and Knobil
was directed by his father to begin with Marks and
Spencer. The latter firm was felt to offer an

excellent training in management. Knobil spent eight
years in the cloth buying department and built up
several valuable connections which have been retained.
In particular the bank with which Marks and Spencer
dealt subsequently loaned Knobil £20,000 to which his
family added a similar amount. The assistant managing
director was formerly the managing director of a
Courtaulds subsidiary, and his contacts in the hosiery
trade proved as valuable as Knobil's.

The location near Leicester was selected as being
the most suitable, as the centre of the hosiery industry and having a concentration of skilled labour. The
actual economic advantages are not clear, however,
since by 1971 'a high proportion of the existing
labour force of 240, had been trained internally'.
The lack of constraint on initial size, and type of
market links, may however, have played a part in the
company's outstanding growth record. By 1968 the firm
employed 34; by 1970, 104; and in 1971, 240. Turnover
in 1971 was over £3 million, and profits were five
times greater than the initial capital investment. In
1971 expansion plans were announced for a new factory
in Leicester, for dyeing and finishing, employing 150-
200 extra workers. It was also intended to train most
of these people internally.

Non-local entrepreneurs. A summary. Among all of the
case studies of firms set up by individuals, the last
is the only one in which the founder had no apparent
prior personal attachment to the company's location.
The other cases without local associations included a
firm set up by a German chemical manufacturer who left
Germany in the 1930s, and another which developed out
of the unusual conditions of wartime. The final two
examples were both large subsidiaries in which locational choice is a process more closely resembling
that of branch plants, than of the firms described
above.

The latter examples are representative of large new
firms and incidentally of an entrepreneurial system

once dominant, and now overshadowed.  Surprisingly
little is known about broad trends in the history of
British entrepreneurship, but it seems likely that the
situation described by Dahmen (1970) also occurred in
Britain.  In Sweden, the first generation of industrial firms in the mid-nineteenth century were formed by
those with capital rather than direct experience of
the trade.  Firms were much larger at inception than
is currently the case.  The second and subsequent
generations of new firms were largely formed by
entrepreneurs with little capital, but sufficient
appropriate experience.  It is possible to discern
this distinction in isolated British company histories
although the second generation came earlier in Britain
than in Sweden.


## 5.5  RATES OF ENTRY OF NEW FIRMS

The process of the creation of new firms has been
shown to be intensely local in geographical terms,
with the location of new firms strongly reflecting the
prior distribution of industrial employment.  The
direct spatial results are cumulative growth, with
continuation in industrial structure, and only occasionally the emergence of a new industry.  The nature
of the process is not in itself enough to be able to
predict future industrial distributions.  What is
needed is a knowledge of how fast the process acts; or
in this context, the rate of entry.

It is estimated that almost 3,000 new firms formed
in the East Midlands between 1947 and 1967 were still
in production in 1967.  The figure for Leicestershire
can be gauged more precisely and is just over 950.
Over half of the firms within the region in 1967 had
been established since 1947, although most of these
were very small.  The overall rates of entry were
about 4 per cent of firms a year, although a significant proportion of these closed before the end of the
period.

Geographical variations in entry-rates will be considered in subsequent chapters. At this point a brief account will be given of the major non-spatial influences. Although not the main focus of interest, non-spatial variations in entry-rates need to be investigated in order to disentangle them from the more purely spatial effects considered later. There are several different non-spatial influences, but most of these can be subsumed within the category of industrial variations. The main exception is that of temporal differences. However, in the spatial analysis in chapter eight, areas are compared over the same time period and this factor can be left aside.

## 5.5.1 The evidence of other studies

Studies of industrial differences in entry-rates have been included in the work of Churchill (1959) for the USA 1950-58, Wedervang (1965) for Norway 1930-48, and of Collins (1972) for Ontario 1961-65. In each case the degree of variation between industries has been found to be greater than that assignable to random chance alone. The frequency distributions of industry rates in each case are approximately symmetrical around the all-industry mean with standard deviations of roughly a third to a half as large as the mean. If the inter-industry differences are greater than random variation the question then arises as to their cause. In general terms some obvious hypotheses can be advanced to account for the observed differences. It would be expected that potential entrepreneurs would set up in business more readily if the prospects of profit and growth were greater, and less readily where initial capital requirements were high. Other factors, working in opposite directions to the previous two, might be the potential risk of closure (usually highest is the easiest-to-enter industries); and low personal prospects in current employment or actual unemployment.(12) The latter factor, observed by Oxenfeldt (1943) suggests higher entry-rates in slow growing industries.

A host of personal and micro-environmental factors may also be important. Contact with entrepreneurs, more common in small firms, may increase knowledge and incentive to be an entrepreneur, for instance. Industries with a preponderance of small firms may have higher entry-rates for this reason, although entry is also financially easier in the same trades. Personality traits will be the most potent discriminator between those who do start their own businesses and those who do not. When investigating industry differences, however, these factors can be expected to cancel out, each industry having a range of personalities. It is possible that industries growing rapidly in one period may attract more adventurous people who later set up their own firms, although Smith's work cited above suggests that entrepreneurs are not necessarily adventurous in other ways, and are usually not in the more mobile (in terms of jobs) managerial grades. We are thus presented with a number of hypotheses suggesting processes some of which act in the same direction, and others in opposite directions. The information available to aggregate studies of entry-rates is incapable of differentiating effectively between hypotheses of this type. Processes acting in the same direction will both produce the same result, while those in direct conflict may be of unequal strength. In the latter case the dominant process will govern the result (e.g. a high or low entry-rate), but this does not mean that the counter-effect is not acting simultaneously.

Despite these difficulties inherent in all hypothesis testing in non-experimental conditions, suggestive evidence can be put forward. Wedervang (1965), for instance, observed a correlation between the entry-rates and the proportion of small plants for thirteen industrial sectors. Calculation using his figures gives a Spearman correlation coefficient of 0.83. The relationship between the entry-rates and growth performance of an industry is less obvious. Wedervang found a strong positive relationship for

135

the recovery period 1933-37, but a negative one for
the depression period 1930-33.  This is due to the
fact that entry-rates remain either high or low to
some extent regardless of industry performance.  A
general change in performance as in the 1930s resulted
in these apparently contradictory results.  These
Norwegian data do however, suggest a tendency within
each industry for entry-rates to rise with a bettering
of performance in the industry as a whole.  These
temporal changes are much smaller in magnitude than
the range of inter-industry differences.  The results
of Collins (1972) for Ontario between 1961 and 1965
contradict those of Wedervang.  Collins finds that for
twenty industrial sectors entry-rate was correlated
with growth in permanent firms (rank 'r' = 0.46), but
uncorrelated with the percentage of small plants
(employing less than eleven people).

5.5.2  Variations between industries in Leicestershire

On the basis of the hypothesis discussed above, the
evidence of the other studies, and the data available,
it is possible to investigate industrial variations in
entry-rates within Leicestershire.  The two relationships tested reflect the ideas that entry-rates are
related to the ease of access to the industry, or to
the rate of growth in the industry.  The latter may
act as a proxy for profitability both in the eyes of
potential entrepreneurs and also as a variable in
analysis.  The measure of entry-rate is not the one
used in other studies i.e. new firms per hundred
existing firms; instead the rate is measured per
thousand employees in the industry at the beginning of
the period.  This measure reflects the process described in previous sections in which the population of
industrial employees is the relevant indicator of the
number of potential entrepreneurs.  A base measured in
numbers of firms (or plants) fails to take account of
the size of the latter.  Moreover, the average size of
plants may itself be an influence on the entry-rate,
and thus should not become inter-twined with the
dependent variable.

136

Data is available for two time periods and for the
various categories of new firms listed in table 5.7.
Short-term survivors are defined as those surviving to
the end of the period in which they were founded.
Long-term survivors are those firms surviving to the
end of the next period. The independent variables are
the following:

(a) the proportion of plants in the industry employing less than twenty people at the beginning of
the relevant period. (This is taken as a measure of
ease of entry).

(b) the average rate of growth in permanent plants
over the relevant period.

(c) the growth of total employment in the industry
(locally) in the relevant period.
The dispersion of entry-rates between industries is
shown in table 5.1.

In each of the regression equations reported below
one or two industries (either rubber or plastics or
both) were omitted where these proved to have extreme
values which would have dominated the regression and
correlation coefficients. All of the appropriate
independent variables were tried, but the only significant equations to emerge were the following:

$$Y_1 = 0.022 \ X_1 - 0.605 \qquad\qquad r^2 = 0.48$$
$$\phantom{Y_1 =} (0.006)$$

$$Y_2 = 0.011 \ X_1 - 0.216 \qquad\qquad r^2 = 0.48$$
$$\phantom{Y_2 =} (0.003)$$

$$Y_3 = 0.008 \ X_2 - 0.180 \qquad\qquad r^2 = 0.46$$
$$\phantom{Y_3 =} (0.002)$$

$$Y_3 = 0.011 \ X_2 - 0.048X_3 - 0.320 \qquad r^2 = 0.59$$
$$\phantom{Y_3 =} (0.002) \quad\ (0.008)$$

$$Y_4 = 0.010 \ X_2 - 0.169 \qquad\qquad r^2 = 0.37$$
$$\phantom{Y_4 =} (0.004)$$

where

$Y_1$ = full entry-rate 1947-55

$Y_2$ = short term survivors 1947-55

Table 5.7

Entry-rates of long-term and short-term survivors

| Industry | MLH (SIC 1958) | Short-term survivors | 1947-55 Long-term survivors | All new firms | 1955-67 Short-term survivors |
|---|---|---|---|---|---|
| Baking | 212-13 | 0.21 | 0.10 | 0.26 | 0.09 |
| Light chemicals | 271-7 | 0.22 | 0.09 | 0.22 | 0.41 |
| Metal manufacture | 311-22 | 0.20 | 0.14 | 0.20 | 0.23 |
| Non-electrical engineering | 331-52 370-99 | 0.60 0.60 | 0.31 0.31 | 0.80 0.80 | 0.43 0.43 |
| Electrical engineering | 361-9 | 0.18 | 0.10 | 0.29 | 0.19 |
| Wool spinning | 414 | 0.18 | 0.12 | 0.24 | 0.05 |
| Hosiery | 417 | 0.30 | 0.14 | 0.41 | 0.44 |
| Narrow fabrics | 421 | 0.11 | 0.11 | 0.11 | 0.10 |
| Textile finishing | 423 | 0.0 | 0.0 | 0.04 | 0.28 |
| Clothing | 441-9 | 0.86 | 0.35 | 1.24 | 0.57 |
| Footwear | 450 | 0.15 | 0.05 | 0.24 | 0.12 |
| Building materials | 461-9 | 0.49 | 0.17 | 0.59 | 0.28 |
| Wood products | 471-9 | 0.82 | 0.78 | 2.29 | 1.17 |
| Cardboard boxes | 482 | 0.72 | 0.44 | 0.96 | 0.18 |
| Printing and publishing | 486-9 | 0.99 | 0.55 | 1.31 | 0.88 |
| Rubber products | 491 | 0.12 | 0.08 | 0.12 | 0.0 |
| Plastic products | 496 | 1.32 | 1.10 | 1.54 | 4.40 |

Note
   Entry rate is defined as number of new firms p.a. per thousand employees at the
   start of the period.

Source of data: Establishment records

138

$Y_3$ = long-term survivors among entrants 1947-55

$Y_4$ = short-term survivors 1955-67

$X_1$ = % of plants employing less than 20 in 1947

$X_2$ = % of plants employing less than 20 in 1955

$X_3$ = growth in total employment 1947-67

The figures in brackets are standard errors. All coefficients are significant at the 0.05 level. These equations suggest that the proportion of small plants, measuring the ease of entry, explains about half of the variation between industries, while rates of growth are in most instances not important. The regression coefficients suggest that a difference between industries of 10 per cent in the proportion of small plants leads to an entry-rate which is higher by about one sixth of the average entry-rate.

The unimportance of growth rates may be due to some deficiency in the measures used, but is not entirely unexpected given the fact that the desire for independence appears to be a more powerful influence on potential entrepreneurs than the desire for profit. Nevertheless, the importance of the growth variables might be expected to be greater on the rate of survival of new firms than on the raw entry-rate, yet the opposite is shown to be true. This does not accord with the commonsense notion that the survival of new firms should be easiest in industries in which markets are expanding fastest. In industries with little expansion new firms have the more difficult task of competing with existing firms in order to make headway. One possible explanation for the inclusion of growth as a negative factor in the equation for long-term survivors may be the following. In most industries there is a turnover of firms with new ones replacing closures. The industries with high turnover are likely to contain most long-term survivors, and these may have been the industries with the slowest rate of growth. This does not, however, explain why growth was not related to the entry-rates for all firms or for short-term survivors. More research is clearly called for.

## 5.5.3 Discussion

The overall conclusion of this exercise is that entry-
rates are quite strongly related to the size structure
of an industry. Industries with many small plants
attract larger numbers of new firms to their ranks
because of ease of entry. However, rates of entry are
not in general related to the performance of the
industry measured in terms of employment growth. Most
important for this study is the fact that differences
in entry-rates between industries are relatively
large and thus industrial structure must be allowed
for when investigating spatial variability.

These results agree closely with Wedervang's findings for Norway, but not with those of Collins for
Ontario, who found no relationship between entry-rate
and size structure, but some association between the
former and employment growth in the permanent firms.
The reason for these contradictory findings may lie in
differences of definition. Collins' figures included
all establishments, branch plants as well as firms.
He states that about one eighth of the new entrants
were branches of United States firms.(13) An unstated
number were branches of Canadian firms. Because
branches are usually established as part of a firm's
expansion, and by relatively large firms, more common
in large plant industries, it is to be expected that
different conclusions will emerge. Indeed, the
expected direction of alteration is towards a diminu-
tion of the size structure association and a strength-
ening of any employment growth effect. This appears
to be what has happened, although no definite state-
ment can be made without a disaggregation of Collins'
figures.

NOTES

(1) New firms are defined as manufacturing concerns

which begin production for the first time and thus exclude branch plants, relocations or changes in ownership. There are two main types of origin for new firms, i.e. establishment by individuals; and establishment as a subsidiary by an existing firm or consortium of firms.

(2)   This point is elaborated upon in Gudgin (1974)

(3)   Collins (1972) p.68. The excess of larger plants is revealed by the sharp breaks in the lines on figure 5.1.

(4)   Four studies are discussed in Oxenfeldt (1943) pp.50-91.

(5)   Of establishments employing eleven or more, 29 per cent employed less than nineteen. The only industries in which the proportion was as low as 10 per cent were tractors, cotton textiles and the following primary processing industries: tobacco, oil refining, sugar refining, general chemicals, iron and steel, glass and paper. A somewhat larger number had under 20 per cent in this category but these included hosiery which is the major industry in Leicestershire.

(6)   In this study the term 'entrepreneur' is used exclusively for those who found firms.

(7)   This point is taken up below, and here it is necessary only to note that the 95 per cent confidence limits for this proportion (using binomial probability) are wide, i.e. 28 per cent and 80 per cent.

(8)   G.E. Oxenfedt (nd) Characteristics of Large New Manufacturing Corporations. Unpublished master's thesis Columbia University pp.49-59 cited in Oxenfeldt (1943) p.91.·

(9)   These companies were all identified from their company reports. It may well be mere coincidence but all three were started in southern England, as were virtually all of the other cases cited in this chapter.

(10)   It has been pointed out (personal communication from P.R. Mounfield) that moving house may provide a source of capital, if the entrepreneur buys a cheaper house, or increases the size of his mortgage. Capital was raised in this way for instance by a former sales manager of a Leicester footwear firm when he

established his own shoe firm in Shrewsbury in 1973.
(11)  This case study is based on accounts in the
Daily Telegraph Magazine No. 293, November 1969;
Leicester Mercury, July 21 1971 and questionnaire
evidence.
(12)  Low prospects or unemployment in an industry may
increase the pressure on individuals to establish
their own firms.  These will often be set up in the
same industry, despite problems of slow growth in
that industry.
(13)  Collins (1972) p.65.

# 6 The growth of firms and plants

There is an obvious need to understand the nature of
the processes of growth in any attempt to explain
aggregate employment change.  The determinants of
growth are, however, an extremely complex matter, and
the object of study of a variety of academic disciplines.  It is not possible to approach the question
of growth in the same way as with the inherently more
straightforward matter of location.  The aims of this
chapter are instead to review the work of economists
and others on the growth of firms, and to test some of
the major hypotheses within the special context of
growth in a single region.  This will provide guide-
lines for the analysis of spatial variation in growth
rates which is undertaken in chapter nine, and will
suggest which variables are most likely to be of
significance.  Of equal importance is the depth which
is added to a spatial investigation through an understanding of the non-spatial processes.  Many geographical patterns are merely the spatial manifestations of
processes in which geographical location plays little
direct part, and it is thus necessary to understand
the processes.  The growth of firms and plants is a
prime example of this.


## 6.1  THE THEORY OF THE GROWTH OF THE FIRM

Research on the growth of firms spans the disciplines
of economics, sociology, business management and
administrative science.  Each of these examines growth
from a different point of interest, and contributes a
different part of the overall picture.  Within
economics in particular there has been a division
between the theoretical and empirical studies, and
although the demarcation is far from absolute, this
distinction will be followed in reviewing the
research.

The traditional theory of the firm says little directly about the growth of firms. The theory leads to the expectation that long-run cost curves will be 'L' shaped, meaning that economies of scale in production exist up to a certain size, but thereafter diseconomies set in. Each specific product market is expected to have an optimum size of plant, and the implication is that most firms will have to operate near to this optimum size in or er to survive. The theory is vague about how firms reach this size, and growth over time is incidental rather than a central issue.

A number of strands of empirical evidence have shown the irrelevance of this theory for explaining growth, and led to the emergence of a new body of ideas directed more specifically at growth itself. The most important empirical evidence has been on the cost curves, and this has in general provided little support for the existence of 'L' shaped cost curves. Instead, 'the majority of studies have concluded that long-run average cost curves are typically "L" shaped' (Lee and Jones, 1974). This means that costs decline rapidly with increasing size, but after a certain critical size the increase becomes much less marked. The lack of any one optimum size opens up the possibility that a range of scales of operation will be encountered. In many industries firms do exist at a wide range of sizes and it has been necessary to account for this fact.

The body of ideas in economics which has become known as the theory of the growth of the firm, centres its focus on the firm as an organisation rather than on units of production.(1) This more realsitic view of the world treats firms as specialist organisations, or as bundles of human resources, which aim to grow, but find themselves constrained by a number of internal and external factors. The work of Downie, Penrose and Marris forms the core of the theory and is largely concerned with these constraints upon firms which are assumed to be attempting to maximise their growth.

Downie (1959) adopted the commonsense stance that rate of growth is related to the efficiency of firms, and went on to suggest the mechanisms by which the two things are related. He suggested that growth requires finance to expand capacity and also price cutting to attract customers from competitors. Access to finance, however raised, will depend on profitability, but price reductions will tend to decrease profits. Hence, the two requirements for growth conflict with one another, and there will be some maximum rate of growth which will be possible at any given level of efficiency.

Subsequent additions to the theory have consisted either of adding new factors into consideration or else articulating the relationships between factors. Penrose (1959) added the constraint of managerial expansion into the theory. She viewed firms as collections of individuals with abilities which influence the form and direction of growth. The abilities and experience of new personnel added to those already in the firm will lead to further potential for expansion, including diversification into new product areas. This type of expansion frees the firm from the limitations imposed by demand for its traditional products. The new restriction in this more open context is the speed with which individuals can be successfully integrated into the firm without its overall efficiency becoming impaired. External constraints of finance and demand are still recognised but constraints on managerial expansion are seen as the major constraint.

Marris (1964) articulated the system of relationships within the theory rather than adding new factors. He described the precise ways in which the financial constraints on growth might operate within the context of the current institutional framework. He maintained that sources of borrowing were strictly limited because of the increasing risk to both borrower and lender as the ratio of borrowed to equity capital increases.(2) New share issues and retained profits are the remaining sources of finance. The success of new issues depends upon the anticipated profitability of the firm, and hence the profitability will impose a constraint on growth. Although profitability also limits the amount of internal finance for growth there is a prior constraint in that some profits have to be paid out in dividends. Unless firms can convince shareholders that low current dividends will entail higher dividends or capital gains in the future, shares will be sold and the threat of takeover will increase. However, rapid growth will entail lower profitability because of the managerial constraints described by Penrose. For all of these reasons the financial institutions impose a constraint on the ability of firms to grow rapidly.

## 6.2 EMPIRICAL INVESTIGATION OF MANAGEMENT EFFICIENCY

The economic theory of the growth of the firm emphasises the constraints which affect all firms in their efforts to grow. There has been much less emphasis on internal differences of efficiency between firms. Given the acknowledged existence of a set of constraints why is it that some firms nevertheless perform better than others? This question has attracted sociologists and administrative scientists more than economists although once again the lines of demarcation are not at all rigid.

One indirect line of evidence from economics has come from Singh and Whittington (1968) who investigated the persistence of growth and profitability over time. They found a strong persistence in profitability between their two time periods, but in the case of growth the association was either weak, or in some industries insignificant. This can be interpreted as indicating that successful managements do exist and continue to be successful through changing conditions. The opposite view, advanced by Rayner and

Little (1966) was that external circumstances swamped managerial differences to produce a random pattern over time in any one firm. However, their study was of growth in profitability, and as Singh and Whittington point out, this is of less relevance to the question in hand than the level of profitability. One final point is that continued high profitability may reflect the persistence of monopoly conditions as well as success in a competitive situation.

The reasons for the relative success of some companies over others, may partly reflect the existence of monopoly power, but this is unlikely to be more than a small part of the overall explanation. Collins and Preston (1961) reviewing the extensive literature on the effects of concentration concluded that there was 'a statistically significant but not always strong association between measures of concentration and the indicators of profitability'. This conclusion was reached in an American context but it is unlikely that the British experience is radically different.

The characteristics of firms which distinguish the successful from the rest are likely to reflect the personality and ability of upper management, and the organisation of the firm. In small firms, where senior management necessarily undertake a significant role in day to day operations, individuals will have a great impact. One example of this comes from L. Sullivan (Sunday Times, 6 February 1977). This concerns a small quoted engineering company - the Weyburn Engineering Co. - making diesel camshafts in Godalming, Surrey. The company was bought by an accountant and a business consultant in 1973. One reason for selecting this company from the many investigated was that it had 'a less than dynamic management'. In the three years after gaining control profits increased 220 per cent to almost £3 million, with shares in 1977 described as 'the starriest single performer on the London share market'. The two owners had a combination of previous commercial success and experience in writing on corporate planning. Together they had a well developed approach to business which apparently contrasted with the previous management and which has made them both rich men.

One characteristic of management which has been widely found to effect growth is that of the age of senior managers. An early mention of this phenomenon came in the Oxford survey of over 800 British firms in 1956, in which Lydall (1959) reported that business-men's ambition for their firms to grow declined with age. Since then the relationship has been reported in several other studies. Child (1973) found that growth but not profitability declined with age, but also that young managers produced more variable growth perfor-mances than their elders. Even in larger firms the age of the chairman or board of directors is found to result in slower and less volatile rates of growth (Hart and Mellors, 1970; Management Today, May 1973 pp.81-3).

In larger firms the ability of senior management will be reflected in the organisational structures adopted by their companies, and it is possible to study directly the effect of different structures upon performance. Child (1973) found some evidence that more profitable companies tended to have less bureau-cratic and rigid organisation, and also smaller proportions of employment in financial activities. Another body of literature cited by Child (1973 p.23) supports the view that different structures are needed for different business conditions, especially with respect to uncertainty. Failure to adopt the relevant structure for a given environment is viewed as being detrimental to a good performance.

One persistent view of business performance is that owner controlled firms will achieve higher profit-ability but lower growth than firms controlled by managers. There is no empirical support for this contention within the UK. Radice (1971) found owner controlled firms to be better in both respects, while

Child (1973) and Holl (1975) both observe no systematic relationship. Similarly contradictory results have emerged from comparable studies relating to US firms.

A footnote to the debate on owners versus managers was provided by a small study which made a further distinction. This study of small firms observed that family firms still managed by their founders grew on average almost twice as fast as those managed by subsequent generations of the founder's family (Merret Cyriax, 1972). This suggestion of cycles of fast and slow growth in family firms was subscribed to by Marshall at the turn of the century. Firms in the same sample which had been taken over and were run by professional management had an intermediate growth performance. It may thus be the case that owner managed firms are more volatile in their growth. Finally, on the topic of individuals the findings of Smith (1967) can be recalled. He reported that his 'opportunist' founders had firms growing at twelve times the rate of the companies founded by his 'craftsmen' entrepreneurs.

## 6.3  EMPIRICAL RESEARCH ON GROWTH

### 6.3.1  Growth and size

A different line of research has had its root in mathematical statistics. One of the few consistent aspects of industrial firms has been the observation that the frequency distribution of sizes of both firms and plants is approximately lognormal in form. Evidence from a wide range of western industrial nations has demonstrated the same fact, and has led to the question 'what probability mechanism generates the lognormal distribution and does a similar process govern the growth and size of firms in the real world?' The statistical theory underlying the distribution was developed by Kapteyn (1903) and later formulated by Gibrat (1957) as the 'law of proportionate effect'. The theory, in brief, is that a large number of individually small and independent influences multiplied together result in the observed distributional form.

The important aspect of the theory is the requirement that the rate of growth should be independent of the initial size. This in turn has led to a large number of attempts to directly test this presumed lack of relationship. Most of these studies have been concerned with large and quoted companies in the UK and USA. The broad consensus has been that rate of growth neither increases nor decreases with size of firm, but that the dispersion of growth performance clearly declines with size, (e.g. Singh and Whittington, 1968; Hymer and Pashigian, 1962). The latter finding accords with intuition in that large firms are usually diversified over a number of markets. They can be thought of as composite entities made up of smaller units, with consequent averaging effects on the aggregate performance.

Three studies using a wider range of company sizes have observed that rates of growth decline with size. Mansfield (1962) observed this in studying long-term growth in three US industries. Wedervang (1965) found the same in his study of all Norwegian firms between 1930 and 1948. Lydall (1959) in a study of British firms employing fewer than 500 reported little correlation between size and growth except for a preponderance of strong growth among the smallest firms. There is evidence, presented in chapter nine, that growth and size are inversely associated in the East Midlands, and thus the evidence of these studies encourages the view that there may be a general tendency for very small firms to grow most rapidly.

It may be the case that very small firms grow more rapidly than large ones, but that among firms which are all relatively large the relationship disappears.

There is some evidence from Aaronvitch and Sawyer (1975) that a substantial amount of growth in large companies comes from acquisition rather than being internally generated.(3) Moreover, the importance of acquired growth increased with size of company except in the very largest size category.(4) There is an implication in this finding that internally generated growth declines with size of firm. If this is the case then it is also possible to suggest that firms too small to be active in takeovers will have the highest rate of internally generated growth, and that this rate may be higher than the rate of total growth (including acquisitions) in large firms.

A final piece of indirect evidence concerns the fact that profits (as a proportion of net assets) appear to be higher among small and private companies than for large and quoted companies. One study was undertaken by the Inland Revenue and is likely to be more reliable than is usual in these matters (Bolton, 1972, p.44). The other was undertaken by Tamari (1968) in connection with the Bolton Report on small firms. The significance of these results is that profitability is usually found to be positively associated with growth, and hence it is likely that growth rates are higher among small firms than larger firms.

6.3.2  Growth and the industrial sector

One of the external constraints which affects the growth of firms is that of demand. The growth of demand available to any one firm, in turn reflects the growth of actual demand, but also the competitive situation in the industry concerned. Both competition and the aggregate growth of demand vary between industries and there is thus a prima facie case for expecting the average growth of individual firms to vary between industries. The situation is less clearcut than it may seem however, since industry differences in the growth of demand may affect closures and entry more than the growth of permanent firms.

151

The empirical evidence on growth of net assets from
the Cambridge study covering the period 1948-60 shows
that differences between industries do exist (Singh
and Whittington, 1968). In the whole period, and also
in the two sub-periods separately, non-electrical
engineering had the highest rate of growth of the four
industries studied. The rank order of the other three
(food, consumer goods, and clothing) were also
maintained. What is more obvious from the figures is
the much larger dispersion within each industry. Indeed, the dispersion is so large that it is not
obvious that the industry averages are significantly
different in the statistical sense, although the
consistency between the two time periods suggests that
the differences are more than random fluctuations.

The variation between individual firms within any
one industry is very wide. The growth of net assets
over a twelve year period ranges from below minus 5
per cent to over 20 per cent. Over 5 per cent of
companies did not grow at all over the whole period.
A very substantial minority in each industry had below
average performances in both periods. With a mean
growth-rate of 8 per cent in both periods (and in the
overall period) the standard deviation of growth was
also of this magnitude in both periods, and only
slightly lower in the period as a whole.

A more limited analysis of growth in capital employed between 1966 and 1971 has been undertaken to test
the Singh and Whittington results at a more detailed
level of industrial disaggregation. The data drawn
from companies with assets in excess of £1 million in
the mechanical engineering industry (NEDO 1972) show
an average growth of capital employed of 7.6 per cent
over the five year period with a standard deviation
of 9.6 per cent. The data was divided into twenty-
nine detailed industries, and using analysis of
variance the industry averages were found to be significantly different.(5) The conclusions to be drawn
from these analyses are that average rates of growth
differ significantly between industries, but that a

very wide dispersion of performance exists within any one industry.

## 6.4 IMPLICATION OF PREVIOUS RESEARCH FOR THE REGIONAL SCALE

The research outlined above indicates that there are constraints of finance, demand, and managerial recruitment which limit the rate of expansion. Differences between firms reflect the abilities of senior management and the way in which the firms are organised. The rate of growth appears not to vary with size, at least among large firms, although it is possible that small firms grow fastest. There is significant variation between industrial sectors, but much greater variation within any one industry.

A complex mixture of factors is thus brought to bear on the growth of firms at any one time. Most of them are unlikely to lead to consistent spatial variations in the rate of growth, but for some factors this is not true. It is these latter factors which must be the centre of focus in any geographical analysis. Industrial structure, and perhaps also the size structure of firms, are two characteristics of regions which are likely to affect growth. It is also possible that regional variations in the quality of management may exist, and if so this would add a further regional dimension. One way in which differences in management quality could arise might be if birth-rates of new firms were geographically variable. In this case some regions would have more founder-managed firms than others, and on the evidence outlined above might then have a greater number of high growth firms. More hypothetically, it is also possible that if such firms are taken over by larger local companies, entrepreneurs might have the opportunity to rise within the larger firm, and thus make a wider impact.

Several factors which are ignored in the general

research on company growth become of potential importance in the context of regional differences. Factor availability is one possibility that may affect growth in firms which have production concentrated in just one, or perhaps a few, regions. Although firms can in theory move location or set up branch plants, there are costs involved in both cases which will tend to retard growth at least in the short term. Regional cost differences may also be of importance. In chapter two it was observed that remote locations may incur distribution cost penalties equal to 1 or 2 per cent of turnover. Other costs were judged to be unimportant except for unit labour costs where it was difficult to see any clear or consistent regional pattern.

A complication which occurrs in the regional context is that any one region contains only a part of many companies when the companies are of any significant size. Any one large company will normally have establishments spread over several regions. The growth of companies, and hence the factors discussed above, are only part of the story at the regional scale. The growth observed in establishments results partly from the growth of local firms, but is also dependent on the degree to which this growth is retained within the region rather than being 'exported' to other regions. In addition, some establishments will be branch plants of companies based outside the region, and growth in their case may be only incidentally connected with characteristics of the local economy.

Although a large proportion of locally based companies may be subsidiaries of major national companies with headquarters outside the region in question, the view is taken here that the growth of such companies depends much more on the subsidiary itself than the larger group of which it is a part. To a large extent subsidiaries (and divisions) can be treated as independent companies, with two important reservations. One is that the financial restraint on independent companies is lessened through membership of a larger organisation, and this will influence their ability to grow rapidly in some cases. It may also enable them to overcome cash-flow problems, and to compete on uneven terms with independent companies. Secondly, subsidiary companies may lose their semi-autonomous status and be converted into branch plants of larger units within the group.

The analysis of growth in a regional context should thus differentiate between companies and branch plants and should also perhaps distinguish independent companies from subsidiaries. In the case of the East Midlands in the postwar period, this has not been fully possible. As a consequence it is necessary to investigate growth in terms of establishments rather than companies. In order to see how the types of findings of research on companies relate to establish-ments an analysis is undertaken, in the following sections, of two of the major influences on growth. These are firstly, the influence of plant size and secondly, that of industrial structure.

6.5   GROWTH AND SIZE OF ESTABLISHMENT IN THE EAST MIDLANDS

6.5.1   Size distributions

Frequency distributions of establishment sizes are usually found to be lognormal in form and the East Midlands is no exception. A lognormal distribution appears as a straight line when drawn out on log-probability graph paper, and figure 6.1 shows that the distribution describes the sizes of East Midlands establishments almost exactly.(6)  The significance of this observation is that the distribution implies that growth and size are independent of one another. Before going on to test this contention directly, the use of the distribution can be explored a little further in a digression to shed light on other aspects of industrial change.

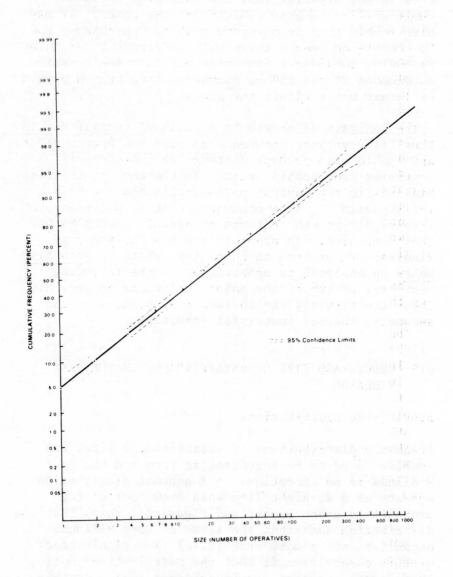

Figure 6.1  Cumulative size distribution of manufacturing establishments in the East Midlands
in 1967
Source of data:  Establishment records

If graphs similar to that of figure 6.1 are
constructed individually for counties within the East
Midlands then a relative deficiency of small plants
appears in three of the cases. This takes the form of
a break of slope in the line on the graph, as in
figure 6.2 which shows the distribution for Derbyshire.
In the Derbyshire distribution a break of slope occurs
at fifty operatives. This indicates a relative
deficiency of small plants, or put in different words
a relative excess of large plants. A similar situation is also found for Nottinghamshire and Lincolnshire. The probable reasons for this are either a
relatively low birth-rate of new firms, and hence,
fewer small plants; or, an influx of relatively large
branch plants from other areas; or both. As will be
shown in chapter eight there is other evidence to
indicate low birth-rates in these three counties.
Also these three counties are the most common destinations for those branch plants which were established
in the East Midlands.(7)

The form of the size distribution may thus shed
light on several aspects of industrial growth
including birth-rates, growth-rates and the importance
of in-moving branch plants. The full utility of size
distributions, in this respect, has yet to be
explored. The potential can however, be seen in
figure 6.3 in which a distinction is drawn between new
firms, new establishments, and permanent establishments. The overall size distribution in Leicestershire conforms closely to the lognormal, but figure
6.3 shows that this is comprised of two elements. The
distribution of sizes of permanent plants is concave
to the left, indicating a relative deficiency of large
plants. The distribution of new plants, in contrast,
has a very marked excess of plants employing over 400
operatives. When branches are omitted from the new
plants this excess disappears. The message to be read
from this graph is that fewer large permanent firms
have been established in Leicestershire than might
have been expected, while more new ones than expected
have arrived. From other evidence it is possible to

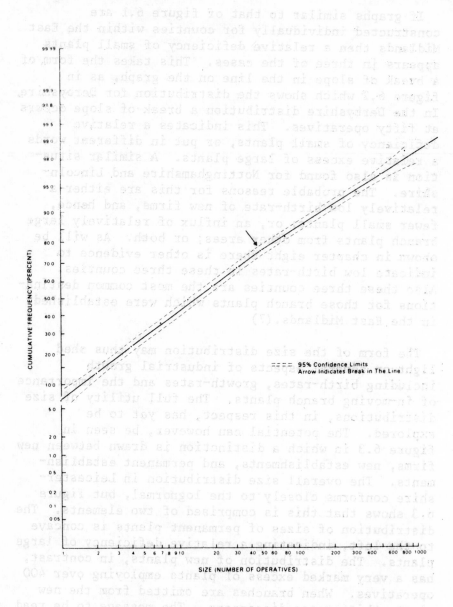

Figure 6.2   Cumulative size distribution of manufac-
             turing establishments in Derbyshire in
             1967
Source of data:   Establishment records

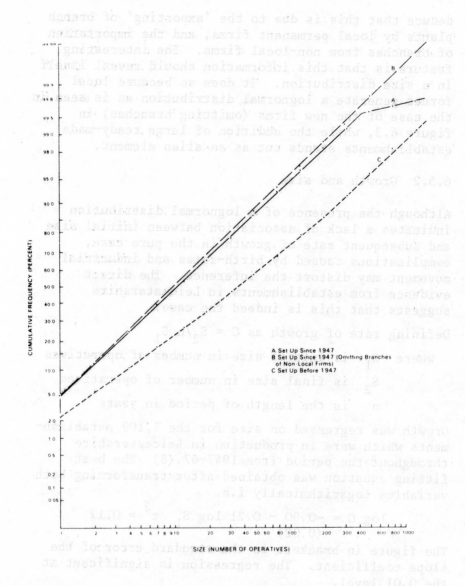

CUMULATIVE FREQUENCY (PERCENT)

A Set Up Since 1947
B Set Up Since 1947 (Omitting Branches
of Non-Local Firms)
C Set Up Before 1947

SIZE (NUMBER OF OPERATIVES)

Figure 6.3  Cumulative size distribution of manufacturing establishments in Leicestershire
in 1967
Source of data:  Establishment records

159

deduce that this is due to the 'exporting' of branch plants by local permanent firms, and the importation of branches from non-local firms. The interesting feature is that this information should reveal itself in a size distribution. It does so because local forces generate a lognormal distribution as is seen in the case of the new firms (omitting branches) in figure 6.3, while the addition of large ready-made establishments stands out as an alien element.

## 6.5.2 Growth and size

Although the presence of a lognormal distribution indicates a lack of association between initial size and subsequent rate of growth in the pure case, complications caused by birth-rates and industrial movement may distort the inference. The direct evidence from establishments in Leicestershire suggests that this is indeed the case.

Defining rate of growth as $G = S_2/n \, S_1$

where $S_1$ is initial size in number of operatives

$S_2$ is final size in number of operatives

$n$ is the length of period in years

Growth was regressed on size for the 1,109 establishments which were in production in Leicestershire throughout the period from 1947-67.(8) The best fitting equation was obtained after transforming both variables logarithmically i.e.

$$\log G = -0.90 - 0.21 \log S_1 \qquad r^2 = 0.12$$
$$(0.02)$$

The figure in brackets is the standard error of the slope coefficient. The regression is significant at the 0.01 level.

The form of this relationship is shown in figure 6.4 in which the curve is superimposed on a semi-logarithmic plot to provide a better visual impression of the relationship. The average rate of growth declines relatively sharply in the low size ranges,

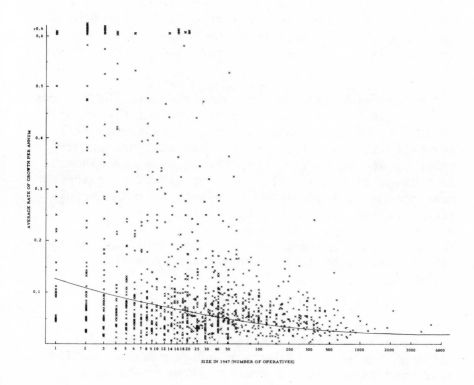

Figure 6.4   Rate of growth and initial size:
            Manufacturing establishments in Leicest-
            ershire 1947-67
Source of data:   Establishment records

but the decrease is less marked thereafter. The
average relationship can be described as negative,
non-linear and very weak. The more obvious characteristics are the great spread of growth-rates and the
way in which this spread declines with size. The
latter is a feature noted in most studies of growth
and size. A further feature is the large number of
establishments which declined over the period (i.e.
those with a growth-rate of less than 0.05). Some of
these are branch plants in which long-term decline is
understandable, but many are independent single plant
firms.

Similar relationships were also observed for the two
sub-periods 1947-57 and 1957-67. The relationships in
these periods were weaker ($r^2 = 0.06$) although still
statistically significant. A final test was undertaken by adding together all the local establishments
of individual firms. This had the effect of removing
most of the individual branch plants from the population, leaving either complete firms, or those parts
of locally based, multi-plant, firms which were
located within Leicestershire. The resulting regression equation, on 1,050 observations, was the
following:

$$\log G = -0.94 - 0.18 \underset{(0.02)}{S_1} \quad r^2 = 0.10$$

This equation is very similar to the previous one,
although the smaller constant and regression coefficient indicate that the average growth-rate is a
little lower for very small establishments and a
little higher for the largest ones. The difference is
slight and would barely show on figure 6.4.

Although the conclusions above refer to plants
rather than to whole firms even in the last case, it
is possible to make some deductions about companies.
The weighted average rate of growth of the establishments in Leicestershire was 0.055 p.a. If the net
addition to employment made by post-1947 branch plants
of local firms is added (minus closures of local

162

branch plants) this increases to 0.058 p.a. If the industrial movement to other areas which originated in Leicestershire between 1945 and 1965 is added, then the rate of increase rises to 0.065 p.a.(9) This rate of growth should represent the average for companies (rather than establishments) omitting growth in subsidiaries acquired during the period. It is quite likely that the latter would substantially increase the observed growth of large firms.

Restricting attention to internally generated growth (i.e. omitting acquisitions) leads to the conclusion that small firms grew faster than large firms. The overall average of 0.065 p.a. is exceeded in table 6.1 by virtually every size category below 200 employees. It is thus obvious that firms employing more than 200 must have rates of internally generated growth below those of small firms. The main deficiency in this deduction is that the large 'firms' include some establishments which are in fact branch plants of non-local companies. In an area like Leicestershire the number of such branch plants is relatively low, and is unlikely to destroy the main conclusion.

The conclusion that growth and size are inversely related, at least when acquisitions are omitted, supports the observations made by Mansfield (1964) and Wedervang (1964), using data on assets and employment respectively. This conclusion is of particular relevance for regions which export relatively little of their growth. In regions like the East Midlands the fact that much growth is exported to other regions means that in the remaining permanent establishments the inverse relationship between growth and size will be even more marked.

One study which found a similar negative relationship between employment growth and size for establishments, was that of Collins (1972) for Ontario between 1960 and 1965. Like the East Midlands study Collins measured size and growth by employment rather than by assets. This study indicated a negative

relationship between size and growth in twenty-five
out of thirty-seven industrial categories, although
the relationship was only statistically significant in
four cases.

Table 6.1

Growth and size of 'firms'* in Leicestershire 1947-67

| Sizegroup (No. of operatives) | Mean | Standard deviation |
|---|---|---|
| 1 | 0.274 | 0.447 |
| 2 | 0.264 | 0.519 |
| 3-4 | 0.160 | 0.211 |
| 5-7 | 0.109 | 0.118 |
| 8-12 | 0.106 | 0.111 |
| 13-19 | 0.128 | 0.183 |
| 20-31 | 0.104 | 0.227 |
| 32-49 | 0.082 | 0.066 |
| 50-79 | 0.077 | 0.070 |
| 80-124 | 0.071 | 0.043 |
| 125-199 | 0.062 | 0.041 |
| 200-315 | 0.058 | 0.035 |
| 316-500 | 0.051 | 0.043 |
| 501-799 | 0.042 | 0.017 |
| 800-1249 | 0.041 | 0.032 |
| 1250-1999 | 0.035 | 0.010 |
| 2000+ | 0.049 | 0.028 |
| Average | 0.113 | 0.216 |

Source of data: Establishment records
    * A 'firm' is defined as all permanent establish-
ments within Leicestershire owned by an individual
company.

In summary the evidence strongly suggests a
generalisation to the effect that growth and size are
inversely related in establishments. The inverse
relationship also probably holds for firms also, as
long as the full range of sizes is included. The
reasons for expecting a higher growth-rate among
surviving small firms are an extension of the more

obvious reasons for expecting greater variability in performance. Since performance is likely to be more variable in small firms, many small firms will close as a result of their markedly below-average performances. These closures are not included in analyses of growth, and instead only the above-average variability is taken into account, while much of the variability in the downward direction disappears from sight. The higher growth-rate will thus result from the fact that only the more successful small firms are taken into consideration. The tendency to observe stronger negative correlations (between size and growth) is not surprising when establishments rather than firms form the units of analysis. Small establishments have relatively unrestricted opportunities to expand, ceteris paribus, in that they can usually move into larger local premises. However, it is more usual for expansion in large firms to be undertaken by setting up branch plants, than is the case with small firms. Large plants forming part of large firms should thus have lower growth-rates than small establishments which can more easily escape the restrictions of their current site.

The fact that an inverse size-growth relationship can coexist with a lognormal size distribution demonstrates the fact discovered in other contexts that it is not usually possible to deduce real world processes from the mathematical processes which generate statistical frequency distributions. Ijiri and Simon (1964) have shown that 'many processes incorporationg comparatively weak forms of the law of proportionate effect will lead to similar distributions'. The analysis of this chapter merely shows that the basic conditions can be even weaker still, and may include a degree of association between size and growth.

## 6.6 GROWTH AND THE INDUSTRIAL SECTOR IN THE EAST MIDLANDS

The work of Singh and Whittington (1968) demonstrated

165

that growth-rates 'differ between industrial sectors'. The purpose of this section is to investigate whether this conclusion holds for establishments as well as for companies. The analysis uses either questionnaire data for the whole region, or establishment records for Leicestershire. In both cases analysis of variance is used to test for statistically significant differences between regions.(10)

Using questionnaire data from 331 establishments on growth between 1947 and 1971, the average growth-rates were found to differ significantly between twelve industrial sectors. Statistical significance in itself indicates little, since even very small differences can be shown to be significant as long as the sample size is large enough. One measure of significance in the non-statistical sense is the intra-class correlation coefficient (Blalock, 1960). A value of unity indicates a perfect association, while zero indicates that no association is present. Using the questionnaire data the value of the coefficient proved to be close to zero at 0.05, indicating that industry differences accounted for only a very small part of the variation between establishments.

A finer industrial breakdown using 72 minimum list heading industries was possible for the 1,109 permanent establishments in Leicestershire (1947-67). Once again the differences between industries were wider than could be ascribed to chance alone (at the 0.01 significance level). The amount of the total variation explained by the industry groupings was as slight as before, giving an intra-class correlation coefficient of 0.05. The situation is as described in figure 6.5, with a key to the industry codes in appendix III. The most obvious characteristic is the very wide dispersion of growth-rates within any one industry. The differences between the industry averages (shown as bars) is much less marked than the range covered by the individual growth-rates (shown as crosses). The industry averages are unweighted arithmetic means, and it should be noted that these

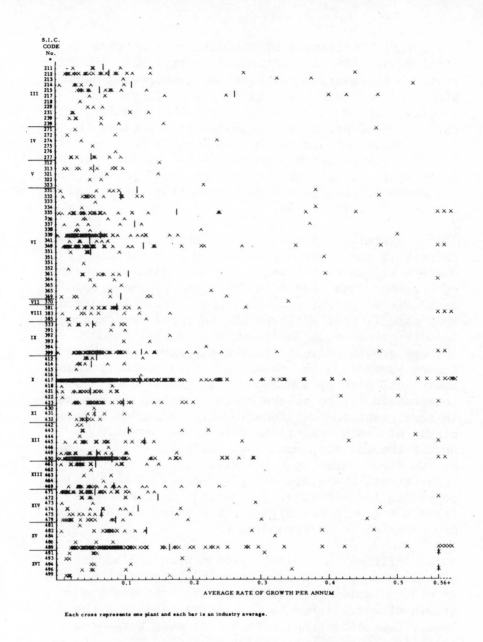

Figure 6.5   Rate of growth and industrial sector
manufacturing establishments in Leicestershire 1947-67
Source of data:  Establishment records

are greatly influenced by the more rapidly growing
small firms. In the footwear industry (MLH 450) for
instance the average establishment, including many
single plant firms, grew by 60 per cent over the
period, although the industry as a whole declined
rapidly by 40 per cent. This occurred because the
large plants containing most employment declined.
Even so they declined significantly less than the
industry at large, and the main brunt of the decline
was absorbed through a high closure-rate and a low
entry-rate of new firms.

A very similar picture of slight variation between
industries but greater diversity within industries
emerges if the twenty year period is divided into two
sub-periods, and also if establishments are grouped
into 'firms' as before. The conclusion to be drawn
from this is that although the national performance of
industries has some influence on the unweighted
average growth of individual establishments, the
impact is small. The chief reason is probably that
individual plants, and especially small ones, are
constrained little by the overall changes in demand.
In some cases the reallocation of production between
plants of individual firms will cause variation
around the industry mean. In the case of small and
medium sized firms in particular, but all firms to
some extent, there are varying degrees of success in
competing for shares of the overall market. Some
firms may expand rapidly in a declining market, others
may contract in an expanding one.

The influence of overall growth upon individual
establishments was tested by correlating national
growth in employment with the unweighted average
growth of establishments in Leicestershire in the
twenty-four industries with ten or more permanent
establishments. The correlation proved weak with an
$r^2$ value of only 0.1 and insignificantly different
from zero. The correlation with the total growth in
employment within each industry was even weaker.
Again it should be emphasised however that this is

due partly to the performance of small firms.  In large firms there is less room for manoeuvre within the constraints set by the general changes in demand.


## 6.7  CONCLUSION

In an analysis of growth within a single region, establishments rather than firms, form the basic units of investigation.  This means that the factors affecting the growth of whole firms are important, but in addition influences on firms' retention of growth within the region must also be considered.  It seems that some of the main empirical results on the growth of firms also apply to a population of establishments, although there are some differences.  In particular, growth declines with size especially in the smallest size ranges.  Also, differences between industries account for very little of the overall variation between establishments.

In an investigation of spatial differences in unweighted growth-rates, neither size nor industrial structure will be of very great importance, unless there are sharp areal contrasts in the latter.  At the regional scale size distributions vary little, and hence, the relationship between size and growth is unlikely to produce a strong spatial dimension.


NOTES

(1)  The following discussion of the work of Downie, Marris and Penrose draws heavily upon the clear account in Lee and Jones (1974).
(2)  The importance of this ratio (known as 'gearing') is shown by its significant role in a discriminant function evolved by R. Taffler which it is claimed will predict business failure with close to complete accuracy (Sunday Times 27 February 1977 p.62).
(3)  The study is of growth 1958-67 in UK companies with assets exceeding £5 million in 1957.  In the 182

manufacturing companies within the sample the average
proportion of 'acquired growth' was 36 per cent.
(4)  The opposite conclusion was reached by Preston
(1973) for growth in very large US companies between
1954 and 1968.
(5)  The growth figures were transformed to logarithmic form.  The industry differences were significant
at the 0.01 level.
(6)  This graphical method of assessing 'goodness of
fit' is viewed as satisfactory by Aitcheson and
Brown (1957).  The confidence intervals were inserted
using a method described by Lepeltier (1969).
(7)  Northamptonshire was the major destination for
in-moving plants but there is reason to expect that
many of these were small transferring companies and
not the relatively larger branch plants.
(8)  Some of these changed their location locally
during the period.
(9)  Figures from the Department of Industry 50 x 50
movement matrix.  The use of these figures here
assumes that all movement was in the form of branch
plants and not transfers.  Rake (1972) estimates that
this is very largely true.  This assumption will tend
to maximise the growth ascribed to large firms.  It is
further assumed that no pre-1945 branches outside the
county were closed in this period.  Since the exercise
is in terms of operatives, while the movement figures
include all employment, it has been (conservatively)
assumed that 80 per cent of this latter employment
consists of operatives.
(10)  Analysis of variance assumes normally distributed observations drawn from populations with the same
variance.  Normality was achieved by logarithmic
transformation.  Equality of variance is more difficult to achieve.  Boneau (1960) showed that unequal
variance seriously distorts results only when
categories have differing numbers of observations.
However, when the higher variances are associated with
large categories, as is the case in this section, significant results are less likely to be found.  The
significant results reported below are thus not likely
to be spurious.  As an additional check a procedure

derived by Box (1954) was used to measure the degree of distortion induced by unequal variance and size groups. This procedure showed that the distortion was not sufficient to give misleading results.

# 7  The closure of firms and plants

In any large population of plants and firms a
substantial proportion close during periods longer
than a few years.  Closures make a significant impact
on employment change and it is necessary to understand
why and how they occur; and why closure rates vary
over space.  The latter question is left for chapter
ten, but the non-spatial aspects of closure are
investigated here.  It is beyond the resources of this
study to investigate the process of closure in depth,
and instead this chapter will review previous research
and test some of the major conclusions within the
context of firms and establishments in the postwar
East Midlands.


## 7.1  FORMS OF CLOSURE

Manufacturing establishments may be closed down
either because the firm itself ceases production, or
because a continuing firm decides to close a branch
factory.  In either case the cause is not necessarily
economic failure.  Firms cease production for a
variety of reasons, voluntary and non-voluntary,
economic and non-economic.  Churchill (1952) states
that for US firms of all types, 'lack of profitability
was by no means the only reason for the sale or
liquidation of a business'.  Wedervang (1964) suggests
that bad health or the death of an owner may cause an
otherwise sound firm to close if it is small or medium
sized.  Even in cases of financial failure complexities are present: 'bankruptcy ... merges impercepti-
bly into various forms of voluntary liquidation or
sale of a business at a significant loss.  Declining
turnover and profitability may be contributory factors
to this outcome but not necessarily, so there is the
not unfamiliar phenomenon of companies overtrading and
being brought down by a shortage of cash'.

(Merrett Cyriax, 1971). Branch plants may be closed
due to internal reorganisation within a company and
closure does not necessarily imply failure in the
sense of unacceptable, or even below average, profitability.

There is some evidence available to indicate the
demarcation lines between financial failure and other
causes as reasons for closure. Churchill (1955) found
that for all US business only half of all liquidations
were made to avoid or to minimise a loss. In a
British study of manufacturing and construction firms
(Merrett Cyriax, 1971) the mortality rate between
1963 and 1970 was 10.1 per cent. Of these, approximately three-quarters were compulsory or voluntary
liquidations (with the former in the preponderance),
while a quarter ceased trading without liquidation.
Furthermore, an additional 4 per cent of the sample
could be classified as financial failures, but were
taken over and did not cease production. A common
cause of both voluntary liquidation and of takeover in
Britain is thought to be problems created by estate
duty on the death of the owner of a small company
(CBI, 1971).

Most closures thus appear to be due to financial
failure, although this does not necessarily imply low
profitability in previous periods. In the case of
branch plants less is known about the factors causing
closure. One study which has however investigated
some of the major reasons for closing branch plants
and subsidiaries is that of Rake (1972) for East
Midlands' companies 1945-71. He found that out of 115
closures, 46 per cent were rationalisations in the
sense that production was moved to other factories, or
was excess to company requirements without a decline
in overall demand. Another 22 per cent were closed
due specifically to declining demand for their
products. Stresses of various types included technological obsolescence, labour problems, and leases
falling due and these were major causes in 30 per cent
of cases.

It is interesting to speculate on the degree to which these factors might be specific to branch plants of multi-plant firms, rather than to independent firms. In fact, it is not clear that any of them are specific in this way. Falling demand and various stresses might lead to closures in the case of independent companies. In the case of rationalisation, closures might have occurred anyway if there is general over-capacity in the industry. The individual establishments may well not be the same, but the overall closure rate may not be affected. Closure by rationalisation is a very visible action of multi-plant firms, but it should not necessarily indicate that branches (or subsidiaries) are more prone to closure than independent companies.

For the analysis of spatial variations in plant mortality, it is important to bear in mind the variety of forms of closure, and especially to avoid the simple equation of high mortality rates with disadvantageous location in the absence of additional evidence.

## 7.2 MANAGERIAL FACTORS IN THE CLOSURE OF FIRMS

In firms as opposed to branch plants it is the smaller ones which are most vulnerable to closure. Within these firms mismanagement, or ineffective management, appear to be the major factors determining which will close and which will survive. This factor can perhaps be separated into two components. Firstly, there is an entry-rate effect. Many businesses are set up in the wrong industry from the start, in the sense that entry-rates are high, and a high proportion of entries will automatically fail. Oxenfeldt (1945) asserts that in the USA (referring to all business not necessarily manufacturing), that entrepreneurs tend to set up firms in the most difficult conditions. High rates of entry are associated with low capital requirements. Low profitability and fierce competition are the result in such industries, and high exit-rates are an inevitable consequence. In such

174

industries a certain proportion of firms are doomed to
failure.  This latter point is echoed by several other
authors.  Beesley (1955) for instance agrees with the
TNEC Monograph (1941) description of entrepreneurs
'marching into ambush', 'naively optimistic, 'inex-
perienced', and 'ignorant of the weapons of trade'.
These factors help to clarify the mechanics of the
association, discussed below, between high entry-
rates and high exit-rates, and also between age and
mortality.

Management inefficiency naturally increases vulnerability to closure in established firms as well as in
those recently set up.  A number of studies have
investigated the importance of this factor and have
elaborated on what exactly it means.  In a study of
100 British firms compulsorily liquidated in 1965,
Brough (1967) found that the official receiver cited
'mismanagement' as a principal cause of failure in
two-thirds of the cases, and 'gross mismanagement'
in 4 per cent.  Not surprisingly none of the directors
of these companies gave this reason.  In a comparable
US study, but one confined to small manufacturing
firms, Woodruff and Alexander (1958) contrasted
successful firms with failures.  They again concluded
that managerial incompetence was the primary underlying cause of failure.
    'The unsuccessful firms in comparison with the
successful ones failed to maintain adequate financial
records, placed less emphasis on the marketing
function, paid less attention to the research and
development of new products, and were generally more
inept in their internal administration.'
Within the general definition of incompetence Woodruff
and Alexander also place 'lack of capital'.  This is
frequently mentioned in bankruptcy proceedings, but in
the view of these authors can be viewed as a symptom
of management inadequacy rather than as a basic cause.

Not all company closures can be blamed on mismanagement in the usual  sense.  Among small firms succession difficulties caused by the departure of the

founder is another factor. Wedervang (1965) expects a substantial exit-rate, of 2 to 3 per cent per annum among private firms due to this cause. Davies and Kelly (1972) are of the opinion that many voluntary liquidations stem from this factor. The root causes of these succession difficulties are several. Firstly, small firms, and particularly first generation firms tend to have highly centralised and personalised management which leads to maximum dislocation and change on succession. Secondly, in this type of management the problem of succession tends not to be given priority, even though it may be foreseen. Thirdly, estate duty may impose financial pressure on a small family business.

Small companies are not the only ones to run into trouble, although business failure and actual closure become less synonomous with increasing size. In Britain recently failing companies like British Leyland, Alfred Herbert and Ferranti have been rescued by the Government, as was Lockheed in America, by the financial community. The assets of large companies are often too valuable to be broken up, and takeovers are a common method of avoiding closure, although in periods of major depression as in the 1930s bankruptcy and closure become more closely related. In some cases part of the assets of a major company may be bought as a going concern while other parts are sold for other uses. One cause of failure which can beset otherwise successful companies, both large and small, is the cash-flow crisis. The failure of Rolls Royce is commonly ascribed to this cause. The company was generally viewed as successful before the RB 211 contract, and once this was broken by going into receivership all creditors and shareholders were repaid in full.


7.3  CLOSURES AND THE BUSINESS CYCLE

One consequence of the general frequency of closures either through mismanagement or other causes is the

curious fact that closure rates appear not to be very
sensitive to phases of the business cycle. Two
studies of prewar closure rates found little evidence
of an association in the UK, West Midlands (Beesley,
1955) or the USA/TNEC, 1941). However Wedervang (1965)
observed closure rates in Norway to be 60 per cent
higher during the depression years 1930-33 compared
with the subsequent four years. The American official
figures on closures (Churchill 1959) show only a loose
correspondence between closure and recession in the
period 1940-59. Two smaller scale studies have found
small companies to be less sensitive to the business
cycle than large ones (Kaplan, 1941; Kinnard and
Malinowski, 1960). This suggestion echoes the observation for growth that macro-economic changes do not
impinge so directly on small firms as on large. The
great variability among small firms means that a great
deal of change, whether growth or closure, takes place
whatever the external conditions.


7.4  CLOSURE RATES AND AGE OF BUSINESS

Studies of the relationship between age and mortality
in manufacturing establishments all point to declining
vulnerability with increasing age. Marcus (1967) suggests two reasons for this phenomenon. Firstly,
entrepreneurs learn with experience and increase their
chances of survival. Secondly, firms which are doomed
to failure from their inception are weeded out within
a very few years.

The only difference between researchers lies in the
estimation of the severity of the 'cull' of young
firms. North American evidence points to the first
five years being the hardest with a levelling off in
mortality rates after this (Churchill 1955). In
particular, the first two years have the highest exit-
rates of all. The American study includes change of
ownership under the heading 'mortality', and this may
explain the apparent levelling out at 80 per cent
mortality, after ten years. This contrasts with the

177

situation for Ontario described by Collins (1972) where the mortality curve levels off at just below 50 per cent after four or five years. Although the inclusion of transfers of ownership in the mortality figures may be expected to have little influence in the first few years, the ratio of takeovers to closures should increase after this. Figures including transfers will in this case continue to show increasing mortality rates past the point at which closure rates stabilise when ownership changes are excluded.

Two European studies suggest a much less severe failure rate among young firms. Wedervang (1965) shows that, for Norwegian firms, age has little effect after twelve years, by which time only half of the firms have been sold or gone out of business. He concludes that, 'it is therefore obvious that American mortality rates are considerably higher than those found for Norwegian manufacturing industries'. Beesley (1955) indicates a similar survival pattern for industrial establishments in the West Midlands. In this study 45 to 50 per cent of plants established in the period from 1923-29 failed to survive until 1938 i.e. at least nine years. The experience of establishments in the East Midlands similarly suggest exit-rates at levels much lower than in the USA. Of all the plants established in Leicestershire between 1947 and 1957, 25 per cent had closed by 1957 and 66 per cent by 1970. In the latter case the age of plants is at least twelve years. The greater longevity of establishments in the European areas which has been studied should be seen in the context of the lower turnover rates (i.e. entry and exit) in these areas. The lower entry-rates and greater longevity may suggest a more cautious attitude to entrepreneurship.

In all of the above studies, where it is possible to deduce detailed trends, exit-rates are almost constant after the early high mortality period. Age appears not to be of importance once maturity is reached. Closures which occur after this period,

Wedervang suggests, are largely 'accidental' and
unrelated to age except in small firms where the death
or illness of the owner may lead to closure.


## 7.5   CLOSURE RATES AND SIZE

As was the case with age, an inverse relationship
exists between exit-rate and size.  Studies from North
America and Norway consistently indicate that smaller
establishments are more vulnerable to closure than are
larger ones.  The same conclusion also holds for
firms.  For both firms and plants the general conclusion seems to be that units employing less than ten
employees have higher than average exit-rates, while
others have lower rates.  In particular, very small
units (fewer than five employees) have closure rates
which are double the average, while large firms or
plants (over one hundred employees) have closure
rates of only half the average or less.  Unlike the
situation for age-related behaviour, the effects of
size do not seem to differ consistently between
Europe and North America although closure rates as a
whole are higher in North America.  Collins (1972)
finds a relationship between size and mortality for
establishments in Ontario which is similar in its
magnitudes to that in the East Midlands during the
postwar period and both of these studies refer to
establishments.  Wedervang (1965) and Kinnard and
Malinowski (1960) both find size effects which
indicate relatively higher mortality rates for very
small firms.  The former also reports that mortality
decreases only slowly with increasing size except for
the very small firms.

The evidence of the studies quoted above suggests
that a similar relationship between size and the
probability of closure exists in several countries and
at different times.  Within the East Midlands reliable
figures were available for Leicestershire alone.  The
overall rate of closure of establishments which were
in production in 1947 was 54.1 per cent.(1)  Using

179

thirty-four size categories, with approximately
logarithmic intervals, the relationship between size
and frequency of closure was found to be the
following (2):

$$Y = 124.54 - 49.45 \; X^{0.1286}$$
$$(2.86)$$

where      Y is the closure rate (%)
         X is the number of operatives in 1947
         the figure in brackets is the standard
         error.

The curve is graphed in figure 7.1 which shows that
the probability of closure over the twenty year
period declined from 75 per cent for a one-man operation down to zero for plants employing over 1,000.

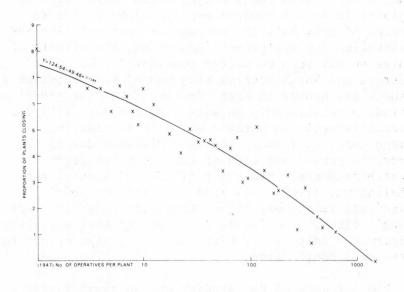

Figure 7.1  Size of plant and frequency of closure in
Leicestershire 1947-67
Source of data:  Establishment records

180

In fact only one establishment employing more than
500 operatives was found to have closed in this
period, and this was predictably in the footwear
industry.  The probability of any one establishment
closing falls to less than one in five with an employment of 300 operatives, and to one in ten with 500.
The form of the relationship is more obvious in figure
7.2 which has been drawn for the lower size ranges
without logarithmic transformation.

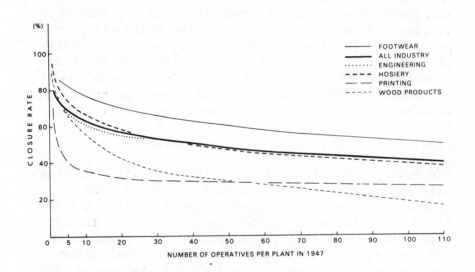

Figure 7.2   Closure rates 1947-67 for major industries
             in Leicestershire
Source of data:  Establishment records

This diagram also shows how the relationship between
size and closure differs between industries.  Most
industries share the same general relationship, but at
varying average levels of closure.

181

The highest rates of closure in Leicestershire were observed in the declining footwear industry, and it can be seen that closures of footwear plants (including many single plant firms) were more frequent in virtually all size ranges compared with other industries.

In any industry, or in manufacturing as a whole, the variety of factors which influence closure can be viewed as a probability process. Factors such as size and age are powerful influences but within any category of size, age or industry the remaining factors will cause random fluctuations. This is seen in figure 7.1 where the figures for individual size categories are scattered randomly along the line of average probability of closure. The probability process can be viewed as a binomial one, and in fact the scatter in figure 7.1 accords with what might be expected from binomial variation. The binomial model is useful in detecting random variations in space, and will be used in this capacity in chapter ten.

7.5.1  The effects of size and age together

The reasons underlying a mortality rate which declines with size partly reflect factors connected with company age, and partly those related to size itself. The disadvantages of youthfulness are mainly associated with inexperience, and because most young firms are also small this factor also affects small firms (and hence small plants). Increasing experience will tend to lead to both expansion in size and to lower vulnerability to closure.

Several characteristics of small firms will tend to lower the chance of survival even among mature small firms. These include the higher cost of obtaining capital, greater difficulty in obtaining credit, and in securing payment of debts especially in time of recession. The smaller financial resources and reliance on a single product or process make small firms less able to emerge successfully from random shocks

182

and accidents. In the case of branch plants, it should cause less disruption for a multi-plant company to close a small branch rather than a large one.

The closure of branch plants is considered in the next section. In this section it is possible to review evidence which attempts to differentiate between the effects of age and those of size alone. Marcus (1967) concluded from his study of US firms that the influence of age on mortality lasted only for the first six years. After this period size had an independent effect on closure but this was only marked for the smallest firms. Wedervang (1964) observed a twelve year period of 'immaturity' among Norwegian firms in the thirties.

Evidence from the East Midlands establishments can only throw an indirect light on this question because dates of entry and closure were not usually known precisely. It was possible, however, to examine the closure rates among those establishments which had been in operation for at least eight years. The closure rates in table 7.1 show that a distinct decline occurred in the frequency of closure with increasing size. Although nearly all of the establishments in this exercise had been established for too long to be described as immature, the relationship between age and size was very similar to that described above for all establishments, including youthful ones. It can be concluded from this that size affects the rate of closure independently of age, and that these effects are marked throughout the range of sizes.

7.5.2  Firms and branch plants

Table 7.2 shows closure rates in Leicestershire for branch plants compared with headquarters establishments and single plant firms jointly. As can be seen, rates of closure for branches decline with increasing size of plant, but no smooth or continuous progression is evident.

## Table 7.1

Closures among mature establishments

| Number of operatives | Closures 1955-67 as a percentage of all plants in 1955 which had survived from 1947 |
|:---:|:---:|
| 1-5 | 57.1 |
| 6-10 | 44.5 |
| 11-15 | 41.3 |
| 16-20 | 36.1 |
| 21-25 | 39.4 |
| 26-30 | 34.1 |
| 31-35 | 22.2 |
| 36-40 | 35.0 |
| 41-45 | 37.5 |
| 46-50 | 32.8 |
| 51-60 | 27.6 |
| 61-70 | 38.0 |
| 71-80 | 20.1 |
| 81-90 | 23.5 |
| 91-100 | 34.8 |
| 101-150 | 23.4 |
| 151-200 | 15.7 |
| 201-250 | 13.8 |
| 251-300 | 13.0 |
| 301-500 | 6.2 |
| 500+ | 0.0 |
| Total no. of plants | 1,789 |

Source of data:  Establishment records

In general, closure rates are near to, or above, 60 per cent for branch plants with fewer than forty employees.  Closure rates are consistently between 45 and 50 per cent for medium sized plants (with 40 to 250 employees), but drop sharply for large plants.  A three-step progression is suggested by these figures corresponding to small, medium and large plants. Large branch plants (with more than 251 employees) have rates similar to those of non-branch plants, and

## Table 7.2

Closure rates for branch plants in Leicestershire 1947-67

| Size in 1947 No. of operatives | All branches | Percentage of initial population of plants | | |
| --- | --- | --- | --- | --- |
| | | Branches of surviving Leics. companies | Branches of surviving non-local firms | All non-branch establishments |
| 1-5 | 57 | 46 | 66 | 70 |
| 6-10 | 73 | 59 | 33 | 61 |
| 11-15 | 80 | 62 | 100 | 58 |
| 16-20 | 47 | 39 | 50 | 49 |
| 21-30 | 73 | 50 | 50 | 44 |
| 31-40 | 64 | 50 | 25 | 43 |
| 41-50 | 46 | 41 | 0 | 45 |
| 51-70 | 46 | 27 | 50 | 35 |
| 71-100 | 50 | 27 | 67 | 36 |
| 101-150 | 46 | 33 | 100 | 41 |
| 151-250 | 50 | 33 | 50 | 22 |
| 251+ | 16 | 15 | 0 | 12 |
| Average | 56 | 44 | 42 | 56 |
| No. of plants in 1947 | 322 | 182 | 50 | 2,108 |

Source of data: Establishment records

Note: It has not been possible to identify closing branch plants of non-local companies which themselves closed down before 1967. Hence closures in the 'all branches' column are probably underestimated.

thus may behave organisationally as if they were
independent firms in respect to closure.  In all other
size categories, however, except the very smallest,
branches have higher closure rates than non-branches.
The smallest branches include small servicing depots
(which are only partly manufacturing) and some
manufacturing departments of large firms located close
to, but not within, the main works.  Such tiny establishments may survive over long periods and account
for the low number of closures in this size category.

Surprisingly, the high rates of closure of branch
plants appears to be due more to entire multi-plant
firms closing down than to the continuing firms
closing one or more of their branches.  However, the
proportions of closures in these two categories were
reversed between 1947-55 and 1955-67.  In the former
period 70 per cent of closures were branches of
continuing firms, in the second period the figure was
only 32 per cent.  The branches of companies based in
Leicestershire tended to have closure rates close to,
or slightly below those of branch plants across the
range of sizes.  There is certainly very little
evidence that branch plants showed any greater propensity to closure than did parent establishments or
single plant firms taken together.  There is evidence
that these branch plants were more resistant to
closure in the higher size ranges that in the lower,
in much the same way as non-branch plants.

It is less easy to generalise about the behaviour
of branches of non-local companies.  The number of
observations is small in any one size category and
this produces erratic results.  There is little
evidence of declining closure rates with increasing
size, except that in the largest size category no
closures were recorded from the five branches in the
category.

Although the finding that branches are no more
prone to closure than other establishments goes
counter to conventional wisdom, there is other

evidence that this represents a general case. Atkins
(1973) analysed closures among the 952 branch plants
set up (across sub-regional boundaries) in the UK
between 1945 and 1961 which were surviving in 1966.
The closures were those occurring in the period
1966-71, thus ensuring a degree of maturity in all
cases. The closure rate of branches was found to be
2.1 per cent and this rate was identical to that in
the parent plants within the same population of
companies. The identity was maintained despite the
fact that the parent plants were almost three times
as large as the branches at the beginning of the
period. The proportion of jobs lost in closures was
slightly higher in the branches however, since the
closing parent factories were only two and a half
times as large as the closing branches.


## 7.6   FREQUENCY OF CLOSURE AND PRIOR RATE OF GROWTH

It is to be expected that firms which close will on
average have grown less rapidly prior to closure than
those which survive. This may also be the case for
individual establishments of multi-plant firms, but
here the connection is less direct. In one American
study it was found that most closing firms had stable
sizes in the five years prior to closure, and that
only a negligible proportion declined in size
(Kinnard and Malinowski, 1960).

This was not found to be the case in Leicestershire,
although in this case there was no distinction between
firms and plants. The analyses measured the growth
between 1947 and 1955 of those establishments founded
before 1947 which closed between 1957 and 1967. Using
the definition of growth described in 6.5.2, the range
of growth-rates is that described in figure 7.3. This
graph should be interpreted along the lines described
in 5.2.1.

The (geometric) mean rate of growth was 0.10 for
establishments which closed and 0.13 for those

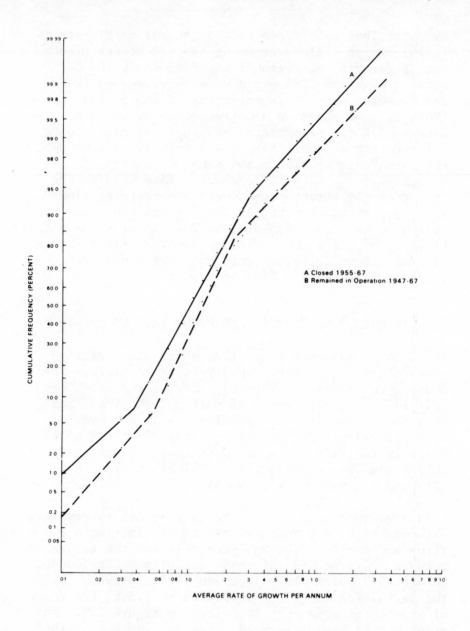

Figure 7.3   Frequency distributions of growth-rates in
Leicestershire 1947-55
Source of data:   Establishment records

188

surviving until 1967. The former average represents
stability over the period, with half of the individual
establishments declining and the other half growing.
The average growth of surviving establishments was 30
per cent higher than that of closures, and the two
populations of establishments can be seen to have
clearly different compositions in respect of growth.

To this extent there is a difference in prior
performance between survivors and closures but not too
much should be made of the fact. Although half of
the closing establishments had declined in size before
1955, it is also the case that 38 per cent of the
survivors did likewise. Conversely examples of very
high growth-rates were present among the incipient
closures as well as among the survivors, although the
high-flyers were relatively more numerous among the
latter. It can be concluded that establishments which
closed performed less well than survivors on average,
but that there was a wide range of experience among
survivors and closures alike. The existence of high
growth establishments which subsequently close may
point out the existence of over-trading as a cause of
failure in firms.

## 7.7  SECTORAL VARIATIONS IN CLOSURE RATES

All of the studies cited above found considerable
differences in closure rates between industries.
There is little point in comparing the industry rates
in detail since the various studies refer to different
periods and to a varied range of economic conditions.
In each case, however, the differences were wider than
could be ascribed to the effects of random variation
around the all-industry average.

The two most likely causes of differences between
industries are the general rate of growth in each
industry and the rate of entry of new firms. Inefficient firms might find survival easier in an industry
which was expanding than in one which was contracting

since, in the latter case, competition could be
expected to be more fierce.  Industries with high
entry-rates will contain larger numbers of young and
vulnerable firms, and perhaps also more poorly managed
firms.

Wedervang (1964) found that in prewar Norway the
rate of expansion had some effect, but that other
factors were more important.  Industries tended to
maintain their relative ranking in closure rates
whatever the economic conditions.  Although some of
the most depressed industries in the depression
period exhibited high rates of closures, the same
industries later expanded most rapidly but maintained
their high levels of closure.  Wedervang also observed
some correspondence between closure rates and entry-
rates but again the association was not strong.  A
closer relationship in this respect was found by
Collins (1972) for plants in Ontario between 1960 and
1965.  The rank correlation for twenty industrial
sectors can be computed from his table (p.170) at
0.33.  It is possible to compute a similar correlation
coefficient for US firms between 1951 and 1955 from
the data of Churchill (1959).  This shows a closer
relationship again, yielding a coefficient of 0.54.

Both of these possibilities have been tested on the
data for closures of Leicestershire establishments
1947-67.  The analysis was restricted to those
industries, listed in table 7.3, which had more than
twenty establishments in 1947.  Table 7.3 shows that
closure rates varied from half of the overall average
up to $1\frac{1}{2}$ times the average.  Some of the industries
with the highest closure rates also have a high
proportion of small firms as in dresses, toys and
games and miscellaneous products.  Conversely some of
the low closure industries are dominated by larger
firms as in narrow fabrics and textile furnishing, but
this relationship cannot be pursued too far.

Table 7.4 shows the correlations between closure
rates, entry-rates and growth-rates as well as the

Table 7.3

Closure rates 1947-67 for industries

| MLH (1957 sic) | Industry | No. of plants in 1947 | Relative rate (all industries = 100) |
|---|---|---|---|
| | Food & drink | | |
| 211 | Grain milling | 22 | 134* |
| 212 | Baking | 36 | 82 |
| 215 | Milk products | 20 | 83 |
| 239 | Soft drinks | 20 | 120 |
| | Engineering | | |
| 335 | Textile machinery | 60 | 89 |
| 339 | 'Other' machinery | 71 | 60* |
| 349 | 'Other' mech. engineering | 113 | 121* |
| 361 | Electrical machinery | 22 | 118 |
| 381 | Motor vehicles | 24 | 69* |
| 399 | 'Other' metal industries | 74 | 114 |
| | Textiles & clothing | | |
| 417 | Hosiery | 434 | 91 |
| 421 | Narrow fabrics | 24 | 54* |
| 423 | Textile finishing | 47 | 71* |
| 431 | Leather | 22 | 134* |
| 445 | Dresses, lingerie, etc. | 106 | 148* |
| 449 | 'Other' dress industries | 26 | 78 |
| 450 | Footwear | 234 | 102 |
| | Building materials | | |
| 461 | Bricks etc. | 33 | 84 |
| 469 | 'Other' building materials | 62 | 119 |
| | Wood products | | |
| 471 | Timber | 66 | 95 |
| 472 | Furniture | 48 | 154* |
| 475 | Wooden containers | 28 | 126 |
| 479 | Misc. wood products | 58 | 121* |
| | Printing & paper | | |
| 482 | Cardboard boxes | 39 | 95 |
| 489 | General printing | 176 | 77* |
| | Miscellaneous | | |
| 494 | Toys and games | 22 | 160* |
| 499 | Miscellaneous products | 30 | 160* |
| | All industries | 2,415 | 100 |

Source of data:  Establishment records

   *  Statistically significant (from average 54.1 per cent) at
      0.05 level

Table 7.4

Industry correlations in rates of entry, growth and closure

| | 1<br>Closure rate<br>1947-67 | 2<br>Entry rate<br>1947-55 | 3<br>Growth of<br>sector<br>1947-67 | 4<br>Growth of<br>surviving plants<br>1947-67 | 5<br>% of plants<br>employing fewer<br>than twenty<br>operatives |
|---|---|---|---|---|---|
| 1 | 1.00 | 0.49 | -0.01 | 0.19 | 0.34 |
| 2 | | 1.00 | -0.15 | 0.29 | 0.29 |
| 3 | | | 1.00 | 0.52 | 0.68 |
| 4 | | | | 1.00 | 0.43 |
| 5 | | | | | 1.00 |

Source of data:  Establishment records:  Dept of Employment

proportion of small plants. Logically, the entry-rate should refer to the period preceding that over which the closures are recorded. This is not possible here and the period 1947-55 is used as a general indication of entry-rates in each industry. It is assumed that the rankings of industries change little between periods. The table demonstrates that size of plant, as measured by the proportion of small plants, is only weakly correlated with the closure rate. The correlation between closure rate and employment growth measured in either way is statistically insignificant. Among the variables considered here only the entry-rate is significantly related to closures across industries, with a coefficient similar in magnitude to those calculated above from the American and Canadian data. The relationship between entry and closure is given by:

$$Y = 40.4 + 0.48 \ X \quad r^2 = 0.24$$
$$(0.23)$$

where        X is the entry-rate (%) 1947-55
             Y is the closure rate (%) 1947-67

A one point increase in the entry-rate raises the closure rate by half as much, but entry-rates account for only a quarter of the variation in closures. There are thus industries characterised by high turnover in firms and establishments and others with low turnover. This situation, which is also described by Wedervang for Norwegian industries, is only part of the story since some industries with high closure rates also have low entry-rates.


7.8   CONCLUSIONS


A wide variety of factors may cause the closure of an individual firm or branch plant. Many of these factors are unlikely to manifest themselves spatially. The major exception is the effect of industrial structure, although regional differences in age and size structure and entry-rate may also have an influence. The last three factors are probably all

closely related with age and size structure reflecting entry-rates.

A final factor is the ownership and control
structure of establishments. The argument is commonly
advanced that branch plants are more prone to closure
than other types of establishment. There appears to
be little hard evidence to support this contention.
A company will often close a branch rather than its
main plant, partly because of skill differences in the
workforces. However, another reason is that branches
are usually (although not always) smaller than the
parent plant, and as we have seen it is a general rule
of all types of factory that closure is more common
among the smaller ones. A counter-force not usually
recognised is the fact that branch plants are often
newer, and may have more modern layout and equipment
as well as room for future expansion. When closures
are required the preference may be to close the main
plant, especially if this is in old and congested
premises, and if skill differences are slight.


NOTES

(1)  The definition of closures omits those establishments which moved locations within the county (see
appendix I), but may include a small number of firms
which moved out of the area altogether. The latter
are unlikely to comprise more than a tiny fraction of
the whole. Rake (1972) attempted to differentiate
between branch plants and complete transfers in
plants set up outside the East Midlands by companies
based within the East Midlands. Of the 155 plants in
this category in the period 1945-65 Rake (p.126)
traced 105 and found only eleven transfers. Hence,
the maximum number of transfers is probably sixty-one,
and the more likely figure is under twenty. This is
only a minute proportion of all closures.
(2)  The equation was fitted using an algorithm
devised by Taylor (1970).

# PART IV

# SPATIAL VARIATIONS IN THE COMPONENTS OF CHANGE

# 8 Spatial variation I: the birth of new firms

Firms which start up in business for the first time
during a given period, or new firms as they are called
here, were shown in chapter four to have contributed
two-thirds of net growth in the East Midlands.  This
is a substantial contribution and it is obvious that
any regional differences in birth-rates will tend to
raise or lower the growth rate of aggregate employment.  In chapter five the process of locating new
firms was found to be a highly localised affair, with
each area having the great majority of its new
independent firms being established by entrepreneurs
from within the same area.  This means that geographical variation in birth-rates is likely to reflect
local characteristics rather than extraneous factors.
A survey of spatial variation may thus be expected to
shed some light on which characteristics of the local
economy are most critical in determining the level of
births.

The degree of spatial variation, as well as the
nature of underlying causal factors, are likely to
vary with the geographical scale under consideration.
A review of several different scales is one way in
which different influences can be identified and
perhaps disentangled from one another.  In this
chapter, four distinct scales will be investigated,
although for the regional scale itself only indirect
evidence is available.

## 8.1  INTERNATIONAL DIFFERENCES IN TURNOVER

There is a little information available to compare
entry-rates between countries, and it is interesting
to use this to provide further information on the
process of establishing new businesses and to place
the British experience in a wider context.  In

general, high entry-rates are associated with high closure rates in a process of business turnover, and consequently in making international comparisons it is most realistic to compare turnover rather than entry and closure individually.

Statistics on turnover are available for several countries outside the UK although all of these are in North America or Scandinavia. The studies, listed in table 8.1 refer to a number of different time periods both prewar and postwar. Since there appears to be a considerable degree of long-term stability in entry-rates, the need to compare across different time-periods is not seen as a particular problem, although care must be taken in drawing inferences. A final problem is that the national studies for the USA and Norway refer to firms, while the single region studies within the UK (Birmingham) and Canada refer to establishments. Also the American statistics of Churchill include changes of ownership as well as true births and deaths. Once again care must be exercised in comparing between definitions.

The usual definition of entry-rate is that obtained through dividing the number of new firms by the total number of firms in the population at the beginning of the period. As outlined in chapter five this definition is avoided in most of the East Midlands analyses because other definitions are more closely tied to the process by which firms are established. In this case, however, the more common definition is used to enable comparisons to be made between studies. Within the East Midlands the only data which include all new firms are those for Leicestershire between 1947 and 1955. In other periods, and areas, the record includes only those new firms which survive to the end of a period, and omit those which open and close within the same period. The Leicestershire figures quoted refer to firms, but expressed as a proportion of the initial number of the establishments.

One influence on the rate of entry is that of

industrial composition. Since composition varies to
an extent between the areas in table 8.1, an unweighted industry average has been calculated in addition to
the all-industry weighted average. Although this
device does not completely irradicate the effects of
differing composition it does do much to lessen them.
Table 8.1 shows that whichever measure is used entry-
rates are considerably lower in the two British
regions when compared with all of the other countries.
The two sets of British figures are very similar to
one another if an average of the two figures for
Birmingham is taken, but this British level is only
half of the average elsewhere.

The figures for Canada refer to establishments and
are thus most directly comparable with those for
Britain. One difference is, however, that Ontario
saw a large influx of branch plants of American
companies during this period. If these are subtracted
from the overall figures then the entry-rates falls to
6.1 per cent (unweighted) and 5.7 per cent (weighted)
respectively. This level is still substantially above
the British levels but interestingly is close to that
of the Hartford, Connecticut area in the North-East
USA. The ratio of (locally based) firms to establishments within Leicestershire was 84:100 in 1967. If it
is assumed that the same proportion was also held in
1947 then the (weighted) average entry-rate for firms
would be 4.3 per cent for Leicestershire. This rate
can be compared directly with that for the USA and
Norway to show that the Leicestershire rate was well
below that prevailing in these countries.

When attention is transferred to the closure figures
it can be seen that high closure rates are generally
associated with high entry-rates, although this is not
always the case. The pattern seems to be that the
North American countries in particular have a high
turnover of firms and establishments, while in
European countries and generally in Britain the turnover is lower. In North America the turnover figures
are very high, with one in twelve firms opening and

Table 8.1

International comparisons of turnover

| | | Date | Entry-rate p.a. Unweighted mean (%) | Entry-rate p.a. Weighted mean (%) | Closure rate (unweighted) |
|---|---|---|---|---|---|
| USA | (1) All USA (a) | 1950-58 | 6.9 | 8.5 | 8.0 |
| | (2) Hartford Conn. economic area (b) | 1953-58 | Not known | 5.8 | 2.6 |
| Canada | Ontario (c) | 1961-65 | 6.5 | 7.0 | 6.1 |
| Norway | (d) | 1930-33 | 6.9 | 7.4 | 4.2 |
| | | 1933-37 | 8.1 | 9.2 | 2.6 |
| | | 1937-48 | 5.0 | 5.9 | 2.1 |
| UK | Birmingham conurbation NW (e) | 1923-39 | Not known | 2.7 | 4.4 |
| | Birmingham conurbation SW | | Not known | 4.5 | 5.3 |
| | Leicestershire (f) | 1947-55 | 3.1 | 3.6 | 3.2 |

Sources of data:

(a) Churchill (1959)     (b) Kinnard and Malinowski (1960)
(c) Collins (1972)       (d) Wedervang (1965)
(e) Beesley (1955)       (f) Establishment records

closing each year. The inclusion of ownership changes may be partly responsible for this, but it is not thought that the distortion is large.

The gap between openings and closures is greater in the American and Norwegian studies than in the British ones in every case. This indicates a growing number of firms and establishments relative to Britain. The evidence suggests that the expansion in number of firms and establishments is related to overall economic growth, as might be expected. Figures for the USA Churchill (November, 1954) show that growth in numbers of firms was only two-thirds of the national average in the North East manufacturing belt, but $1\frac{1}{2}$ times or twice this average in the West and South East both of which were developing relatively rapidly. It is also the case that Norway was industrialising rapidly between 1930 and 1947 (Holm 1966) and this may explain the very rapid growth in numbers of firms over this period.

Despite the limited evidence, there is a strong suggestion that turnover rates may be a culturally determined phenomenon, with the gap between entry and closure rates influenced by the general economic performance. The areas which are culturally closest to Britain among these studies, i.e. Ontario and Hartford are most similar in levels of entry. In the USA as a whole, and in Ontario, it seems doubtful that the number of firms was growing much faster than in Leicestershire (which was a relatively rapidly expanding part of the UK). A similar comparison can be made for Sweden. Dahmen (1971) investigated changes in Swedish manufacturing between 1919 and 1939 and concluded that half the firms in 1939 had appeared since 1919. This proportion of surviving entries is almost exactly the same as that experienced in both Leicestershire and in the East Midlands as a whole.

If we conclude that expansion in the number of firms (or establishments) is determined by the rate of economic expansion, does it matter whether this is achieved through a high level of turnover or a low level? It is not easy to answer the question although there are reasons for preferring a high turnover. At the very worst, a high turnover may reflect an incautious attitude to business in which a large number of firms are unwisely established, only to fail within a short space of time. It seems doubtful that such a situation would do much harm. The productivity of those employed in the short-lived experiments may be lower during the experiment than it otherwise might have been, although even this is by no means clear. An advantage of a large number of short-lived firms might be the pressure exerted on the survivors to keep their efficiency up and prices down. A queue of willing applicants for a given market must have some salutary effect, even if the range of relevant markets is limited to those industries which are already competitive through high turnover. Short-lived firms will provide employment and this will be of benefit in conditions of labour surplus. Relatively short-lived establishments in Leicestershire employed (on average) 7,000 people during the period 1947-67.

If the high entry-rates do not reflect large numbers of rash decisions then the conclusion is different. It may be the case that the prevailing attitudes to entrepreneurship are less favourable in Britain than elsewhere, and if so, then lower numbers of individuals of average or even high business competence may be setting up firms than in other countries. Although a high proportion of companies are still forced out of business, the survivors may be better managed than in Britain. Another aspect of importance is that high entry-rates may promote a high rate of technical innovation. Even if this is not the case high entry-rates may still lead to a faster change of industrial structure than would otherwise be the case. It is not obvious that the extra new firms are in newer industries but if this were so then the growth of new industries is boosted. The optimum position is reached when the new firms enter new, growing and high productivity industries, while closures are

concentrated in older declining trades.  There is,
however, no obvious mechanism which would result in
this happening.  The more likely situation is that
high entry and closure rates are concentrated in the
same industries.


8.2   REGIONAL VARIATIONS IN ENTRY-RATES WITHIN THE UK

Unless the Midland regions have exceptionally low
entry and closure rates, it seems that the UK is a low
turnover country by international standards.  This
most probably reflects less favourable attitudes to
entrepreneurship in this country compared with others.
The question raised in this section is whether systematic differences in entry-rates exist between regions'
within the UK.  There is some reason to think that
average attitudes to starting businesses may vary
across the country but if geographical differences are
discovered, other factors are likely to be more
important.

   Unfortunately, there is little information available
at the regional scale on which an assessment can be
based, although the next few years will bring changes
in this respect.  In the last section it was seen that
prewar entry-rates in the West Midlands were very
similar to those in the East Midlands.  Another source
of information is for London between 1962 and 1966
(Strategic Plan for the South East, 1976).  The
figures in table 4.34 of the Strategic Plan show that
in manufacturing, 12.4 per cent of the establishments
in 1966 had not existed in 1962.  This represents an
entry-rate of survivors of 4.7 establishments per
1,000 employees per annum, and compares with an
equivalent figure of exactly the same magnitude for
Leicestershire in 1957-67.  It is not known if the
London figures include moving establishments, as well
as genuinely new ones, but they are likely to include
fewer branch plants.  The period is longer in the case
of Leicestershire, and this fact is likely to increase
the London figure relative to that of Leicestershire.

There is little published information available for other regions, although figures in Cameron (1972) allow an entry-rate to be computed for new firms in the Clydeside conurbation between 1958 and 1968. The data includes all firms employing more than five people which were opened sometime during the period. The annual entry-rate appears to be only 75 per cent of that in Leicestershire over approximately the same period.(1) Not too much weight can be placed behind this comparison, however, since small variations in definitions, completeness of records, and especially the rigour with which the lower size cut-off is adhered to, can all give rise to substantial distortions. Further careful research is necessary, but nevertheless the sets of figures given above were both counted (and not estimated) from data originally collected by official agencies. This is the only available comparison between an Assisted area and a Non-Assisted area, and as far as can be discerned the entry-rate is higher in the latter. Although the comparisons are very crude, and involve problems of both definition and dates, the figures point tentatively towards the conclusion that while entry-rates in South and Central England do not vary widely, the rate for industrial West Scotland may be lower.

Another way of approaching the question of regional variations in birth-rates is to use an analogy with human population. Countries with high human birth-rates tend to have age distributions with high proportions of children. It will also be the case that populations of industrial firms with high entry-rates have high proportions of young firms. There is no regional information available on either age of enterprises, or indeed of any aspect of enterprises as such. Instead the argument has to be translated into terms of size rather than age, and establishments rather than firms. Given that we know that new firms are nearly all very small, then a high birth-rate of firms implies a large addition of small firms. Also the vast majority of new firms operate only one establishment, and hence a high birth-rate implies a large addition of small establishments. Even if many of these close within a short space of time, they will still be apparent in any cross-sectional size distribution.

This hypothesis implies loosely that it is possible to infer birth-rate differentials from cross-sectional distributions of establishment size in that a large proportion of small plants will imply a high birth-rate of new firms. Table 8.2 shows that the proportion of small establishments is highest in the South East region.

Table 8.2

Size distributions of establishments by region

| Region | Employment size group | | | | | |
|---|---|---|---|---|---|---|
| | 11-24 | 25-99 | 100-199 | 200-499 | 500-999 | 1,000+ |
| North | 35.2 | 32.2 | 11.4 | 13.0 | 4.4 | 3.9 |
| Yorkshire & Humberside | 41.3 | 33.0 | 12.1 | 9.2 | 2.7 | 1.7 |
| East Midlands | 38.1 | 35.5 | 12.7 | 9.2 | 3.0 | 1.5 |
| East Anglia | 42.1 | 33.6 | 10.0 | 9.1 | 3.4 | 1.6 |
| South East | 47.8 | 33.4 | 8.6 | 6.4 | 2.3 | 1.5 |
| South West | 42.5 | 33.8 | 10.9 | 8.3 | 2.8 | 1.7 |
| West Midlands | 41.9 | 32.9 | 10.9 | 8.9 | 3.1 | 2.3 |
| North West | 39.1 | 34.5 | 11.3 | 9.5 | 3.2 | 2.4 |
| Wales | 36.3 | 32.4 | 13.4 | 11.2 | 3.6 | 3.0 |
| Scotland | 40.8 | 34.7 | 11.1 | 8.0 | 3.2 | 2.3 |
| Northern Ireland | 27.4 | 41.4 | 14.6 | 12.4 | 2.5 | 1.8 |
| UK | 42.4 | 33.8 | 10.6 | 8.4 | 2.9 | 2.0 |

Source of data:  Business Statistics Office, Business Monitor PA 1003, 1971

It is also high in Southern England as a whole and in the West Midlands, but low in all of the Assisted

205

areas except Scotland. Before it is possible to infer
the spatial distribution of birth-rates from the
pattern in table 8.2 it is necessary to take two
precautions. It is possible that the geography of
establishment size reflects industrial composition
more than it reflects differences in birth-rates. To
examine this possibility, the proportion of establishments in the smallest size category was calculated for
each region and each individual industry (at SIC Order
level), and the average was taken across the industries. These unweighted averages, shown in table 8.3,
provide a measure of birth-rate which is relatively
free of the effects of industrial structure.

Table 8.3

Proportions of small * establishments in UK regions

| | % of all plants employing 11+ | |
| | Weighted % | Unweighted % |
| --- | --- | --- |
| North | 23.7 | 23.4 |
| Yorkshire & Humberside | 27.5 | 26.8 |
| East Midlands | 25.2 | 26.5 |
| East Anglia | 28.0 | 29.4 |
| South East | 33.5 | 32.0 |
| South West | 28.7 | 28.7 |
| West Midlands | 27.4 | 26.4 |
| North West | 26.2 | 25.9 |
| Wales | 23.4 | 22.7 |
| Scotland | 27.3 | 26.6 |
| Northern Ireland | 20.2 | 23.7 |

Source of data:  Business Monitor PA 1003, 1971
    * Establishments employing between 11 and 19
      people

  Table 8.3 shows that there is relatively little
difference between the weighted and unweighted proportions.  The main differences due to industrial
structure occur in the East Midlands, East Anglia and
Northern Ireland which have relatively few small plant
industries, and in the South East and West Midlands

where the converse is true. The pattern of unweighted
figures shows that the Southern regions have the
highest proportions of small establishments regardless
of industrial structure. These are followed by the
Midland regions Yorkshire and Scotland each with an
almost identical proportion. The remaining regions
which are all or partly Assisted areas have the lowest
proportions.

The evidence thus far suggests that the proportion
of small plants declines northwards and westwards
within the UK. Before we can infer that birth-rates
do likewise, a further problem must be resolved. The
direct link between birth-rates and size distributions
only holds in a population which is generating its own
size distribution. A large influx of establishments
of any particular size from outside will cloud the
issue. This is important because the postwar period
has seen a large-scale movement of branch plants to
Assisted areas from companies based elsewhere.

It can reasonably be assumed that all moving establishments employ more than nineteen people. This
assumption can be used to recalculate the proportions
of very small establishments while omitting those
plants involved in industrial movement.(2) As an
extreme case all surviving moves since 1945 are subtracted from each region in table 8.4. The second
column in this table is calculated by dividing the
actual number of small establishments by the number
of indigenous large plants. This proportion is then
multiplied by the ratio of the unweighted to the
weighted mean to make allowance for industrial
structure. Even in this relatively extreme case the
largest proportions of small establishments remain in
the three Southern regions.(3) There is little
variation over the rest of the country except that the
Assisted areas have somewhat higher levels than the
Non-Assisted areas. It should also be noted that the
Southern regions retain their high proportions even if
account is taken of the moves out of those regions.

Table 8.4

Proportions of small establishments by region     Unweighted %

| Region | Establishments employing 11-19 as % of all establishments employing 11+ | | |
| | Including in-moving plants | Excluding all postwar in-moving plants | Excluding moves 1966-71 |
|---|---|---|---|
| North | 23.4 | 27.6 | 26.0 |
| Yorkshire and Humberside | 26.8 | 27.7 | 27.0 |
| East Midlands | 26.5 | 27.7 | 27.5 |
| East Anglia | 29.4 | 37.7 | 32.9 |
| South East | 32.0 | 33.4 | 32.2 |
| South West | 28.7 | 31.4 | 29.7 |
| West Midlands | 26.4 | 27.1 | 26.6 |
| North West | 25.9 | 27.1 | 26.2 |
| Wales | 22.7 | 30.3 | 24.7 |
| Scotland | 26.6 | 28.9 | 27.8 |
| Northern Ireland | 23.7 | 28.2 | 26.1 |

Source of data:  Dept of Industry

Omitting all moves in the preceding quarter of a century is likely to over-compensate for the effects of industrial movement. A large proportion of moves occurred in the early postwar years and by the 1960s these can be viewed as indigenous rather than immigrant establishments. That is, they had been at their destinations for long enough to have taken part in the generation of new firms. A more realistic assumption is that only recent in-moving establishments have played no part in generating new, and hence small, firms. The final column of table 8.4 repeats the exercise described above, but in this case only with surviving establishments in 1971 which had moved since 1965. In this case the three most Southerly regions clearly have higher proportions of small establishments. The Assisted area regions have the lowest proportions, with the notable exception of Scotland where the proportion compares favourably with the Midland regions.

After making due allowance for potential complications it seems safe to say that the South East and neighbouring regions have the highest proportions of very small plants. Following the train of reasoning outlined above, this observation can be used to suggest that birth-rates are the highest in the South East. It also seems likely, although by no means proven, that they are lowest in the Assisted area regions other than Scotland. The conclusion is tentative, and more evidence is plainly needed. The intriguing result of these calculations is, however, that the regions which can be inferred to have the lowest birth-rates are also broadly those with the poorest records of indigenous employment growth. The pattern of birth-rates also coincides with what might be expected from a study of the spatial variation observed at a smaller scale within the East Midlands. That variation is outlined in the next two sections, along with a discussion of the likely determinants of the regional pattern.

## 8.3 SUB-REGIONAL VARIATIONS WITHIN THE EAST MIDLANDS

The proportion of firms founded between 1948 and 1970 was estimated for each East Midland county using the methods described in appendix III. The estimates refer to 'new' firms which survived until 1970 and do not include firms which were both opened and closed within the period. The entry-rates are listed in table 8.5 alongside the estimated average size of the firms in 1967.

Table 8.5

Estimated entry-rates between 1948 and 1970

|  | Number of new firms in 1970 per 1,000 manu- facturing employees in 1948 | Average No. of employees per firm 1970 |
|---|---|---|
| Leicester- shire | 6.7 | 22 |
| Nottingham shire (a) | 7.1 | 20 |
| Derbyshire (b) | 4.0 | 28 |
| Northampton- shire | 6.7 | 21 |
| Lincoln- shire (c) | 3.1 | 30 |

Source of data:  Questionnaire survey, Dept of
Employment

Notes
    (a)  Excluding Newark and Retford
    (b)  Excluding Chesterfield
    (c)  Including Newark and Retford

A sharp contrast is immediately obvious in the figures. Leicestershire, Nottinghamshire and North-amptonshire all have entry-rates near to seven firms per 1,000 employees. In Linclonshire and Derbyshire the figures are close to half of this level. The reasons for the sharp difference could be many faceted but one feature which both areas have is that the main towns are dominated by heavy engineering firms. (4) The conjecture that the experience gained in the large establishments found in these areas may be relatively inappropriate for those who might otherwise set up new firms is supported by other strands of evidence. Firstly, a similarly sharp contrast is to be found within Leicestershre, where Loughborough had an entry-rate which was significantly below that of Leicester. Loughborough is also a town in which manufacturing employment is dominated by a single, large, heavy engineering concern. Secondly, Beesley (1955) found a similar contrast in his investigation of entry-rates in the prewar West Midlands. The zone within his area which had low entry-rates was typified by large assembly plants. The other zone contained mostly small component manufacturers and was found to have an entry-rate which was almost 70 per cent higher (table 8.1). Although the area with high entry-rates also had a higher rate of closure the difference in closure rates was more muted than that with entry-rates.

Two small additional pieces of evidence can be advanced to support the theory that dominance by large plants has the effect of depressing entry-rates. The first comes again from within Leicestershire where the establishment-based data allows a much more detailed analysis. Market Harborough is a small country town some ten miles from Leicester, in which almost a third of employment in manufacturing in 1947 was within a single large clothing factory. The entry-rate was very low in the ten years after 1947. However, by 1957 the dominant plant had declined very substantially, and in the following decade the entry-rate increased markedly.

The second point is drawn from questionnaire evidence, reported in chapter five, on the trade in which founders established their firms. All of the areas listed above as having low entry-rates also had below average proportions of firms set up in the same trade as that in which the founder had previously worked. In two cases, those of Newark-Retford and the Erewash Valley the proportion was significantly below average in the statistical sense. Other areas with below average proportions were Derby, Lincoln, Kesteven (including Grantham), and also the two coal-field areas of Mansfield-Worksop and the Leicester-shire-Derbyshire coalfield. In the latter cases single large firms were locally important, but there were also a higher than average proportion of immi-grant firms and branch plants. The particular contention here is that large plants tend to provide less relevant experience for potential entrepreneurs. This prevents some people from starting their own firms, but in other cases may force those with unquenchable resolve to start in a product area with which they have no direct association. As a result low entry-rates become associated with a low degree of continuity between previous occupation and the product of the new firm.

Although most of the large plants mentioned in this context are in engineering this may only be a coinci-dence. It is probable that the largeness of the organisation is itself a major contributory factor. The narrow experience gained as a 'small cog in a large wheel' may be a factor which inhibits those who might otherwise be considered to be potential entre-preneurs. A second possibility is that assembly plants somehow inhibit would-be entrepreneurs in ways only incidentally connected with their large size. The occupational structure is likely to differ between assembly and other plants and this may hold the key.

Large size in itself is intuitively more likely to be responsible for low birth-rates. The wider experi-ence of working in a small firm may be the relevant factor, but the increased confidence obtained through knowing and working with actual founders or at least managing directors must rate as a potentially impor-tant factor. The fact that several cases were encountered in which foremen of recently founded firms set up their own firms suggests this factor to be at

212

work, even if it is not the dominant force. Chain reactions of this type certainly merit additional research. Differences in job security between small and large firms are another possible influence. Pension schemes in large firms may deter some potential founders from taking the plunge into independence. Conversely, the greater likelihood of small firms closing may provide an impetus for entrepreneurs, especially as it was shown in chapter five that some catalytic event was normally necessary to trigger off the final decision to start a firm.

A separate line of reasoning altogether is that large firms may dominate local labour markets and force wages up to levels too high for the incipient new firm. There is no way to discriminate effectively between this 'external-constraint' type of factor and the entrepreneurial supply factors listed above, without further research. It can be said, however, that labour factors are more likely to inhibit growth or endanger survival, than to actually reduce entry-rates per se. The greater work satisfaction sometimes reported for small organisations may also compensate for the lower wages paid by small firms.

The significance of the former interpretation of the observed differences in entry-rate is that many areas in Britain which are dominated by heavy metal and engineering industries, large plants and branches have had slow growth and hence need Government assistance. If regions like the North East, South Wales or West-Central Scotland have entry-rates only half as large as those in the Midlands or South East then this could result in net growth of manufacturing employment at levels of 35 per cent below the latter areas, since two-thirds of net growth in the East Midlands was contributed by new firms.

There is reason to expect a shortfall in growth of 25 rather than 35 per cent, however, if the size of the new firms is considered. In the East Midlands, the three counties with high entry-rates had average sizes of new firms in 1970 at close to twenty-two employees in each case (table 8.5). In Derbyshire the figure was higher, at twenty-eight employees, and for Lincolnshire the average was thirty employees. On the basis of these five observations it seems that the average size of new firms may increase inversely, but less than proportionately with entry-rate. In the case of Lincolnshire, for instance, an entry-rate which was only 46 per cent as large as that for Leicestershire, was combined with an average size 36 per cent larger to give an employment total of just under two-thirds of that in Leicestershire. New firms contributed nearly 30 per cent of the gross new employment (as defined in chapter four) in Leicestershire but only 20 per cent in Lincolnshire. Ceteris paribus, this factor would have the effect of reducing net growth in industrial employment by about one quarter.

Within the East Midlands the lower birth-rates have not had a marked effect on aggregate employment performance because of the equilibriating effects of labour shortages. Permanent firms have in many cases expanded through setting up branch plants in other areas, and consequently the lower pressure exerted by low entry-rates upon labour availability appears to allow these firms to retain more of their expansion within the local area. In addition, externally based firms have taken up any slack in labour supply. In areas without such labour shortages, these factors do not apply and a low level of employment generated in new firms will lower the overall growth of employment. If net growth in regions like Wales, West-Central Scotland and the North were to be reduced by as much as one quarter through this factor, then it will go a substantial way towards explaining the persistent differences of indigenous growth between assisted areas and the rest.

## 8.4   ENTRY RATES AT THE LOCAL SCALE

### 8.4.1   Employment exchange areas

The reasoning advanced in the previous sections to
account for spatial variation in entry-rates, implies
that differences will exist between areas below the
sub-regional scale.  Since firms are set up close to
the previous workplace of the founders, then the
differing characteristics of individual labour catchment areas will cause varied levels of entry.  It
should be noted, however, that it is difficult to draw
meaningful conclusions about entry at scales which are
smaller still.  For instance, at the intra-urban scale
the location of home or previous workplace will have
only a loose influence on the siting of new firms.

Analysis at the local scale is only possible for
areas within Leicestershire.  Complete records of all
entries are available for the period 1947-55, but
thereafter only for survivors to 1967.  New firms
include those which were subsidiaries in 1967, but as
noted above, the great majority of these had been
started as independent concerns.  The entry-rates for
surviving new firms in individual employment exchange
areas are given in table 8.6.(5) The entry-rates are
expressed in two forms.  The base using employment in
1947 is adequate as long as employment does not rise
rapidly over the period.  However, if employment in
permanent firms, or in mobile establishments, rises
rapidly, then the initial employment does not
adequately measure the true stock of potential entrepreneurs.  This is most clearly shown in the case of
the Oakham area, where a large branch more than
doubled total employment near the start of the period.
The 1947 base indicates an extreme birth-rate, but
the 1967 base provides a figure much more in line with
the rest of the county.

The example of Oakham illustrates the point made in
8.2 that incoming branch plants probably play a part
in generating new firms.  Two other cases in which

Table 8.6

Rates of entry and employment in surviving new firms

| Employment exchange area | Entry-rate 1947-67 per 1,000 employed | | Average size of new firms in 1967 (No. of operatives) | Employment in new firms as a % of total employment in 1947 |
|---|---|---|---|---|
| | In 1947 | In 1967 | | |
| Leicester | 8.3 | 8.0 | 16.3 | 13.5 |
| Coalville | 6.5 | 4.5 | 15.8 | 10.3 |
| Loughborough | 4.3 | 3.9 | 16.0 | 6.9 |
| Melton | 7.2 | 5.4 | 13.1 | 9.4 |
| Oakham | 33.3 | 7.8 | 28.9 | 95.7 |
| Market Harborough | 8.3 | 9.8 | 14.4 | 12.0 |
| Hinckley | 5.5 | 5.9 | 23.6 | 12.9 |
| Average | 7.3 | 6.9 | 16.9 | 12.4 |

Source of data: Establishment records

rising total employment affects the birth-rate calculation are also evident in table 8.6. In both cases it is reasonable to take an average of the two figures, producing a value of 5.5 for Coalville, and 6.3 for Melton. Similarly, the average rate for the whole county is 7.1.

The entry-rates within Leicestershire are above average in Leicester itself and also in the two rural areas of Oakham and Market Harborough. The lowest rates are to be found in the North West of the county, in Loughborough and Coalville and to a lesser extent in Hinckley. Explanations of this pattern will be deferred until later in this section, except to say that the low rate in Hinckley reflects an industrial structure strongly dominated by hosiery and footwear. Both of these industries have a low proportion of small plants and hence low entry-rates. The new firms which do appear in these industries are typically larger than average and this is reflected in the higher average size of new firms in Hinckley (table 8.6).

The average size of new firms varies little among the remaining areas except in Oakham, where the figure is inflated by a single large firm. The average size of new firms is measured in number of operatives in table 8.6 to conform with the practice elsewhere in this study. The average figure for all employees is twenty-three. The smallness of this size emphasises once again that it is the number of new firms which is of significance rather than their individual employment, or even the size of the largest. In Leicestershire, 927 new firms had survived until 1967.

The amount of employment in new firms is a function of both the entry-rate and the size of the new firms. Since there is no marked inverse association between entry-rate and average size in these figures, the areas with low entry-rates also have relatively low aggregate amounts of employment generated by new firms. The only exception is Hinckley where the larger average size compensates for the low entry-rate. The generated employment is measured as a proportion of total jobs in 1947, to avoid the distorting effects of subsequent growth in permanent firms and branch plants. In the Loughborough area the new firms generated employment at a little over half the average rate, but there is little variation between most of the other areas except Oakham.

The amount of employment in new firms can be viewed as the outcome of two probabilistic processes. One of these is the process of setting up a new firm. As indicated in chapter five a large number of influences bear on each individual decision, and consequently each decision can be viewed as if it were governed by random chance. An adequate model of this random process is the Poisson. This predicts the probability of any particular number of firms being set up within an area, given a (small) general probability. This is an adequate rather than ideal model because it assumes an equal propensity among employees to set up a new firm. This is unrealistic since some people are more likely than others to establish a firm whatever the circumstances.(6) The Poisson model is still extremely useful even if it does not precisely describe the pattern of birth-rates. The utility derives from the fact that it becomes possible to identify those areas in which the birth-rate could not have arisen by random chance assuming an even propensity to start a firm among all employees. In table 8.6, the value for Leicester is significantly above the overall mean at the 0.01 level, while those of Loughborough and Hinckley are significantly below average. The other areas have birth-rates which could have arisen by chance on the assumptions of the Poisson model. The interpretation of these differences is that either the stock of potential entrepreneurs differs between areas or else conditions are such as to induce differing numbers of potential entrepreneurs (from a population with uniform entrepreneurial propensities) to set up firms. The latter interpretation seems the

218

intuitively more acceptable. In this case it is
necessary to explain what conditions produce high
rates in Leicester and low ones in Hinckley and
Loughborough. The most probable cause is industrial
structure and this will be examined in detail in
8.4.2.

The second probability process is that governing the
growth of firms once they have been established. This
would be complicated to model because of the lack of
independence between successive time periods.
However, the evidence of table 8.6 suggests that the
weighted mean size varies little between areas except
where industrial structure intervenes. It seems
reasonable to view growth as a random variable with a
mean that is spatially uniform at this scale once
structural differences have been allowed for.

8.4.2  Local authority areas

The apparent importance of new firms in employment
growth makes it worthwhile to investigate spatial
variations in greater detail. The existence of
establishment records within Leicestershire, makes it
possible to distinguish between industries and sub-
periods. It is also possible to adopt a finer areal
mesh. The areas used below correspond to the local
authority units prevailing before the reorganisation
of 1974, and are described in figure 8.1. These
separate urban areas from rural areas. It is not the
purpose here to analyse intra-urban variations, and
thus the areas in and around Leicester have been
amalgamated to form 'Greater Leicester'. This latter
area conforms loosely to the 'journey to work area of
Leicester' in 1966. It is thus the area within which
most of the firms founded by Leicester employees will
be located.

Table 8.7 shows entry-rates for two time periods.
In the first period all new firms have been recorded,
while in the second only survivors to 1967 are
included. These firms which survive until the end of

219

the period in which they opened are called short-term
survivors.

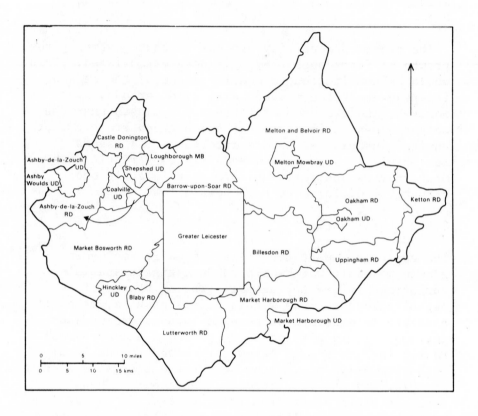

Figure 8.1   Local authority areas in Leicestershire
in 1967

The short-term survivors from the earlier period are
also included for comparison.  A number of consistent
patterns emerge from table 8.7.  These are:

(a)  Entry-rates are consistently above average in
Leicester and its immediate hinterland (Greater

Table 8.7

Entry-rates for local authority areas within Leicestershire

| Areas | Firms entering 1947-55 | | | | Firms entering 1955-67 | |
| | All new firms | | Short-term survivors | | Short-term survivors only | |
|---|---|---|---|---|---|---|
| Greater Leicester | 6.8 | *** | 4.7 | ** | 5.8 | ** |
| Rem. Blaby RD | 9.6 | * | 9.6 | * | 17.7 | *** |
| Rem. Barrow RD | 5.0 | NS | 4.3 | NS | 2.4 | *** |
| Rem. Billesdon RD | 0.0 | NS | - | | 23.5 | * |
| Loughborough CB | 1.6 | *** | 1.4 | *** | 2.9 | *** |
| Shepshed UD | 1.6 | ** | 1.6 | NS | 4.6 | NS |
| Coalville UD | 2.5 | *** | 2.1 | * | 2.1 | *** |
| Castle Donnington RD | 8.6 | NS | 8.6 | ** | 14.0 | *** |
| Ashby de la Zouch UD | 2.0 | NS | 2.0 | NS | 7.5 | NS |
| Ashby d la Zouch RD | 1.4 | * | 1.4 | NS | 6.4 | NS |
| Ashby Waulds UD | 0.0 | ** | - | NS | - | NS |
| Market Bosworth RD | 10.2 | ** | 8.3 | ** | 5.7 | NS |
| Hinckley | 3.9 | *** | 3.1 | ** | 3.9 | ** |
| Lutterworth RD | 7.1 | NS | 4.1 | NS | 1.7 | ** |
| Market Harborough UD | 3.3 | * | 2.9 | ** | 10.0 | *** |
| Market Harborough RD | 2.1 | NS | 2.1 | NS | 7.3 | NS |
| Melton Mowbray UD | 12.1 | ** | 11.0 | *** | 5.3 | NS |
| Melton and Belvoir RD | 2.5 | ** | 1.9 | NS | 4.7 | NS |
| Oakham UD | 40.5 | *** | 34.7 | *** | 6.9 | *** |
| Oakham RD | 26.3 | NS | 26.3 | NS | 96.8 | *** |
| Uppingham RD | 9.4 | NS | - | NS | 6.3 | NS |
| Ketton RD | 8.6 | NS | 5.7 | NS | 1.5 | NS |
| Average | 5.7 | | 4.2 | | 5.3 | |
| No. of firms | 726 | | 529 | | 710 | |

Source of data: Establishment records
Entry-rates are no. of new firms per 1,000 employees
Significance levels:  * - 0.10 level
                     ** - 0.05 level
                    *** - 0.01 level
                     NS - not significant

221

Leicester);

(b) Entry-rates have a tendency to be above average in rural areas adjacent to major cities. This is true of Blaby and Market Bosworth in the case of Leicester, and also of Castle Donnington which is close to both Nottingham and Derby;

(c) Consistently below average rates in Loughborough and in the neighbouring towns of Coalville and Shepshed, and also in Hinckley;

(d) Most of the rural market towns have above average rates, including Melton, Oakham, Lutterworth, and also Market Harborough in the second period.

How are these patterns to be explained? A number of observations can be made immediately. The importance of the small spatial scale is evident in two ways. Firstly, the rural districts close to large towns act as overspill areas in that available premises may be taken up by urban entrepreneurs. Disused railway buildings, and quarry or farm outbuildings are all types of cheap premises which can serve industrial needs in rural areas. A second factor is that some longer distance commuters live in these rural areas, but work in the urban industries. These may actively prefer locations close to their homes. Two rural areas close to Leicester do not have high entry-rates. One of these (Barrow) is highly industrialised but has an unfavourable industrial structure with much employment in footwear. The other, (Billesdon) is very rural with few premises suitable for industrial use. At the larger scale of the employment exchange area or of sub-regions these effects cancel out and disappear from view.

These overspill and commuting factors may also explain the somewhat higher rates in market towns. The availability of premises was increased by the run-down of rural crafts and services. The increase in car ownership over the period is likely to have increased commuting to these relatively pleasant environments especially among professional and managerial workers.

The more significant variations cannot be explained in these terms, and the next step is to investigate the effect of differences of industrial structure. This could be achieved by some algebraic manipulation which expresses actual entry-rates as a residual from that expected, on the basis of industrial composition. However, with entry-rates of only a few firms per 1,000 employees, not many industries have enough employees in each area to enable meaningful comparisons to be drawn. Instead, entry-rates were calculated for four major industries separately.

The results are summarised in table 8.8. In Greater Leicester entry-rates are above average in virtually all columns, but only in engineering in the early period is the higher rate statistically significant. This probably means that the highly significant entry-rates for all industry in Leicester are partly the result of industrial structure but this is not the whole explanation. In Blaby and Market Bosworth, both close to Leicester, there is evidence that high birth-rates are not primarily due to industrial structure, but this does not seem to be the case in the other 'hinterland' areas i.e. Castle Donnington.

The investigation of individual industries enables those areas with low birth-rates to be separated into a number of categories. In Hinckley, Shepshed and Coalville industrial structure is the major influence. Each of these towns specialises in industries which have relatively high barriers to entry. In Hinckley these are footwear and hosiery, in Shepshed hosiery alone, and in Coalville elastic web. In each case the average size of factory is large, for the industries concerned, and this may account for low birth-rates within individual industries. The birth-rate in engineering is significantly high in Hinckley, perhaps reflecting its proximity to Coventry.

Loughborough is in a category almost on its own, although neighbouring Barrow has the next worst pattern of low birth-rates across industries.

Table 8.8

Entry-rates by local authority areas: a summary

| | Firms entering 1947-55 | | | | | | | | Firms entering 1955-67 | | | |
| | All new firms | | | | Short-term survivors | | | | Short term survivors only | | | |
| | All Engin-eering | Hosiery | Footwear | Printing | All Engin-eering | Hosiery | Footwear | Printing | All Engin-eering | Hosiery | Footwear | Printing |
|---|---|---|---|---|---|---|---|---|---|---|---|---|
| Greater Leicester | +*** | + | S | + | +*** | + | S | + | +*** | + | + | + |
| Rem. Blaby RD | +** | +*** | S | - | +** | + | - | +· | +*** | + | - | +· |
| Rem. Barrow RD | +** | - | - | + | + | + | S | - | -*** | + | -* | S |
| Rem. Billesdon RD | S | S | + | | | - | S | S | +* | - | | + |
| Loughborough CB | -*** | -*** | S | S | -*** | -*** | S | -*** | -*** | -*** | S | - |
| Shepshed | -** | -** | +* | S | | | S | | +*** | -*** | S | S |
| Coalville UD | -*** | S | S | S | -* | -* | S | -* | -* | +** | S | S |
| Castle Donnington RD | + | - | + | + | +** | +** | S | +** | +*** | +*** | | |
| Ashby UD | - | S | | S | | | S | | + | - | | S |
| Ashby RD | S | S | S | S | | | S | | S | S | | S |
| Ashby Waulds UD | -* | S | | | | | - | | - | | | |
| Market Bosworth RD | +** | S | S | S | +** | +** | S | +** | S | + | + | S |
| Hinckley UD | +** | + | -** | S | -** | -** | S | -** | +** | - | -* | |
| Lutterworth RD | + | + | | S | | | S | | -** | S | S | |
| Market Harborough UD | -* | - | S | S | +** | +** | S | +** | +** | +*** | S | -* |
| Market Harborough RD | - | + | S | + | | | S | | +*** | +*** | +*** | + |
| Melton Mowbray UD | +** | + | S | S | +*** | +*** | S | +*** | S | - | S | S |
| Melton RD | -* | + | S | | -** | -** | S | -** | S | S | S | |
| Oakham UD | +** | +** | S | S | +** | +** | S | +** | +*** | S | S | S |
| Oakham RD | + | S | | | + | + | S | + | +*** | | | |
| Uppingham RD | S | +*** | S | S | S | S | S | S | +*** | | | S |
| Ketton RD | + | S | S | | - | - | S | - | S | | | |

Source of data: Establishment records

Entry-rates are no. new firms per 1,000 employees

Key to symbols  + above average   Levels of significance (Poisson)   *  0.10
              - below average                                          **  0.05
              S same as average                                       ***  0.01

Loughborough fails to experience above average birth-rates in any industry, and is below average in most (including the residual industry category not included in table 8.8). Industrial employment in Loughborough is dominated by one of Leicestershire's largest factories. This is an electrical engineering factory now split between four divisions within the Hawker-Siddely group. The fact that so much employment is in electrical engineering, reduces the likelihood of new firms, since this industry has lower birth-rates than other major branches of engineering. Nevertheless, it is not necessarily true that skills learnt within an electrical engineering factory are not relevant to other branches of engineering. Hence, Hawker-Siddeley employees may have sufficient experience to begin firms in mechanical, instrument or general engineering.

Among the smaller areas in Leicestershire entry-rates are close to average in most industries, although they are high in engineering for almost all rural areas and market towns. In Market Harborough a strong tendency to high birth-rates can be observed in the second period. Two possible influences may be at work in this case, in addition to that mentioned in 8.2. One is the growth of commuting to Leicester as discussed above: the other is the growth of Corby New Town some ten miles away. It is likely that existing, cheap, premises were in extremely short supply in Corby, and Market Harborough is one of the nearest established centres. Also industrial links between Corby and Market Harborough can be seen beyond the confines of the new firm sector. One of these is a divisional headquarters for Golden Wonder Crisps Ltd who have a large plant at Corby, and the other is a small engineering subsidiary of York Trailers Ltd who again have a major works in Corby.

8.4.3  Major influences on entry

In small areas, at the local scale, significant variations in rates of entry are probably due to overspill from the main towns. The more important variations in the main towns are partly due to industrial structure, but additional factors are also operating. Within Leicestershire the above average birth-rates in Leicester itself and the low rates in Loughborough have not yet been adequately explained. It is of course possible that Loughborough entrepreneurs were setting up firms in Leicester, but there is no reason to expect that this was happening. Ignoring this thought, three main possibilities present themselves, all reflecting the processes involved in establishing a new firm.

Size of establishments. One of these, discussed at length in 8.2 is the influence of size of plant. It has been argued that large factories will inhibit the spawning of new firms, and this may be an important factor in the case of Loughborough.

The evidence of table 8.9 does suggest that Loughborough has an unusually large amount of employment in large plants.

Table 8.9
Size of establishments: major centres

|  | % plants employing 1-20 (Leics. = 100) | | | % of employment in large plants |
| --- | --- | --- | --- | --- |
|  | All Eng. | Hosiery | Footwear | 250+ |
| Greater Leicester | 98 106 | 110 | 121 | 46 |
| Loughborough | 92 84 | 78 | - | 67 |
| Hinckley | 71 113 | 78 | 38 | 42 |
| Coalville | 76 70 | 120 | 0 | 58 |
| Shepshed | 71 146 | 80 | 0 | 15 |
| Barrow R.D. | 77 117 | 78 | 62 | 44 |
| Market Harborough | 106 97 | 63 | 63 | 53 |
| Average | 62% 63% | 40% | 29% | 47 |

Sources of data: Establishment records, Dept of Employment

Nor is this due to a single extreme case. Larger than average establishments are common in hosiery, printing, chemicals and non-electrical engineering, as well as in electrical engineering. It is difficult to suggest why this should be so, and there probably is no simple explanation. Coalville is another town with more large plant employment than other areas, and again entry-rates are low, although industrial structure is partly responsible here. Market Harborough also has rather more large plant employment than most areas, but this is mostly due to a single clothing factory. In other industries there is a relatively high proportion of small plants.

The figures on the proportion of small plants given in table 8.8 are difficult to interpret without running the risk of circular argument. There is certainly some correspondence between high proportions of small plants and high entry-rates. Loughborough has relatively few small plants. Hinckley has a considerable shortfall of small establishments in footwear, the one industry in which its birth-rate was conspicuously low. Above all there is a tendency for Leicester to have more than average numbers of small plants in the major industries.

The problem is to decide whether a lack of small plants lowers entry-rates or conversely whether low entry-rates in the past depress the proportion of small establishments. All that can be said here is to note the correspondence between the two, and to tentatively view this as support for the a priori expectation that employment in small plants aids the generation of new firms.

Local linkages. Differences in the degree of local linkage between firms may affect entry-rates. The amount of subcontracting work put out locally by existing manufacturers is likely to be of special importance, given that a large number of new firms begin life by taking on contracts from established manufacturers. Using data collected by postal questionnaire to East Midlands firms (appendix II) a picture of subcontracting linkages has been assembled. In particular, two trends are noticeable. Firstly, there is a clear distinction between manufacturing towns and rural areas in both the amount of subcontracting and in its degree of local concentration. This contrast, shown in table 8.10 reflects to an extent the differing locations of branches and parent plants.

Table 8.10

Subcontracted work put out by East Midlands factories

| | Sample size | % of plants putting out work | % putting out work to local firms |
|---|---|---|---|
| Major towns (Nottingham, Derby, Leicester, Mansfield, Lincoln, Northampton) | 472 | 54 | 35 |
| Other industrial towns (Newark, Loughborough, Hinckley, Corby, Kettering, Wellingborough, Erewash Valley towns) | 142 | 55 | 39 |
| Rural areas | 98 | 35 | 17 |

Source of data: Questionnaire survey

The second effect was one of a decreasing tendency to put out work to local firms (i.e. those within thirty miles) with increasing distance from the main manufacturing belt running north-south from Mansfield to Northampton. Lincolnshire (Kesteven and Holland) averaged only 12 per cent to local firms, while Newark, on its boundary, had 15 per cent. These figures provide a background against which to view the specific figures for Leicestershire given in table 8.11.

This evidence again sheds some light on the variations in entry-rates. Two areas with apparently low levels of local subcontracting, Loughborough and Coalville, are both areas with below average entry-rates.

Table 8.11

Subcontracting by establishments in Leicestershire

| Local authority areas | Sample size | % of plants putting out work | % putting out work to local firms |
|---|---|---|---|
| Leicester CB, adjoining RDs, and Lutterworth RD | 170 | 58 | 41 |
| Loughborough and Shepshed | 12 | 63 | 33 |
| Hinckley UD | 19 | 74 | 53 |
| Coalville UD, Ashby UDs, RD | 19 | 16 | 11 |
| Melton UD, RD, ) Rutland )16 Market Harborough UD, RD) | )16 | 50 | 25 |

Source of data: Questionnaire survey

Hinckley's high level of local subcontracting reflects its tight concentration in two industries. This pattern of subcontracting in Hinckley does not, however, lead to above average entry-rates in hosiery or footwear. The rural areas to the south and east of Leicester have higher levels of subcontracting than rural areas elsewhere in the East Midlands. Taken together the level is not much lower than that for the area as a whole, excluding Leicester itself. Thus there is no real evidence that lack of subcontracting work would have a marked depressing effect on rural entry-rates relative to the areas outside Leicester. The subcontracting put out by plants within Leicester, should in contrast lead to higher entry-rates here than elsewhere, assuming that a distance decay effect keeps a high proportion of the work within Leicester as opposed to nearby rural areas.

The information available here is indicative but by

no means conclusive. The volume of subcontracted work
is unknown, as is its variability over time. In
addition, the definition of the term 'local' (thirty
miles) is too coarse to permit hard and fast judge-
ments. However, the figures, such as they are, do
suggest that the effect of subcontracting linkages is
to inflate entry-rates within Leicester and to make
them relatively lower than elsewhere, with the exception of Hinckley. The actions of the few largest
employers may be critically important, and it is
possible that where these are large assembly plants
(as in Loughborough) the amount of work put out
locally is low. Without further work this cannot,
however, be substantiated.

## Entrepreneurs from non-manufacturing backgrounds

The fact that large non-manufacturing employment sectors may generate additional entrepreneurs in manufacturing may explain some of the residuals in the
pattern of new firm creation. In particular, Hinckley
and Loughborough have two-thirds of their workforces
in manufacturing compared to 54 per cent in the
Leicester Employment Exchange Area and much less
elsewhere (table 8.12). Figures from the 1951 Census
using a finer areal disaggregation showed that much
the same relative pattern existed at the beginning of
the period also.

Table 8.12

Manufacturing employment as proportion of total
employment 1967

| Employment Exchange Area | |
|---|---|
| Leicester | 54.4 |
| Loughborough | 65.7 |
| Hinckley | 67.4 |
| Coalville | 32.3 |
| Melton | 33.2 |
| Market Harborough | 43.3 |
| Oakham | 17.8 |

Source of data: Dept of Employment.

The lowest proportions of all were in Rutland excluding Ketton, and these tended to have positive values

for new firm creation. At the other extreme, Loughborough and Hinckley had much higher proportions in
manufacturing (and thus less in other sectors) than
the other industrial towns. The evidence thus points
to the conclusion that a relatively large non-manufacturing employment sector is associated with higher
than average rates of entry. Using manufacturing
employment to predict numbers of new firms may thus
lead to over prediction in towns like Hinckley and
Loughborough and under prediction in some rural areas,
and also perhaps in Leicester.

The amount of employment in industrial wholesaling,
and in other non-manufacturing industries closely
allied with manufacturing, is probably the most important aspect. It has not been possible to separate
these activities from less relevant service trades in
order to examine the figures. Nevertheless, it is to
be expected that such activities are concentrated in
the major cities. Within Leicestershire, it is
Leicester itself which is most likely to gain from
manufacturing firms set up by those who formerly
worked in service trades allied to manufacturing.

Summary. Although the examination of these three
factors has not been rigorous, it does suggest a
series of conclusions. In each case the factors would
tend to inflate entry-rates within Leicester, and
conversely would tend to deflate entry-rates in
Loughborough. In other cases the forces would not
act in a single consistent direction and in some cases
would tend to be self-cancelling. Hinckley, for
instance, appears to have a relatively large amount of
local subcontracted work which should raise entry-
rates, but on the other hand has an industrial structure dominated by large plant industries, and contains
only a small proportion of non-manufacturing employment. The evidence is suggestive, but further work is
needed if the above observations are to be confirmed.
This should preferably be on other areas, but at the
same spatial scale. Only with a number of replicated
studies will it become possible to put some quantitive

measure on the force of each factor.

NOTES

(1)  The entry-rate from Cameron (1972) is obtained by dividing the 353 new firms by the average number of establishments (2,402) giving a rate of 14.7 over ten years.  The figure for Leicestershire was made as comparable as possible.  The lower size threshold of five employees presented some problems since only initial and final employment figures were generally available.  The final figures were adopted for surviving new firms and initial figures for those closing within the same period.  The Leicestershire figures also referred to operatives only, and a threshold of four operatives was adopted, to approximate to the Clydeside threshold of five employees.

(2)  The numbers of moves between 1945 and 1965 which survived until 1966 is obtained from Howard (1969). The number of moves between 1966 and 1971 which survived until 1971 is known from unpublished tables provided by the Department of Industry.  In order to obtain the number of moves 1945-66 surviving until 1971, average closure rates were calculated from Atkins (1973) and applied over the period 1966-71 to those plants which moved before 1961.  Numbers of survivors among plants moving between 1961-66 are available from Department of Industry figures.

(3)  The high figure for East Anglia probably results from a number of firms employing less than nineteen transferring the short distance from the London area into the region.

(4)  In the Lincolnshire figures the towns of Lincoln, Newark and Grantham all fall into this category.  In Derby, Rolls Royce and the British Rail workshops strongly dominate the local employment structure.

(5)  The location of these areas is shown in figure 4.1.

(6)  The Negative Binomial distribution will provide a better model when entrepreneurial propensities are variable between employees.  This more rigorous

formulation will be explored in future work.

# 9 Spatial variation II: the growth of firms and establishments

This chapter deals with the important topic of spatial differences in the employment growth of permanent firms and establishments. These are defined as units which survive through some given time period. Even in the relatively long twenty year period used through most of this study, permanent establishments still contained four out of every five jobs. Permanent firms include almost all of the major companies, over periods of this length, and their contribution to employment is consequently the most critical element in change over time. The evidence from the East Midlands suggests that about a quarter of the jobs in 1947 were lost through closures.(1) New firms and in-moving establishments were unable to make up this loss, and hence only the expansion within the permanent establishments turned a potential decline in employment into a healthy growth.

It would be preferable to analyse the growth of firms separately from the question of how this growth is distributed among the establishments of multi-plant firms. However, even if sufficient data were available, there are some severe conceptual problems concerned with definitions of functional units within large corporations, and concerned with identifying the spatial origins of growth in large multi-regional or multi-national firms. In this study the conceptual problems have generally not arisen, largely because of the lack of sufficient data, with which to investigate the multi-regional firms. Most of the available information is on establishments and hence the investigation is of growth within individual factories. The causes of spatial variation within establishments can be due either to those factors affecting companies, or to those affecting the location of growth within companies. At the regional scale the latter question focuses on the forces which cause the 'export' of jobs to other regions in the form of new branch plants, or of differential growth in establish-ed plants. In the following investigation of growth variations at the regional scale, the various problems involved with multi-regional firms are circumvented by confining attention to those companies in which production is largely concentrated within a single region. These are referred to as single region companies, although this description is not completely accurate.

The ultimate focus of interest in this study is at the regional scale, but growth is analysed at a number of spatial scales since each one may throw some light on the processes which operate at adjacent scales. The greater availability of data at the intra-regional scale means that more work is carried out at this level, but nevertheless the intention is primarily to reflect on factors which may also be operative across regions.

## 9.1 GROWTH AND PROFITABILITY AT THE REGIONAL SCALE

The possibility exists at the regional scale within the UK to analyse variations in the growth of single region companies. This can be done using financial data, and in this section company results are investi-gated for a single industry, mechanical engineering, in the period 1966-71.(2) Before looking at the figures it is worthwhile reflecting on what pattern might be expected from the discussions of production costs in chapter two. The main conclusion of that chapter was that transport costs were higher in peripheral regions for industries distributing to national markets. It is also possible that unit labour costs differ between regions, but the available information was ambiguous on this point.

If higher transport costs are experienced in some regions, what effect will this have on companies? The higher costs can be borne in one or more of three

235

possible ways. Firstly, unit labour costs may be lower indicating either that wages levels are lower than average for the same work, or that productivity is raised through superior capital equipment or management methods. Secondly, profits can be lower. Lower profits may either result in lower dividends, or lower retained earnings or both. In the former case there is a higher likelihood of takeover with the possibility of some loss of control in the region concerned. In the latter case, there will be an increased cost of financing investment, with the consequence that investment levels, and perhaps future growth, may be lower. Thirdly, the higher costs may be reflected in higher prices, in which case there is likely to be some loss of competitiveness. This in turn will depress the rate of growth in the long term.

There is no evidence that unit labour costs are systematically low, where transport costs are low, and hence we can expect lower profitability or lower growth or both, in more remote regions. The analysis in 2.2 suggested that costs might be 1 or 2 per cent higher (as a percentage of sales) in remote regions. The next step is to examine whether any correspondence exists between the pattern of costs, and spatial variation in profits or growth within the mechanical engineering industry. In order to do this, firms were allocated to regions by using the registered office of the company. Branch plants and subsidiaries were traced through trade directories as far as possible. In cases where there were more than a small minority of plants outside the home region the firms were designated as multi-regional and not tied to any one region.(3) Profit is before tax and before payment of interest charges, it includes dividends, interest, royalties and rents receivable. Financial results are always open to question, particularly in the case of subsidiary companies, but differences between companies in accounting procedure are not a serious hindrance in this analysis, unless there are systematic variations across regions.

The figures in table 9.1 show a marked decline in
profitability away from the South East.  The pattern
is similar to that of distribution costs in figure 2.2
except that Scotland lies above most of the other
peripheral regions.

Table 9.1

Average profitability in the UK mechanical engineering
industry by regions 1970-71

| Region | No. of firms | Mean profit/sales % | Standard error |
|---|---|---|---|
| South East | 75 | 9.4 | 0.7 |
| South West | 7 | 9.4 | 2.9 |
| East Midlands | 17 | 8.4 | 1.6 |
| West Midlands | 30 | 7.8 | 0.7 |
| East Anglia | 8 | 7.5 | 1.6 |
| Scotland | 22 | 7.3 | 1.6 |
| North West | 47 | 6.4 | 1.1 |
| Yorkshire and Humberside | 33 | 5.5 | 1.4 |
| North | 7 | 5.5 | 3.9 |
| Wales | 7 | 5.3 | 3.0 |
| Multi-regional firms | 16 | 6.9 | |
| UK | 271 | 7.6 | 0.4 |

Source of data:  NEDC for mechanical engineering
                 industry (1972)

The differences between regions were not statistically
significant in an analysis of variance.(4)  However,
the value for the South East is significantly different (at the 0.05 level) from that of Scotland and of
the regions with lower average profitability than
Scotland.  Moreover, the spatial pattern of profitability is highly significant.  The rank correlation
between profitability and distance from London is, for
example, 0.8.

The mechanical engineering sector includes a somewhat heterogenous collection of industries serving a
variety of markets.  Although the differences between
all of the twenty-nine product groups identified by
NEDC (1972) are not significantly different in the
statistical sense, there are significant differences
between individual groups.  It is thus necessary to
examine the possibility that differences in the
composition of product groups may underlie the
regional variations in profitability.  To test the
possibility each company's profitability was expressed
as a deviation from the median (5) profitability
within its product group.(6)  The regional pattern of
average deviations is displayed in table 9.2  The
pattern is similar to that of table 9.1 in that
Southern regions still have the highest profitability
while Assisted Area regions (other than Scotland) lie
at the foot of the table.

Table 9.2

Average profitability as a residual from industry
median by regions

| Region | Residual profit/sales % | Standard error |
|---|---|---|
| East Midlands | +1.62 | 1.6 |
| South East | +1.34 | 0.7 |
| East Anglia | +0.49 | 1.7 |
| Scotland | +0.03 | 1.3 |
| West Midlands | −0.01 | 0.6 |
| North West | −0.52 | 1.0 |
| South West | −0.56 | 2.6 |
| North | −1.26 | 3.7 |
| Yorkshire and Humberside | −2.02 | 1.3 |
| Wales | −2.70 | 2.8 |
| Multi-regional firms | 0.23 | 1.1 |

Source of data: NEDC for mechanical engineering
                industry (1972)

The principal difference between the two tables is in

the position of the South West region which falls in relative position, once allowance is made for its industrial composition.

The standard errors are large in table 9.2 and not too much store can be placed on the precise ranking of regions. The differences between the South East and both Wales and Yorkshire are however, statistically significant. The range of profitability between the best and worst placed regions is similar in magnitude to that suggested above for distribution costs. There is thus a suggestion in these figures that the impact of higher distribution costs is being absorbed through lower profits, except perhaps in the case of Scotland. This would be a most important conclusion if it could be verified. The evidence here is limited to a single industry over a short period, and further studies are necessary to reach a firm conclusion.

Before enquiring whether other studies have in fact discovered a similar pattern, one further test is necessary. The profit/sales ratio has the disadvantage that differences in costs of materials between industries may make this an unsuitable indicator of company performance. A more conventional measure of performance is the ratio of profits to capital employed. The latter includes all issued share and loan capital, reserves, minority interests in subsidiaries, and short-term loans, and goodwill. Again there are differences between companies in accounting procedures, but unless these are consistent between regions they are unlikely to affect results.

The figures in table 9.3 show the decline in profitability outwards from the South East is just as marked using this measure as it was before. All Assisted Area regions have below average levels of profitability, as has East Anglia (which in figure 2.2 was shown to have distribution costs as high as those for Wales or the North). Once again with the exception of Scotland the pattern accords with the geography of

Table 9.3

Profit - capital ratios in mechanical engineering by region

| | Average profitability 1966/77 | Standard error | Average profitability 1966/71 as a deviation from industry medians | Standard error |
|---|---|---|---|---|
| South East | 15.7 | 1.2 | +1.4 | 1.1 |
| West Midlands | 14.9 | 1.5 | +1.8 | 1.6 |
| East Midlands | 14.9 | 3.1 | +2.6 | 3.1 |
| South West | 14.4 | 3.2 | -0.4 | 3.9 |
| North West | 12.5 | 1.5 | +0.3 | 1.5 |
| Scotland | 12.3 | 2.4 | -0.9 | 2.0 |
| East Anglia | 12.2 | 3.4 | -0.7 | 3.4 |
| Yorkshire and Humberside | 11.4 | 1.3 | -1.1 | 1.3 |
| North | 10.3 | 3.9 | -1.4 | 3.6 |
| Wales | 9.4 | 3.0 | -2.0 | 2.3 |
| UK | 13.9 | 0.6 | +0.7 | 0.6 |

Source of data: NEDC (1972)

distribution costs shown in 2.2. The regional differences are not statistically significant, although there are significant differences between the South East and several lower profitability regions. (7) Again, the spatial pattern is highly significant even if the magnitude of the overall differences is not.

If the regional profitability figures are examined on a year by year basis between 1966 and 1971, the pattern described above still remains. The Assisted Area regions have below average profitability levels in every year, with the single exception of Scotland in 1969/70. It is very noticeable that the variation between regions increases every year from 1966-71. (8) In 1970/71 the difference between the regions is in fact statistically significant at the 0.05 level. The reason for this widening gap is unclear, although the most likely causes are the worsening economic climate into the recession of 1971, and inflation. There is little sign of the effects of the Regional Employment Premium in the annual figures, although the profit ratio for Scotland increased sharply after 1968, while those of Yorkshire, and the Midlands fell especially in 1969/71. There was no apparent change in the other Assisted Area regions.

The regional profitability averages expressed as deviations from industry medians are also shown in table 9.3. The differences are far from statistically significant, but the geographical pattern remains much as before. The pattern conforms even more closely than previously to the pattern of distribution costs, since in this case the two Midland regions have higher levels of profitability than the South East.

Despite its strategic importance in assessing the value of alternative locations, very little research has been done to compare the average growth or profitability of firms in different regions. Two exceptions are the studies of British regional differences by Nicholson (1956) and by Hart and MacBean (1961).

Nicholson's study used net margins per head as a measure of profitability, and compared for each region the numbers of trades lying above and below the national average margin for that trade. His calculations for 1948 showed that the number of trades above the national average declined northwards and westwards from the South East region, the South East having 60 per cent and Scotland 28 per cent. Hart and MacBean compared both profitability and growth for a matched sample of firms from Scotland and the rest of the UK. They concluded that on each test Scottish firms performed less well than the rest, but that the differences were never statistically significant.(9) Hart and MacBean concluded from their study that there was no firm evidence to suggest that Scottish firms were less profitable than any others. It is true that differences were not statistically significant, but it is also true that three independent studies have all shown Scottish firms to have lower profitability than those in the South of England or in the Midlands. The differences are slight in comparison to the wide variation between firms in any one region (hence the lack of significance), but as demonstrated above the geographical pattern is significant even if the magnitudes per se are not. The evidence appears to suggest that regional variations do exist, and that they are not peculiar to the late sixties nor to the mechanical engineering industry.

The fact that profitability has been found to vary between regions does not lead to clear expectations about variations in growth. Lower profits may enable competitive pricing, but may also give rise to less investment, and consequently to lower growth in the long run. The figures for growth in capital employed between 1966 and 1971 are shown in table 9.4. The presence of extreme values presents problems in this case and an arbitrary decision was made to exclude all values of larger than four times the national average. The regional differences in table 9.4 are not significant at the 0.05 level, but are significant at the 0.07 level. This gives a one in fourteen chance of

Table 9.4

Regional differences in growth-rates within the mechanical engineering industry

| Region | Growth in capital employed 1966-71 | Standard error | Growth of capital as deviations from industry medians |
|---|---|---|---|
| East Anglia | 9.1 (12.1) | 4.4 | +2.9 (+5.8) |
| South East | 9.0 (9.3) | 1.0 | +1.3 (+1.5) |
| Scotland | 6.9 (8.2) | 2.5 | +0.5 (+1.5) |
| North West | 6.6 | 1.2 | +1.0 |
| West Midlands | 6.3 (7.2) | 1.8 | -0.9 (0.0) |
| South West | 5.3 (9.1) | 3.9 | -1.7 (+2.4) |
| Wales | 4.8 (15.3) | 7.2 | +0.2 |
| Yorkshire and Humberside | 4.8 | 1.4 | -1.1 |
| East Midlands | 4.8 | 1.4 | -1.3 |
| North | 2.9 | 3.0 | -2.6 |
| UK | 7.6 | 0.6 | |

Source of data: NEDC (1972)

Note

Nine extreme values (over four times as large as the UK mean) have been omitted. The figures in brackets indicate growth without these omissions. Standard errors are for growth without omissions.

error, and can be accepted as indicating a true difference between regions.(10)  The difference between the South East and every other region (except East Anglia) is significant.  There is little difference between the other regions, although the value for the North is significantly below those of Scotland, the North West and the West Midlands.

The third column in table 9.4 has the growth figures re-expressed in the form of deviations from the industry medians.  This device should have the incidental effect of making some allowance for differences in market concentration between product groups. The differences between regions are not large and in several cases the figures are influenced by the remaining extreme values.  On the whole, however, the rank ordering of regions is little changed.  The South East and East Anglia remain at the top of the list and the Northern region remains at the bottom. There is probably little significance in the differences between the remaining regions. There would seem to be some differences in growth between regions, with a little evidence that firms in the South East, and perhaps also East Anglia, were growing faster in this period, than were firms in other regions.

In conclusion the figures above suggest that higher distribution costs in peripheral regions may have the effect of reducing profitability.  The correlation between profitability (adjusted for industrial structure) and a measure of distribution costs is good although not perfect.  A mere correlation between the two does not of course necessarily indicate any causal connection.  However, the differences between the Midland regions on the one hand and the major Assisted Areas regions on the other is of roughly the right order of magnitude for this hypothesis.  It is also difficult to imagine other circumstances (other than coincidence) which could underlie the observed pattern. Certainly there is no evidence that unit labour costs are systematically lower in the remote regions.

One measure of unit labour costs is obtained if net output is divided by labour costs. This can be done for 1968 but not for other years in the period 1966–71. The figures in table 9.5 show that in 1968 unit labour costs were high in Scotland but low in Northern Ireland and the North.

Table 9.5

Unit labour costs in mechanical engineering

| Region | Labour costs/net output | | |
| | 1968 | Average 1963 & 1968 | Index 1963–68 (UK = 100) |
|---|---|---|---|
| Northern Ireland | 0.51 | 0.52 | 95 |
| South East | 0.51 | 0.53 | 96 |
| East Midlands | 0.52 | 0.54 | 97 |
| Wales | 0.54 | 0.54 | 97 |
| West Midlands | 0.55 | 0.56 | 101 |
| North West | 0.54 | 0.56 | 101 |
| Yorkshire and Humberside | 0.56 | 0.57 | 102 |
| East Anglia | 0.52 | 0.57 | 102 |
| North | 0.52 | 0.57 | 102 |
| South West | 0.60 | 0.58 | 105 |
| Scotland | 0.58 | 0.61 | 110 |
| UK | 0.54 | 0.55 | 100 |

Source of data: Census of production

Unit labour costs are influenced by changes in both output and wages and are known to fluctuate from year to year. To make some allowance for these variations an average has been taken of the figures for 1963 and 1968. This average does not coincide with the period 1966–71 but is intended as a rough indication of conditions in the 1960s. Its value will depend on the nature of annual fluctuations in the sixties, and this is unknown.

The average figures indicate that the lowest unit labour costs occurred in Northern Ireland and the

South East, while the highest were observed for Scotland. In each case these positions were maintained in both 1963 and 1968. Among the remaining Assisted Areas regions, Wales had below average costs while those for the North were above average. In both of these cases there were marked differences between the two years. Apart from the fact that unit labour costs appear to be genuinely low in Northern Ireland, there is no clear evidence that they are generally low in peripheral areas. In Scotland the opposite appears to be true, and in this case both transport costs and labour costs were higher than average. This is not fully reflected in the figures on profitability and growth, and one reason may have been the influence of the Regional Employment Premium in the second half of the period. Such an explanation does imply, however, that REP was put to different uses in Scotland than in Wales or the Northern region.

Lower profits can be expected to depress growth in two ways. Firstly, it is more difficult to finance growth from retained earnings. It is also more difficult to raise external finance with a poorer profit record. The relationship is likely to be complex, and few studies demonstrate a very high correlation between growth and profitability. Nevertheless, some relationship is usually found for companies and we can expect this to hold for regional averages also. The figures presented above for growth within mechanical engineering give some support to the notion that peripheral regions have a poor growth performance, but the evidence is not strong and in particular the two Midland regions have low growth values.

It is not easy to consider profitability and growth jointly. As a crude attempt however, the regions were ranked from one to ten, for profitability and growth separately, and the average rank was calculated.(11) The highest average rank was for the South East and all of the regions in the top half were in the South or Central England except for the North West. The low ranking regions included all of the Assisted Areas,

(including in this case the South West). Although it
has not been possible to demonstrate with confidence
that growth varies systematically between regions,
there is a prima facie case that this is the case for
mechanical engineering. Profitability and growth,
considered jointly, demonstrate a core-periphery
pattern. In the case of profitability there is strong
evidence of such a pattern, and this in itself would
tend to indirectly suggest that long-term differences
in growth would be observed. Although this section
has been concerned with growth in assets rather than
of employment, the two things are usually related.
The fact that firms in the South East appear to grow
faster on average than those in Assisted Areas in
terms of assets indicates (but it does not prove) that
the same is true of employment.


9.2  GROWTH AND EMPLOYMENT RETENTION AT THE SUB-
     REGIONAL SCALE

Differences between regions in rates of company growth
appear to be relatively small. This leads to the
expectation that intra-regional differences will be
negligible, except perhaps for random fluctuations at
the very local scale. There is the possibility that
the regional differences mask a greater heterogeneity
at smaller scales, perhaps distinguishing conurbations
from other areas. However, there is no strong reason
to expect this, especially within the East Midlands
(with which this section is concerned) since there
are no large conurbations.

   The employment data used in this section makes it
necessary to concentrate on establishments rather than
firms. In this context there is much more reason to
expect sub-regional variability. Differences in
labour supply and perhaps also the differential appli-
cation of government policy in granting IDC certificates are likely to be the major factors which lead
firms in some areas to retain less of their growth
in local factories compared with firms in other areas.

Another factor which may influence the local retention of employment growth is the availability of premises in the light of government restrictions on new buildings. Firms in large cities are more likely to have factories which are impossible to expand by physical extension. If large new industrial buildings are prohibited and no alternative premises are available, then either growth is foregone or more probably branch plants are established in other areas. For some types of expansion the acquisition of an existing company may be feasible, but increasing demand will generally require the expansion of total capacity within any particular industry.

9.2.1 Unweighted rates of growth

Spatial variation in growth rates within the East Midlands has been examined first at the county scale and secondly at a coarse sub-county or 'district' scale.(12) The data are compiled from the responses to the 330 questionnaires which supplied information on employment in both 1947 and 1970. The mean growth rates per annum for the establishments in each county are given in table 9.6. Growth is measured, as in chapter six, as the ratio of final size to initial size divided by the length of period in years.

Table 9.6

Mean growth-rate of manufacturing establishments in the East Midlands 1947-70

| County | No. of plants | Mean growth-rate p.a. |
|--------|---------------|------------------------|
| Nottinghamshire | 73 | 0.112 |
| Derbyshire | 48 | 0.135 |
| Leicestershire | 116 | 0.140 |
| Northamptonshire | 58 | 0.100* |
| Lincolnshire | 35 | 0.104 |
| East Midlands | 330 | 0.125 |

Source of data: Questionnaire survey
   * Significantly different from regional mean
     at 0.05 level

248

The values in each case are close to the overall mean, and an analysis of variance performed in the figures, with the counties as groups, indicated that differences of this magnitude could have arisen by chance. On an individual county basis, however, the value for Northamptonshire is significantly below the regional mean of 0.125 obtained from the questionnaire responses. This may indicate either a low rate of growth in firms, perhaps due to the poor industrial structure, or else to a low rate of in situ growth, perhaps due to shortage of labour. In chapter six it was shown that growth varies between industrial sectors. In Northamptonshire 60 per cent of employment was in the footwear industry in 1948 and this industry has since declined substantially. Hence the more likely causes of slow growth in Northamptonshire are those connected with industrial structure.

The pattern of growth in districts is mapped in figure 9.1. The differences between areas were not revealed to be statistically significant in an analysis of variance, but with eighteen districts there is an opportunity to look for a geographical pattern, even when the overall differences are small. The figures in figure 9.1 have all been drawn from the questionnaire survey, and this means that sample sizes fall below ten in several rural areas, increasing the chance that sampling variation will dominate the map. Something of a core-periphery pattern can be discerned, although this is weak, in that the major city, Nottingham, records a below average value (perhaps because of urban congestion). Sampling fluctuations could very easily cause differences of this magnitude, however, and no stress can be placed on individual values.

Some credence is given to the notion that urban congestion affects growth by the relationship between frequency of locational change and urban size. Replies to the question 'has this establishment ever moved to a different location within thirty miles?', revealed that movement had occurred in twice the

249

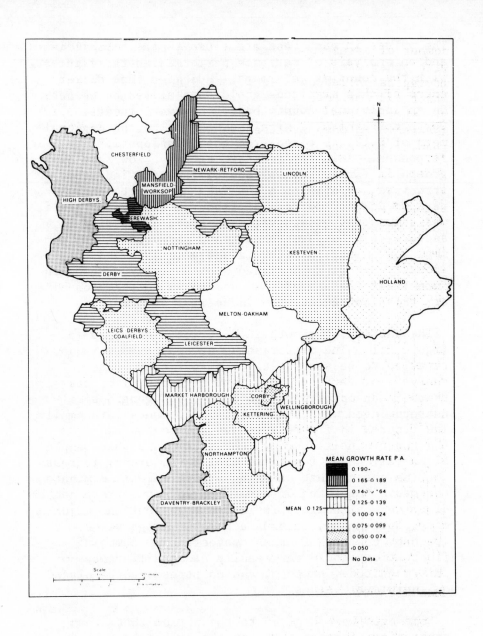

Figure 9.1   Mean growth-rates p.a. for establishments
1947-70 by districts

Source of data:   Questionnaire survey

250

number of cases in cities and large towns compared
with other areas.  In general the growth-rates of
moving establishments were much higher than those
which did not move.  From these facts it can be inferred that in the large cities it is more usually
necessary to move premises in the course of growth
than is the case in less urbanised areas.

The low growth values in several of the peripheral
rural areas in figure 9.1 is due partly to their
higher incidence of branch plants.  Using questionnaire evidence again there was a sharp contrast in
growth between branch plants and other establishments.
The recorded values were as follows:

| | | |
|---|---|---|
| Single plant firms | 0.13 | (208 plants) |
| Parent plants | 0.14 | (73 plants) |
| Branch plants | 0.09 | (49 plants) |

The growth-rate for branches is just over half that
for parent plants, and the difference is significant
at the 0.01 level.

It is not possible to examine vigorously the pattern
of growth in figure 9.1, chiefly because the sample
sizes are too small to permit controls for size
structure and for industrial structure.  Nevertheless,
a rough interpretation can be attempted.  The availability of labour was greatest on the Nottingham/Derby-
shire coalfield during this period, and it appears
that available labour may have allowed firms in Derbyshire and North Nottinghamshire to retain more of
their growth within those areas.  Shortages of labour
were most acute in Leicestershire and Northamptonshire.  There is no hint in the figures that labour
shortages restrained local expansion in Leicestershire
more than elsewhere.  However, in Central Northamptonshire the combination of a declining industry (in
employment terms) and a shortage of labour is apparent
in the low rates of growth.  Beyond this, and the
other points made above, there is little more that can
be said, since small sample sizes in some areas lead
to higher sampling fluctuations.

251

## 9.2.2 The retention of employment growth

The rates of growth reported in the previous section were all unweighted averages, and consequently small establishments made a major contribution to the figures. In the growth of employment it is the large establishments which have the major impact, and in this context the weighted growth figures are more important. The questionnaire responses are not sufficiently reliable to estimate weighted growth-rates and no progress can be made in this regard. It is possible, however, to say something about the rate of retention of growth.

Permanent firms in each county can change size in a number of different ways. They can expand (or contract) their employment at existing (permanent) establishments. Alternatively, they can open new branches, either within the same county or elsewhere. Also they may close pre-existing establishments. Finally, they may grow through acquisition, although we will not be concerned with acquisition here. The total growth of permanent companies cannot be reliably estimated, but it is possible to arrive at satisfactory figures for employment in branch plants set up since 1948. The most adequate base against which to compare employment in branches is the 1967 employment within permanent establishments in each county. This gives a good idea of the aggregate employment size of those companies which were involved in setting up the branch plants. This population of permanent plants will contain a few long established branches of non-local firms, but the great majority of plants are likely to be those operated by locally based companies.

The figures for total employment in table 9.7 includes the estimates for permanent establishments, and local branch plants set up since 1948 (see table 4.4), plus employment in branches which were established outside each county by local companies.(13) The figures show that Leicestershire companies had

252

Table 9.7

Employment in permanent plants and 'new' branch plants 1967

| County | Total employment | Percentage of employment in 'new' branches | | |
|---|---|---|---|---|
| | | Local branches | Non-local | Total |
| Leicestershire | 161.3 | 6.2 | 8.7 | 14.9 |
| Notts./Derbys. (a) | 237.6 | 4.0 | 4.0 | 8.0 |
| Northamptonshire (b) | 60.6 | 6.6 | 6.8 | 13.4 |
| Lincolnshire (c) | 48.3 | 2.1 | 7.5 | 7.5 |

Source of data: see text

Notes

(a) Excluding Newark, Retford and Chesterfield
(b) Excluding employment in steelworks
(c) Including Newark and Retford

253

had the highest proportion of their employment in branches, and also the highest proportion in branches located outside the county. The next highest proportion was for firms in Northamptonshire, but in this case relatively more employment was in branches within the county. The remaining counties had similar totals in branches but a much higher proportion of employment in Nottinghamshire/Derbyshire was retained within the area in local branches.

The interpretation of these figures appears to be relatively straightforward. The highest proportions of employment in branches occur where labour shortages were greatest. Very low unemployment levels and high female activity rates prevailed through the whole period in both Leicestershire and in central Northamtonshire. Firms in these areas have high levels of employment in branches, although the pockets of labour available in north and south Northamptonshire enabled branch plants to be set up within the county in that case. In the north the development of Corby New Town led to an influx of steelworkers, whose wives and daughters became available to work in the branch factories which arrived to take up the opportunity. In the Nottinghamshire/Derbyshire area the proximity of the coalfield to the major towns meant that a relatively large pool of labour, particularly female labour, lay within commuting distance of existing factories. In other cases, branches could be established relatively close to parent plants. There was less need than elsewhere to set up branches outside the county, although in some cases government building restrictions made this necessary.

The behaviour of companies in Lincolnshire is less easy to understand. Unemployment levels were relatively high by East Midlands standards in the early part of the period, although seasonal fluctuations were large, due to the needs of agriculture. The female activity rate was average for the region, although it lay below that of the major textile areas. The labour situation is reflected in the low proportion of employment in branch plants. However, it is surprising that so much of the branch plants employment is outside the county, especially since Leicestershire firms were regularly locating about one in ten of their branches within Lincolnshire. Only small numbers of jobs are involved and lack of accuracy in the estimate may be the cause; but another possibility is the low density of the rural population. This is a strong disadvantage if the need is to establish large branches. The main industry of Lincolnshire is engineering and it is likely that the branch plants were larger than the small hosiery and footwear factories established by Leicestershire firms.

This discussion has been couched in the static cross-sectional terms of employment in 1967. It is possible to convert this into terms of employment change with judicious use of assumption. The growth of firms based in Leicestershire could potentially have taken place largely by expanding (or failing to close) existing establishments more than was the case in other counties. The shortage of labour in that area makes this an unlikely proposition, and it seems safer to assume that expansion in this form was at the very least not greater in Leicester than elsewhere. The same can be assumed to be true of Northamptonshire. Using this assumption it can be concluded that relatively more of the growth generated by local firms was retained within the county in the case of Nottinghamshire and Derbyshire. Least was retained by Leicestershire firms. The causes in each case appear to reflect labour availability, although government policy measures are likely to have exerted pressure in the same direction, especially after 1963.


## 9.3 RETAINED GROWTH AT THE LOCAL SCALE

One of the paradoxes in considering the growth of firms is that growth may vary at the regional scale, is unlikely to do so at the sub-regional scale, but

is again likely to be important at the local scale.
The reason in the last case is that small areas
contain relatively few firms and random variations in
company performance may have a considerable effect on
aggregate employment change.  In small areas, it is
also unlikely that all of the establishments of any
sizable company will all be located within the area.
At the local scale the question of how growth is
distributed spatially between parts of any one firm
assumes as much importance as the question of the
amount of growth in total.  In this section growth is
examined for local areas within Leicestershire.  There
are no data on the total growth of companies, and
instead the analysis concerns growth solely in local
establishments.  The period is 1947-67 as in previous
chapters, and permanent establishments are once again
defined as those surviving throughout the period.

The relative importance of locally retained growth
to total growth (excluding acquisitions) can be seen
in the following figures.  Just over 19,000 new jobs
were created either by net in situ expansion of
permanent establishments or by branch plants established within Leicestershire since 1947 by local
firms.(14)  In addition, locally based firms created
an estimated 14,000 jobs in other areas between 1947
and 1966.(15)  This gives a total of approximately
33,000 jobs, of which 30 per cent were in permanent
establishments, (16) another 30 per cent were in
local branches, and a final 40 per cent were exported
to other regions as branch plants.  This growth was
generated largely by permanent locally based firms,
but also by some permanent branch plants of external
companies.  Of the new jobs created by these firms
and establishments, leaving aside any acquisitions
they may have made, only three-fifths occurred within
the county.  This is the context within which we now
examine variations in the growth which did occur
locally.

## 9.3.1 Variations in the rates of local growth

The rates of growth of both establishments and firms are shown in table 9.8 for each employment exchange area. The values for Leicester, Loughborough and Hinckley are in each case very close to the average, while those for the other areas are somewhat below it. Although these differences are real ones, in that they occurred for the whole population of plants and are not based on samples, it is nevertheless likely that they are due to chance. A 't' test indicated that each of the values was not significantly different from the mean, even at the 0.10 level. This can be interpreted as meaning that given the wide variation between growth-rates of individual plants or firms, the observed area averages are relatively small. It can be concluded that random differences existed between the average local growth-rates of the seven areas. The next step is to see how this was translated into employment.

## 9.3.2 Growth-rate and size of plant

The figures in table 9.8 were unweighted averages. Again, the weighted averages are of more significance to employment growth due to the importance of large firms and establishments.

Table 9.8

| Average growth-rates in permanent plants 1947-67 | |
| --- | --- |
| Employment exchange area | Growth-rate of establishments |
| Leicester | 0.11 |
| Coalville | 0.09 |
| Loughborough | 0.12 |
| Melton | 0.07 |
| Oakham | 0.07 |
| Market Harborough | 0.09 |
| Hinckley | 0.11 |
| Average | 0.11 |

Source of data: Establishment records

The weighted averages in the final column of table 9.9 tell a rather different story from their unweighted counterparts. In table 9.8 all values were greater than 0.05 indicating that most establishments grew rather than declined.

Table 9.9

Employment growth in 'permanent' establishments 1947-67: numbers of jobs

| Employment exchange area | In situ growth | Leicestershire branch plants generated from within E.E. area | In situ plus local branches No. | % of 1947 total |
|---|---|---|---|---|
| Leicester | 5,769 | 7,461 | 13,230 | 22 |
| Coalville | 2,320 | 209 | 2,529 | 59 |
| Loughborough | 1,953 | 816 | 2,769 | 20 |
| Hinckley | 800 | 690 | 1,490 | 15 |
| Melton | -214 | 11 | -203 | -10 |
| Oakham | - 6 | 2 | - 4 | - 5 |
| Market Harborough | -682 | 25 | -657 | -25 |

Source of data:  Establishment records

The new figures show that decline in overall employment occurred in the three rural areas.  There was only slight variation in growth between the three largest centres, but in the coalfield area (Coalville) the rate was almost three times as high.

In both Leicester and Hinckley about half of the growth, which is included in table 9.9, occurred in branch plants.  In the case of Loughborough the proportion was a little less, but in the rural and coalfield areas relatively little employment went into local branch plants.  This pattern probably reflects labour availability once again, although the local effects of government IDC restrictions is not known. A secondary factor may be the size of town.  The inner areas of Leicester are the most densely built-up part of Leicestershire and these probably offer least opportunity for physical extensions to individual factories. Hence Leicester has the highest proportion of its local expansion in branches. The great majority of these branch plants remained within the Leicester employment exchange area, and many were little more than detached departments.

Figure 9.2 shows that for in situ growth the large establishments generally declined, although in Coalville the large establishments performed unusually well.(17) In the Coalville area the twenty-four establishments employing in excess of 100 grew by an aggregate of 76 per cent compared with an aggregate decline in employment in large plants elsewhere.

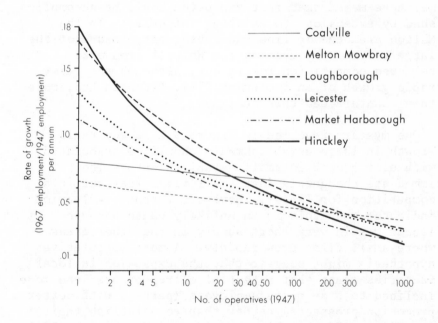

Figure 9.2  Rate of growth and size of manufacturing
            establishments in Leicestershire 1947-67
Source of data:  Establishment records

In most of the areas, the rate of growth declines with initial size in rather similar ways, but two areas stand out in exhibiting very different relationships. These are Melton and Coalville. In the case of Coalville the slope coefficient for the regression line is significantly different from the county average at the 0.05 significance level, but for Melton the difference is not statistically significant. The cause of the distinctiveness of Coalville is once again likely to reflect labour conditions. As the one coalfield area within Leicestershire, the local availability of labour was easier, chiefly because of a female participation rate which in 1948 was 25 per cent compared with 40 per cent in the surrounding textile area. This, it seems, relieved local firms of the need to look elsewhere for labour. The dispersed low-density settlement pattern additionally may have meant that most expansion could be accomplished by extensions to existing factories. In the Melton area the decline and subsequent closure of the largest local employer at the Holwell ironworks relieved competition for labour, although the later rapid growth of an immigrant firm, Petfoods Ltd, more than counteracted this decline.

One mystery revealed in figure 9.2 is why rapid growth in large establishments should be associated with slow growth in small establishments. The immediate thought is that small firms lost out in a competition for labour. However, further reflection indicates that this is an unlikely cause because labour was in very short supply in the other areas where small firms grew rapidly. A more speculative hypothesis might suggest that the expansion in local factories meant that potential entrepreneurs were more inclined to stay on as employees (perhaps with better promotion prospects) rather than to establish their own firms. If this happened in periods prior to 1947, and also affected the more dynamic entrepreneurs to a greater extent than others, then fewer fast growing new firms would have opened. The implications for the period under scrutiny here would be a shortage of rapidly expanding small firms.

There is some reason for thinking that labour conditions are not the only factor which differentiates
Coalville from the other areas in the context of
employment growth. Leaving aside the rural areas we
can examine the combined growth in Leicester, Loughborough and Hinckley. Figures are available for
employment in branch plants set up outside Leicestershire during the period, but only for these areas and
Coalville together. The maximum employment growth
figure for Leicester, Loughborough and Hinckley
occurs, if it is assumed that all external branches
originated in these areas, while none of the total
came from Coalville. Adding the employment in
external branches to the local growth shown in table
9.9 would result in a combined (weighted) growth-rate
of 37.5 per cent for these three areas. This is still
considerably below the rate in Coalville, and it seems
that firms in Coalville did achieve higher rates of
total growth.

One possible reason for this result might be related
to acquisitions. Rake (1972) shows that most acquisitions undertaken by East Midlands firms were for
purposes of diversification, buying into markets, or
to gain control over suppliers, customers or competitors. In some cases however, the aim was to expand
productive capacity especially when this had to be
done quickly. It is possible that this motive for
acquisition comes to the fore more frequently in
conditions of greatest labour scarcity. If so, then
firms in the Coalville area may have had less reason
to pursue growth directly through acquisition, with
the result that more growth was generated internally
to the firms concerned. One potential cause which
does not seem to have been of relevance is that of
industrial structure. The mix of industries was very
similar to that of neighbouring areas in its growth
potential, although not in the nature of its products.

If Leicester, Loughborough and Hinckley can be

considered to form a coherent group of areas, while Coalville is in a category of its own, then the rural areas constitute a third group. The common factor in this group is the small number of permanent establishments. In each of the three cases only thirty or less plants were involved, making it possible for extreme random fluctuations to greatly affect the amount of local employment generated. All three areas registered net decline in the employment within permanent establishments, and in each case one or two firms dominated the figures. As it seems unlikely that the permanent firms involved here set up branch plants outside their areas, the declines are most probably due to the bad luck of having in each case a large declining firm or firms. In the Market Harborough area, although five out of the six firms initially employing more than 100 declined over the period, the net decline of nearly 700 jobs is very largely due to the decline in the single largest firm.

It seems that two factors differentiate the three groups. The first is the initial employment size. Areas with few firms can gain or suffer from fluctuations which may be considered random in a geographical sense. In areas with relatively large numbers of firms, the random fluctuations are likely to be evened out, but here a second factor comes into play. Some of the employment growth may be exported through branch plant formation, and the degree to which this has happened has probably depended on the local availability of room for expansion, premises and particularly labour. The interplay between branch plants and acquisitions as a direct means of achieving growth has largely been ignored in this chapter, but there is some suggestion above that it may play some part in causing differential growth at the local scale.


9.4  CONCLUSIONS

It is not clear, from any of the sections in this

chapter, that the growth of firms varies between regions. However, there is evidence from mechanical engineering that this may be the case for single region companies. It is always possible that the results obtained are unrepresentative of a wide section of manufacturing, but the figures are sufficient to suggest that his is an area of research which merits extensive attention.

At smaller scales the influence of market demand and technological change which underlie the effects of industrial structure, very probably play a role in growth, but in this study the data has been insufficient for these to be detected. Instead attention was focused on a question which is probably more important at these spatial scales, at least when labour is a scarce resource. This is the question of how much growth is retained within an area, rather than being 'exported' elsewhere in branch plants. Wide variations were found between areas, and in each case the major discriminating factor is likely to have been local labour conditions.

NOTES

(1) A small proportion of these were branches of locally based permanent firms.
(2) The data is drawn from Company Financial Results 1966/67 - 1970/71. Economic Development Committee for Mechanical Engineering. HMSO.
(3) Sixteen out of 271 firms were designated multi-regional. In some cases subsidiaries of the companies themselves were not traced. However, if these are widespread across regions or countries they will tend to weaken any regional differences. Hence, the regional contrasts discussed below may be underestimated. A similar analysis using the same data has since been undertaken, independently by K. Ingham (Ingham, 1975). He included rather more cases as single region companies and there were also some other discrepancies in the allocation of companies to

regions. These affected individual results but the overall conclusions were broadly the same.

(4) The calculated F value was 1.29 compared with $F (11,259) = 1.83$. The 0.05 significance point was computed using the Box (1952) procedure to allow for the effects of heteroscedasticisty. The 0.05 point in this case was 4.2.

(5) Medians were preferred to means due to the existence of extreme values in some industries.

(6) This method assumes no interaction between location and industry. This lack of interaction has been confirmed by Ingham (1975).

(7) The calculated F value is 1.2, which is not significant at the 0.10 level.

(8) This is measured by the F statistic which increases in value from 0.80, through 0.96, 1.04, and 1.33 to 1.90.

(9) The paper of Hart and MacBean (1961) has been subject to criticism on its methodology by Smyth (1961). However, in a reply to Smyth, Fisher (1962) demonstrates that the Hart and MacBean methods were correct.

(10) The convention of working to a 0.05 level of significance is purely arbitrary, and should not be adhered to if this is to the detriment of common sense! As a precaution the analysis of variance was run again using logged values. In this case the significance level fell to the 0.15 level.

(11) In both cases this was done with figures expressed as deviations from industry medians.

(12) Districts are amalgamations of local authority areas constructed so as to include towns along with their hinterlands.

(13) The latter estimates are constructed from Department of Industry figures by taking employment in 1966 for moves which occurred 1952-65 plus that in three-fifths of the moves 1945-51.

(14) The only figures available for 1947 were for operatives. The number of non-operatives in that year was estimated using national proportions.

(15) It is assumed that all external branch plants were established by permanent firms rather than new

firms.   This is very likely to be a correct assumption.
(16)   Some of the permanent establishments moved
location within the country.
(17)   Decline is indicated on figure 9.2 by a growth-
rate of less than 0.05.

# 10 Spatial variations III: closures

It was indicated in chapter seven that closures come
in many forms.  Independent firms may close through
financial failure or other causes.  Branch plants are
closed sometimes for reasons akin to financial failure, but in other cases because multi-plant companies
decide that advantages lie in concentrating production, even if this means the closure of profitable
factories.  Another type of closure which should be
distinguished from the first one listed above is that
which derives from a high entry-rate.  New firms are
sometimes formed at a rapid rate but many fail to
survive more than a few years.

These distinctions are important in a regional
analysis because the spatial incidence of each type
may vary, sometimes for unrelated reasons.  In some
cases, when demand rises only slowly, or at least more
slowly than labour productivity, then closures will
affect companies as a whole in the relevant industries.  A high incidence of closures might be expected
to coincide with decline or slow growth in surviving
companies and plants.  In other cases, conditions may
be conducive to company rationalisation involving
closures, even though demand is rising faster than
productivity.  If the closures fall more heavily on
branch plants than on parent factories, then regions
with high proportions of the former will suffer most.
Finally, areas with high entry-rates may also have
many closures.  The large numbers of small firms
involved in such turnover will often mean that there
are more closures of this sort than any other.  Hence,
regions with high entry-rates are likely to have the
largest absolute rate of closure.

It is possible to argue that a distinction between
closures and other forms of employment decline is
relatively unimportant, and that only the overall

266

magnitude of decline is significant. This is probably
an erroneous view for two reasons. One relatively
minor reason is that closures will typically occur
suddenly and dramatically, while the shedding of
labour by continuing companies can be more gradual.
If individual closures are large, then the re-employ-
ment prospects of employees may be made more difficult
by the sudden increase in unemployment of people with
similar skills.

A more important reason is that the form of decline
may have subsequent effects on future employment
growth. The point is best made by assuming that a
particular industry has employment declining at a
certain rate due to the interaction of world demand
and technological change. If the industry is
dominated by large firms with large plants, what form
will the employment contraction take? Large firms are
normally much more resistant to closure than small
ones and it is more likely that contraction will be
achieved through declining size in continuing companies than by closures. Similarly, if the plants
operated by the companies are large, then these will
be difficult to close, and again contraction is more
likely than closure. Regions with declining industries of this type will change relatively little in
the process of contraction. Employment will decrease,
but the same factories remain. Also, unless the
decline results in mergers within the industry, the
management of the firms is likely to change relatively
little.

A second situation might occur in an industry with
neither very large firms or establishments, nor large
numbers of very small ones. In this case, an overall
contraction is likely to include closures. Entire
companies may close, and continuing companies may
close individual factories. In both cases, closure is
more likely than with very large firms and plants.
The closure of companies releases premises as well as
labour, and is likely to discrimate between more and
less efficient management. In a declining or slow

growing market, competition will be fierce, and the survival of only the more successful management teams may leave the surviving firms more able to withstand continued competition, for example, if this comes from foreign competitors with lower labour costs or better equipment. It is thus possible that regions with this type of declining industry may find that average management standards become higher than in regions with large plant industries.

A related factor is that industries which are dominated by medium sized firms may find that more closures occur than can be directly attributed to the market conditions. This may be part of the normal changes which occur in such industries with new firms replacing older ones as time progresses. In the regional context, it does not necessarily follow that the slack created by these closures is taken up by firms in the same region. If foreign competition is fierce, then some of the slack may be taken up by firms outside the country, especially if the competition have some advantage not available to domestic companies. Regions with these industries may find that their employment contractions take place more rapidly than would otherwise be the case. In postwar Leicestershire, for instance, the footwear industry containing few of the largest companies declined rapidly, even compared with footwear nationally. This was in part due to its concentration on women's footwear which faced particularly strong competition from abroad. However, it is possible that the decline in this branch of the industry was hastened by the way in which it was organised predominantly into medium sized companies.

A rapid decline achieved through closure can be beneficial from a region's point of view as long as there is overall pressure on resources. If labour and premises are released rapidly by declining industries, and taken up by other growing sectors, then the industrial structure will change quickly. This allows more rapid adaptation to changing economic conditions and, in the long term, would lead to a relatively buoyant economy. This may well describe the East Midlands in recent decades. The major industries thirty years ago were in textiles, clothing and footwear. Each tended to have slowly growing demand, combined with a lack of dominance by very large firms. The industrial structure has changed rapidly since the war, with faster growing industries taking up both labour and premises made redundant by closures. In some cases, the new industries have been related to the old, as in plastics, in which the switch from wooden heels to plastic in making shoes provided one way in which plastics knowledge was introduced into the area. Although it is difficult to prove, decline may stimulate invention and enterprise where both the declining and new industries are able to produce potential entrepreneurs and allow new firms to be established.

A final type of industry might be one with large numbers of small firms and few barriers to entry. In these industries, there will be many closures above the number required by market conditions, due to the turnover in companies. Areas with a high rate of turnover may be most likely to produce ultimately successful firms and to gain large proportions of the market irrespective of whether it is growing or declining. In this way, a high closure rate may become associated with a successful sconomy. The association is, of course, an indirect one, since the high birth-rate of new firms would be responsible for both the economic success and for the high rate of closures. In Leicestershire, to continue the example above, the growth in employment from 1948-67, relative to the national performance, was notably best in those industries with low barriers to entry. This was true of wood products, printing and paper products, miscellaneous industries (including plastics) and for engineering as a whole. These industries also had high closure rates in several cases, but it is unfortunately not possible to gauge how these rates compared with those in other areas.

The work outlined in chapter seven showed that industrial structure and size structure were the two regional characteristics most likely to influence the rate of closure. There was little evidence, on the other hand, that the structure of ownership and control made much difference in itself. The remarks in previous paragraphs are intended to indicate that the influence of all three aspects may interact in a complex way, to produce the superficially paradoxical conclusion that a high closure rate may be beneficial to economic progress. The study of ways in which industrial change is achieved through closure, growth and decline is an important subject about which little is known. Other than the work of Dahmen (1970) for interwar Sweden, little research has been undertaken, and virtually none in Britain.

Although these questions are important for a regional investigation, a project which uses a data set based in a single region is in a poor position to investigate them. Little progress has been made in this study, except at the local scale. Before describing this, it is worth reviewing one important piece of work on closures within multi-regional companies in the late 1960s.

## 10.1 CLOSURES WITHIN UK MULTI-REGIONAL COMPANIES

Atkins (1973) has analysed rates of closure 1966-71 for virtually all British companies which established a branch plant outside their area between 1945 and 1960. Areas in this context are the sixty zones into which the country is divided by the Department of Industry for this and other purposes. The branch plants had all been established for at least six years, and the influence of the early build-up period of branches is thus left out. Twelve classes of company were distinguished dependent on the location of branch and parent company respectively between Development Areas, Intermediate Areas and Non-Assisted Areas. The Development Areas were those of 1973,

270

i.e. Scotland, Wales, Northern Ireland, the Northern
Region, parts of Cornwall and Merseyside.  The Intermediate Areas were mainly within the North-West
Region and Yorkshire and Humberside.  Figures derived
from Atkins' work are shown in table 10.1.  The
period was one of contraction in UK manufacturing
industry, but the table shows that branch plants were
a more stable element than parent plants in the same
companies.  The closure rates were similar, but the
parent plants which closed were over twice as large
on average as the branches.  Moreover, the reduction
in the size of survivors was 9 per cent for parents,
but under 1 per cent for branches.

The major interest here lies in the geographical
pattern of closures.  The spatial units form a core-
periphery configuration with the Non-Assisted Areas
as the core, and the Development Areas constituting
the outer periphery.  The closure rates for the branch
plants were similar in all three types of area.
Although the Development Area branches had a slightly
larger initial size, there was little difference in
this respect which could distort the figures.  The
size of the closing plants is not revealed, but it can
be seen in table 10.1 that the proportionate employment loss in branches, through closure and changes in
survivors, increased from the core areas out to the
peripheral ones.  The performance of parent plants
showed a reverse trend with the highest rates of both
closure and employment contraction in the Non-Assisted
Areas.

There was a slight tendency for branches in Assisted
Areas to have a higher propensity to close than their
parents.  However, their total employment declined
less, and the period saw a net transfer of jobs from
the parents to the branches.  This was even more
marked in those cases where both branch and parent
were located in Non-Assisted Areas.  The period was
one of dispersion within multi-regional companies.  It
seems likely that the parent plants which were being
run down were mainly located in conurbations and city

Table 10.1

Closures in UK branches and parent plants

| Location | | Closure rate | | Growth of employment | |
| --- | --- | --- | --- | --- | --- |
| Branch | Parent | Branches % | Parents % | Branches % | Parents % |
| DA | DA | 11.4 | 12.1 | +10.2 | -12.7 |
| DA | IA | 17.3 | 13.2 | -16.4 | -24.6 |
| DA | Non.Ass. | 12.7 | 9.4 | -11.7 | -14.4 |
| All DA Branches | | 13.8 | 10.6 | -11.9 | -16.2 |
| IA | DA | 14.3 | - | -13.4 | -17.7 |
| IA | IA | 12.9 | 11.1 | -8.6 | -17.1 |
| IA | Non.Ass. | 9.2 | 10.0 | +1.2 | -12.5 |
| All IA Branches | | 11.1 | 9.7 | -2.7 | -14.3 |
| Non.Ass. | DA | 25.0 | 25.0 | -23.6 | -22.6 |
| Non.Ass. | IA | 22.2 | 14.8 | +7.2 | -14.7 |
| Non.Ass. | Non.Ass. | 12.0 | 15.8 | +0.2 | -19.4 |
| All Non.Ass.Branches | | 13.2 | 16.0 | -0.5 | -19.4 |
| Average | | 13.0 | 13.1 | -6.1 | -17.2 |

Source: adapted from Atkins (1973)

centres, probably in old and congested premises.
Their closure and contraction has resulted in what has
now become known as the inner city problem.

The overall contraction in this population of multi-
regional firms amounts to 165,000 jobs. The branch
plants bore only a small proportion of this, but the
decline in their case was effected very largely
through closures and hardly at all through changes in
survivors. Among the parents' plants, where the main
contraction lay, the pattern was different. Over 70
per cent of the employment loss was achieved through
contractions in survivors. The contrast is quite
marked and suggests that branches have more rigid
employment levels than parent plants. If contraction
is needed, then closures will result rather than
adjustments to employment levels as in main plants.
The difference in relative sizes may have a strong
influence, since the parent factories employed on
average almost three times as many people as did the
branches.

The major conclusion of relevance to this chapter
is that branch plants closed at very similar rates in
the different types of area. This occurred within the
context of a general dispersal of employment from
parent plants to branches, and especially to branches
in Non-Assisted Areas. The existence of government
regional policies probably played a significant part
in the overall dispersion, but the last point shows
that stronger forces were at work and these were
probably connected with the disadvantages of inner
urban locations.

10.2  CLOSURES OF ESTABLISHMENTS AT THE LOCAL SCALE

The major influences on the rate of closure were
shown in chapter seven to be those of industry, size
and age. Ownership status appears to be a relatively
minor factor, although this need not follow in all
situations. Using the information for Leicestershire,

it is possible to examine the pattern of closure at
the approximate scale of labour catchment areas.
There is little information on the age of firms and
establishments and this has not been investigated.
However, age will be strongly reflected in the size of
establishments, which has been measured. In addition,
no attempt will be made to control for ownership
status. The rates of closure are shown in table 10.2.
In the area as a whole, over half of the establishments which were in production in 1947 had closed by
1967. The closure rates in the three larger industrial areas, Leicester, Loughborough and Hinckley,
were all close to the average for the county. The
size of closing establishment was also close to
average in Leicester and Loughborough, but in Hinckley
the prevalence of footwear and clothing firms meant
that closures were substantially larger. The proportion of employment lost in closing establishments
reflects not only the rate and average size of
closures but also the size of survivors. The predominance of large permanent establishments in Loughborough resulted in the closures having a relatively
small impact despite the fact that they were as
numerous and as large as elsewhere. Large factories
were less dominant in Hinckley with the result that
closures were important, and accounted for a third of
the 1947 employment.

The Coalville area has a below average closure rate,
but the closures were average in size, and the overall
employment lost is only a little below the level for
the whole county. The relatively small number of
establishments, and the variable size composition of
survivors has led to considerable variability among
the rural areas. High exit-rates in Oakham and Melton
included many small rural crafts which employed very
few people. These had a larger relative impact in
Oakham because there were few large factories. The
most conspicuous figures in table 10.2 are those for
Market Harborough. The closure rate is the only one
which is significantly different from the overall
level.(1) Moreover, the average size of closures was

274

Table 10.2

Rates of closure of establishments in Leicestershire, 1947-67

| Employment exchange area | Closure rate (% of establishments in 1947) | Average size of closures in 1947 (No. of operatives) | % of 1947 employment in closures |
|---|---|---|---|
| Leicester | 54.8 | 24.4 | 27 |
| Coalville | 46.2 | 25.6 | 24 |
| Loughborough | 52.0 | 24.9 | 17 |
| Melton | 63.5 | 13.6 | 22 |
| Oakham | 65.0 | 6.1 | 37 |
| Market Harborough | 34.1 | 8.7 | 5 |
| Hinckley | 55.5 | 39.4 | 32 |
| Average | 54.1 | 25.3 | 26 |

Source of data: Establishment records

very small and the impact on the local economy was minimal.

The crude rates of closure and the average sizes vary quite widely between areas at this scale, although less so among the larger towns. Much of this will be due to differences of size structure and industrial structure, and the next step is to make allowances for these factors. As with the entry-rates in chapter eight, it is possible to examine the pattern in considerable local detail, and this is done below.

The method used in this section to make allowance for the effects of size and industry is to calculate an 'expected' number of closures in each area. These values are then compared with the actual rates to produce residual closure rates. The areal units used are amalgamations of four square kilometre grid cells. They were constructed so as to be relatively small, but to contain a minimum of ten establishments, which is sufficient to demonstrate statistical significance at the 0.05 level. An additional criterion was that urban and rural areas should be kept separate. The 'expected' values are computed as follows. A relationship between size and frequency of closure was fitted, using the algorithm of Taylor (1971), for the five industries with more than 150 establishments in 1947.(2) The form of the resulting relationships is described algebraically in Gudgin (1974) and graphically in figure 7.2. In addition, a joint equation was derived for the remaining industries which included half of all establishments. The relationship for individual industries among the remaining establishments was increased or decreased by a constant, equal to the difference between the mean closure rate in that industry, and industry in Leicestershire as a whole. From these equations, a probability of closure was derived for each establishment in each area. The sum of these probabilities gave the expected number of closures.

276

The pattern of residual values (i.e. differences between actual and expected closure rates) is described in figure 10.1(a). The location of areas on this map can be seen by comparing it with figure 8.1. The general impression is one of randomness with a juxtaposition of high and low values, except perhaps in the rural eastern areas, where the rates are either average or high. The closure of establishments can be viewed as a random process, especially once the major general factors have been excluded. The best simple model for closures is the binomial which, given some general probability, can be used to measure the significance of observed numbers of closures and non-closures. The mean probability in any single area is taken as the expected rate of closure. This is equivalent to using a binomial model in which the probability is variable, being a function of size and industry.

It is possible to use this technique to examine the possibility that the pattern in figure 10.1(a) is composed mainly of random variations around the expected values. The randomness can be removed to look for underlying regularities by 'filtering out' from the map only those residuals which are statistically different from expectation. This is done in figure 10.1(b). As can be seen, only a small number of areas have closure rates which can be judged to be significantly different from expectation, even using liberal levels of significance. Some of these remaining areas may well be merely the realisation of unlikely random events.

The pattern in the centre of the map consists of three areas in the suburbs of Leicester with low closure rates and one in the city centre with a high rate. The significance of these values is low but there are a priori reasons for viewing this as illustrating general factors. A differentiation between city and suburbs was also reported for Toronto by Collins (1971), and is probably due to a bias in the selection of locations by growing firms. Many

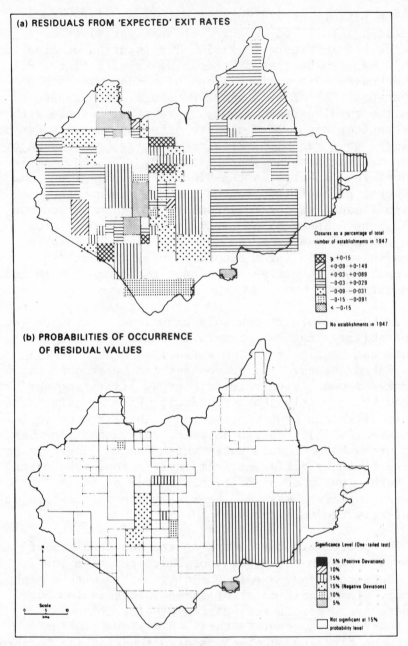

**(a) RESIDUALS FROM 'EXPECTED' EXIT RATES**

Closures as a percentage of total
number of establishments in 1947

≥ +0·15
+0·09 · +0·149
+0·03 · +0·089
−0·03 · +0·029
−0·09 · −0·031
−0·15 · −0·091
< −0·15

No establishments in 1947

**(b) PROBABILITIES OF OCCURRENCE
OF RESIDUAL VALUES**

Significance Level (One · tailed test)

5% (Positive Deviations)
10%    "    "
15%    "    "
15% (Negative Deviations)
10%    "    "
5%    "    "

Not significant at 15%
probability level

N

Scale
0   5   10
kms

Figure 10.1   Residual closure rates and their
probabilities in Leicestershire 1947–67
Source of data:   Establishment records

278

firms with city centre locations are forced to move as
they grow, and many choose less congested sites in
suburban locations. As a result, growing and
successful firms tend to be over-represented in the
suburbs, and less successful ones in the centre. City
centre redevelopment schemes often provide a shock
which some small firms do not survive, but this may be
due to the fact that relatively unsuccessful firms are
concentrated in these area.

Aside from this intra-urban contrast, there is
little in figure 10.1(b) which suggests that there are
consistent factors influencing exit-rates other than
the influence of size and industry. An exception may,
however, be illustrated by the case of Market
Harborough in the south west of Leicestershire, which
has a low closure rate that is significant at the 0.05
level. Until the mid-1950s, a third of all employment
in this town was within a single large clothing
factory. It is argued in chapter eight that dominance
by large plants will reduce the birth-rate of new
firms. This, in turn, will result in low rates of
closure. It is thus hypothesised that low entry-rates
prevailed in Market Harborough in the 1930s and 1940s,
resulting in relatively few closures in the period
under study here. Similarly, low closure rates are
seen in figure 10.1(a) for many parts of north west
Leicestershire including Loughborough. Large plants
were also dominant in these areas, but less so than in
Market Harborough, and consequently the low rates are
not significantly different from expectation.


10.3  CONCLUSION

It has not been possible to directly observe the
pattern of closures at the regional scale. Nevertheless, the evidence of previous sections does allow a
number of inferences to be drawn. It is known that
both size structure and industrial structure influence
the rate of closures, with age structure and entry-
rates as additional influences. At the local scale

279

of variation within Leicestershire, size and industry appeared to be the major factors, although some influence of entry-rates was apparent through the remaining random pattern.

It is likely that the same processes acting at the local scale will also act at the regional scale. The difference comes in the structural characteristics which exist in other areas. The Development Areas tend to have a larger proportion of employment in industries which are declining or growing slowly. These could give rise to high rates of closures especially of larger establishments, but the importance of large plant industries may well mean that decline is borne by size adjustments in survivors more than by closures. The major impact of closures is probably seen in areas with declining industries without dominance by very large establishments. The textile and clothing industries are prominent examples, and consequently the Intermediate Areas, in which these are concentrated, probably have high rates of closure.

Paradoxically, the highest crude rates of closure may occur in the Non-Assisted regions. These have larger numbers of small establishments perhaps reflecting higher entry rates. If so, then the closures will occur mainly among smaller firms, and be due to high rates of turnover. It is argued above that high closure rates are likely to give rise to economic vitality, other things being equal, because they cause more rapid changes in companies and industries. The Development Areas may have populations of establishments, including branch plants, in which indigenous change is relatively slow compared with the textile areas, or the Non-Assisted Areas. The effect of regional policy is to introduce new establishments and industries into Assisted Areas. In the short term, these will bring beneficial changes in several respects, but in the long run may not result in the vitality which comes from the ability to change quickly.

NOTES

(1)  Using binomial probabilities, the value is
significantly different from 54.1 at the 0.01 level.
(2)  These were hosiery (MLH 417), miscellaneous
light engineering (MLM's 349 and 399), footwear
(MLH 450), printing (MLH 489) and wood products
(MLH's 471-9).

# 11 Acquisition and ownership

The previous three chapters have explored spatial
variations in a number of processes which together
make up employment change. These did not include
acquisition, although this an important element of
locational and growth behaviour when seen from the
point of view of individual companies. This chapter,
serving as a footnote to the main study, has the aim
of providing a rationale for excluding acquisition
behaviour, and at the same time exploring those areas
of industrial activity where it is potentially of
most importance.

The principal reasons for not regarding acquisition
on a par with the location and growth processes of
previous chapters is that acquisition per se does not
constitute a real change in employment. It merely
reorganises the way in which jobs are controlled by
companies. Although a number of secondary employment
repercussions may materialise, it is not obvious that
these are best explained from the point of view of
acquisition, rather than from the vantage point of
some component process (e.g. closure) which includes
all firms. A second important consideration is that
there is no strong reason for believing that acquisitions will exhibit any consistent spatial influences.
Acquisitions of most types are made for reasons which
do not usually have a strong spatial content. Firms
are usually bought for non-locational characteristics,
except for a few acquisitions in which local knowledge
plays an important part.

The effects of acquisition should be separated from
those of ownership status, although the two are
obviously connected. The direct effects of acquisition can be viewed as those which occur within a short
period of the actual purchase or merger. After this
settling in period, the acquired company becomes a

non-independent part of a larger industrial group, with a status which may vary from that of a virtually autonomous subsidiary company to one of a branch plant largely controlled from other locations. An investigation of changes following acquisition has not been a part of this research, but a very detailed study of this aspect has been made by Rake (1972). By coincidence, his study was concerned with companies based in the East Midlands over the postwar period up to 1971, and the following four paragraphs are based on his findings.

The employment consequences of acquisitions mainly lie in the effects on closure and in situ growth, although occasionally branch plants are formed by subsidiary companies as a consequence of post-acquisition expansion. Rake found that about half of the acquisitions were made in order to expand capacity or existing markets. The other half involved diversification of various kinds, with a minority undertaking backwards or forwards integration. Some of these purposes were best served by buying up a company and transferring production to some existing factory within the group. Twelve per cent of acquired establishments were closed within two years of acquisition. The size of these closures is not revealed, but it seems probable that they were relatively small. A further 16 per cent of establishments were closed more than ten years after acquisition.

An important question is how the closure rates demonstrated in these acquisitions, and in post-acquisition subsidiaries, would compare with the situation if no acquisitions had occurred. Many closures after the initial two year period in Rake's sample took place for reasons which would be likely to cause the same fate among independent companies. Declining demand, technological obsolescence and unprofitability due to labour or management problems were prominent reasons of this kind. Although independent companies might have had a stronger stimulus to seek some solution to these problems, the subsidiary companies potentially have access to greater financial resources to overcome difficulties. The typical outcome of these conflicting pressures is unknown, and without a careful study taking account of size and industry it is impossible to say whether subsidiary establishments have a greater propensity to close than independent companies. However, if there is no clear evidence that branch plants are more readily closed than parent plants, it seems unlikely that this would be true of subsidiary companies.

The closure of establishments immediately after acquisition appears to be clearly due to the acquisition itself, but further reflection shows how the situation is more complex. Many such closures reflect over-capacity within industries. Companies are often bought to extend the market of the purchaser and consequently they are closed with production being transferred to existing factories. In such situations the over-capacity would presumably cause closures even without acquisition, with smaller and thus weaker companies, in the most vulnerable position. The closures may not necessarily involve the same companies, but there is no clear reason why the long run spatial pattern should be different. The fact that a quarter of all acquisitions had been sold due to the retirement or death of the owner suggests, however, that many of the same companies may have closed.

The performance of surviving companies after acquisitions may well be influenced by the newly acquired status of a subsidiary company. The overall perspective will often change from the narrow one of a smaller independent company to the wider one of a larger group. Moreover, the finance for expansion is more readily available in some, but not in all, cases. Rake found that for his sample, equal numbers of acquired companies grew or declined by more than 20 per cent. A further third changed little. In the longer term, about one third were commercially integrated into the wider group presumably losing most of their autonomy. Another third were not integrated at all, and the rest were integrated in intermediate degrees. Most of the post-acquisition changes involved only in situ changes in size. A minority, however, were re-equipped to produce different products, and a few others engaged in a variety of locational changes.

Again, it is very difficult to say whether the performance of surviving subsidiary companies in the early post-acquisition years differs from that which would be experienced by independent companies. The availability of relatively large financial resources for successful subsidiaries suggests that performance might be more variable among subsidiaries. However, the existence of a wider base for comparing success within industrial groupings, and the ability to exchange management personnel between companies suggests that on the contrary, performance would be less variable. Again, only a carefully standardised comparison is likely to discover whether subsidiaries are likely to be generally more successful than independent companies or vice versa.

A laissez-faire policy towards subsidiary companies appears to be commonly employed after acquisition. However, the retirement of the original owner, or some major reorganisation within the acquiring group often reduces the autonomy of subsidiaries. The behaviour of Courtaulds Ltd in the hosiery industry provides an example of this. Independent hosiery companies were acquired over time, but especially in the 1960s when strong competition between the UK textile giants led to policies of forward integration to secure markets for output. Most of the acquired companies retained their pre-acquisition form although some internal rationalisation did occur. In 1975, however, a hosiery division has been formed with its headquarters near the centre of the industry in Derbyshire. The subsidiary companies, some of which have lost their individual identity, now have a co-ordinating administrative level between themselves and the main Courtaulds administration in London. The progressive loss of local autonomy over time is probably a general trend which is intensified with each merger boom. The extreme position (which is not necessarily reached by all subsidiaries) occurs when all production is in branch plants with little local control, and a large divisional headquarters exists in which all but day to day decisions are taken. The importance of such a trend is often viewed to have three aspects. Firstly, there is the direct effect on the geography of production. Secondly, there is the effect of spatial concentration of administrative employment, which incidentally includes most of the more highly paid jobs, and will cause larger multiplier effects on the economies of receiving regions. Finally, the concentration of control into some regions may bias the spatial distribution of future investment.

The spatial consequences of major rationalisations and reorganisations are unclear. One common feature is that small units peripheral to the major factories are closed down. If the principal factories are widely distributed, then the closures might also be widespread. However, if independent companies have historically grown faster in one region than in others, then more acquiring firms may be based in that region. In this case, the peripheral closures will be concentrated in regions which are distant from this centre of acquisition. There was some evidence in the study described in Crum and Gudgin (1976) that divisional administrations were concentrated in the South East region for this reason. In the same study, divisions of large companies were divided into two types – those consisting of branch plants and those consisting of subsidiary companies. Employment in the latter was concentrated in the South of England, while much more employment of the former was in the more peripheral regions. The reasons for this are unclear, but may reflect a tendency for organisations based in the South to rationalise production more when factories are widely spread across the country.

There is clear evidence that the formation of large

industrial groups in the past, in which acquisition has played a major part, has led to the concentration of administrative jobs in the South East region. Crum and Gudgin (1976) estimated that there were 100,000 - 150,000 more white collar employees in that region than would be expected, given the number and industrial distribution of operatives. Most of these were in corporate (i.e. top) headquarters or in the headquarters of individual subsidiary companies. The intermediate level of the divisional headquarters appears to be much less important in the UK than, for instance, in North America.

The final asserted consequence of the continuing trend towards centralised control is that future investment will reflect the location of top decision makers. In this case, it may be necessary to distinguish between the location of operational control and the location of ultimate authority. Corporate headquarters of UK companies typically contain under 2 per cent of total UK employment within their respective companies and often the figure is less than 1 per cent. Yet white-collar workers comprise about 25 per cent of all employment in manufacturing, and hence, the great majority are employed outside the corporate headquarters. The major functions of corporate headquarters are those of financial co-ordination and broad policy formation. The operation of industrial matters is a lower level function in most cases. Investment decisions are certainly vetted at the top levels in virtually all companies but the major impetus and direction appears to come from below. Granick (1968) asserts that in US companies, much operational control resides in divisional headquarters. His view of British companies, which is supported by the author's own investigations, is that control in British companies is more decentralised. The main stimulus on the location of investment probably comes from the headquarters of subsidiary companies. If these are concentrated in some regions, then this is probably the long-term outcome of superior enterprise, and growth in those regions in the past, plus the history of industrial movement spurred on by regional policy which has attracted very large numbers of branch plants (but not headquarters) to the development areas. Although loss of local control by a region over its own production may have important long-term consequences for the type of investment which is made, there is little evidence at present that the volume is reduced.

One important consequence of the concentration of ownership and control may be that entry-rates are depressed in those regions which end up with most branch plants and least parent establishments. It has been argued in previous chapters that this association does exist, although it may be due to the large average size of branches and the routine nature of their production, rather than to their lack of local autonomy. The latter may, however, be reflected in the success of new entrants, i.e. there is some evidence that firms founded by entrepreneurs from white-collar occupations are much more successful than those of founders with manual backgrounds. The concentration of industrial white-collar employment into Southern regions may thus lead these regions to have more of the most dynamic new firms.

Most of manufacturing industry is now under the control of large multi-regional, indeed multi-national companies. The question of ownership status and the acquisition which leads to loss of independence, has a wide ranging significance. The arguments advanced in the preceding paragraphs do not, however, suggest that newly acquired companies, or companies of differing status within the spectrum of ownership and control, should form the primary components in the accounting framework adopted in this study. Much location and growth activity has essential features which are common to both independent and subsidiary companies. Branch plants are a common way to expand total capacity in both cases, and the factors bearing on the location of branches will differ little between the two types. The rate of growth, and the division

of contraction between closures and in situ decline
similarly do not seem to primarily reflect ownership
status. None of this is to say that ownership and
acquisition are aspects of no consequence. This is
clearly not true, but on the other hand, they would
appear to be of secondary rather than major significance. It was suggested in chapter three that
distinctions of ownership and control should form the
second tier of disaggregation in devising components
for an accounting framework. It has not been possible
to analyse this second level to any great extent in
this study, but it is hoped that in the future more
progress will be possible.

To finish this discussion, let us examine briefly
the geography of one large multi-regional company in
the light of some of the processes on which this
study has been based. The company in question is the
Baker Perkins Group Ltd which manufactures machinery
for the food, printing, laundry and other industries
and is one of the top 300 manufacturing companies in
the United Kingdom. The company, which is described
in a comprehensive history by Muir (1968), consists of
a core company, Baker Perkins Ltd, and several
subsidiaries. The group headquarters and major
factory is at Peterborough. The two original companies were formed by an American and a Canadian
respectively, both in London. The main factories of
the original companies were moved to Peterborough in
two stages, one in the last century, one in the 1930s.
Two early subsidiary companies also contributed to the
growth at Peterborough, in that they were both closed
and had their production transferred from Shropshire
and Edinburgh respectively. The current factories in
the UK are as follows.

| Branches | Subsidiary company | parent plants |
|---|---|---|
| Newcastle | Gainsborough (Lincs) | Basingstoke (3 |
| Gateshead | Leeds (2 companies) | companies trans- |
| Saxilby (Lincs) | West Bromwich | ferred from |
| Skegness | Glasgow | London) |
| | Stoke | Luton |

The branch plants were set up by Baker Perkins Ltd, or by its subsidiaries prior to acquisition. In both cases, they were established in accessible areas with available labour during conditions of labour shortage shortly after the last war.

The subsidiary companies were almost all started on a small-scale by men who had previously lived in the same area. With the two exceptions mentioned above, the location has not been changed as a direct consequence of acquisition. In most cases, the location is still close to that originally chosen. The main exceptions are the companies founded in London. All of these have dispersed to towns within fifty miles, three of them having been amalgamated into a single company now located in Basingstoke. The dispersion has spanned almost an entire century, with wage differences being initially significant, but general urban congestion later assuming the principal role. In addition, the subsidiary companies have retained a high degree of local autonomy, although in some cases the original subsidiaries had been amalgamated into new companies. The corporate head office staff at Peterborough is relatively small. The company now has a widespread geography of production. However, the factors which have influenced the distribution pattern are mainly those which are important in the location of new independent firms and branch plants. The present company has assumed its present locations by default rather than by design. Many large companies are similar locational confederations with little conscious choice in choosing locations to reflect the nature and existence of the present organisation.

A final note which emerges from the Baker Perkins case study refers to the results of Scottish enterprise. Four companies acquired by Baker Perkins were founded by Scottish entrepreneurs but only one remains in Scotland, and this is the most recent acquisition having been founded only in 1953. The others reflect a range of circumstances. One was closed with its production transferred to Peterborough. Another had concentrated production at its London branch before acquisition. In the third case, the founder had migrated to the Midlands, where he worked for several years prior to setting up his own firm. This leakage of the fruits of enterprise may be an unusual occurrence, but it is more likely to be representative of a general process by which ideas and success from peripheral regions are drawn towards national core areas. At least two of the companies among the East Midlands cases were also started by Scots who had migrated southwards.

# 12 Conclusions and implications

This study has been about two things.  One has been
the methodological question of how to approach the
investigation of regional differences in the growth of
indigenous employment.  The other has been a study of
postwar growth in a single region which achieved an
above average performance in spite of a poor industrial structure.  The two are intertwined in that the
methodology has been applied to the region which
consequently acts as a case study of the approach.
Nevertheless it is appropriate to reflect on what has
been achieved under the two headings separately.


12.1  REVIEW OF THE COMPONENTS APPROACH

Much regional analysis within the UK context has
concentrated upon the importance of industrial
structure as a determinant of growth.  Despite the
fact that the mix of industries in a given region can
be a potent influence on growth, this factor has been
relegated to a position of secondary importance in
this study.  The reason lies in the fact that measurement of the influence of industrial structure is an
end rather than a beginning, it provides little scope
for furthering understanding beyond the measurement
itself.  The nature of the links between structure and
growth are not clarified; nor are the non-structural
factors identified.

The approach in this study has instead emphasised
the need to disaggregate total change into component
parts.  The choice of components is a critical one,
and it was argued in chapters two and three that,
since locational cost constraints are slight at the
UK scale, the components should reflect types of
decisions on the location and growth of companies.
Decision makers have increased freedom of action when

released from the mandatory pressures of large spatial differences in costs, and the easiest means to progress is to identify the factors bearing on the different types of decision. The types of decision selected were respectively those connected with the initial location of new firms, relocation, growth, and closure. The method involves taking each of these mutually exclusive components and investigating firstly its importance in overall growth, secondly its nature as a process, and finally the causes of spatial variation within it.

What then can be said on this way of looking at regional change after applying it as far as data permitted? The most obvious conclusion emerges immediately after performing a disaggregation of overall change. The individual components are generally much larger than the net change, and the latter is seen to be little more than the residual balance between larger counteracting components. This discovery, obvious though it is in retrospect, strongly reinforces the feeling that explanatory efforts must be directed below the level of aggregate change, and specifically at the level of meaningful and coherent components.

Once the disaggregation is performed then further progress is a straightforward matter. In the case of the growth of permanent firms and plants industrial structure was found to be one factor as expected, but others were also apparent. There was a strong suggestion that distribution costs affect average profit levels (and hence also growth in the long run) between regions. Within the study region, labour supply constraints were the major influence on how much growth was retained within individual areas rather than being transferred to alternative plants belonging to the same company. There was also a suggestion that urban density might affect the degree of retained growth through limitations imposed on the physical expansion of individual factories.

New firms were found to be much more important than previously suspected, and the major factors influencing variations in birth-rates were connected with barriers to entry as reflected in the size structure and type of industrial processes characteristic in different areas. There is also evidence that the occupational structure of manufacturing employment influences the growth potential of new firms through the supply of greater numbers of middle-class founders. Rates of closure were considerably influenced by industrial structure, but size structure and entry rates played a part as well. No progress was made in this study towards measuring regional variations in closure rates, although the evidence on profitability suggests that a regional dimension may exist over and above any effect of industrial structure.

Finally, the major influences upon industrial movement (apart from government policy measures) are principally associated with labour supply and distance from parent plants, although access to raw materials and proximity to markets are important in a minority of industries with relatively high transport costs. The influences on industrial movement are known primarily from the work of others, although some original work not reported here was undertaken. It is interesting to note that the wealth of research on industrial movement which has been conducted over the last fifteen years is an example of attention being concentrated on a coherent component of change rather than on the totality of change. Those who have contributed to the movement studies have been remarkably successful, but movement is only one component and needs to be integrated with the others to build up an explanation of overall changes.

Through the investigation of each component separately, a set of causal factors is accumulated, each viewed as having some influence on growth. Industrial structure (indicating the type of product) is one factor and size structure, occupational structure, and process type are others.  Labour supply, urban density and the availability of local demand and raw materials are also involved.  This list contains some unexpected factors in addition to those which are widely discussed as being of considerable importance.  The main advantage comes not however in adding new factors to an ever expanding list, but in identifying where they fit into the system of industrial change, and in measuring their importance.  These points can be illustrated with an example.  Size structure and type of industrial process appear to affect entry rates.  Within the East Midlands, Derbyshire had a low reported entry rate and this can be estimated to have led to a shortfall of 2,500 jobs over twenty years.  These two factors have thus been identified as affecting a particular aspect of growth, and have had their importance measured (even if only roughly) in terms of numbers of jobs. The components of change approach allows this sort of procedure to be carried through for all of the factors identified. Only a fraction of this task was undertaken in this study, but there appears to be no major obstacles in the way of further progress.  To complete this section let us return to the beginning and look at what light has been shed on the role of industrial structure in employment growth.

The effect of changes demand and productivity within a region's initial industries (which is what is usually meant as the effect of industrial structure) influence the growth and closure of existing factories.  The initial mix of industries also has an effect on the birth-rate of new firms but this influence is different from the former.  A favourable structure for one is not necessarily favourable for the other.  Finally, industrial structure in itself has no direct effect on industrial in-movement.  The latter fact is obvious and yet investigations of employment change almost never separate mobile and non-mobile industry when analysing the effects of industrial structure.  This failure to make an obvious separation illustrates the benefit to be

295

gained from thinking in terms of components rather
than aggregates.

The fact that structural influences on plant growth
and closure differ from those on entry-rates of new
firms has implications on the timescale over which
change is analysed. In the short term, changes within
existing firms and plants are all important. The
longer the period, however, the more important become
differences in birth-rates of new firms. Hence the
role of industrial structure will change as the timescale changes. Both effects are in some sense aspects
of industrial structure, but an analysis of how
structure affects individual components of change
reveals the greater complexity which lies beneath the
surface.

A final point related to industrial structure was
discussed in chapter ten. It was argued there that
employment decline which occurs largely through
closures may have beneficial effects when compared
with decline occurring through the medium of size
changes in factories which do not close. The former
process may differentiate more successfully between
more and less efficient managements. If so, then
regions in which the declining industries contain
predominantly small and medium-sized firms, which are
more prone to closure, may end up with a more
efficient set of firms better equipped to counter
future problems. This possibility is merely speculative at present, but again serves to illustrate the
greater subtlety which derives from thinking in terms
of separate components. In this case the distinction
is between growth (and decline) as against closure.
The example can also be reversed to suggest that
expanding industries will affect regions differently
if the expansion occurs within industries having low
barriers to entry. In this case regions with high
entry-rates may be able to capture the lion's share of
the extra employment, in a way that would not be
possible if the expansion occurred in industries with
high barriers to entry.

In summary the components of change approach provides much greater potential for identifying those factors which lead to differences in growth rates, and for observing the ways in which they act upon growth. Equally the approach has the important attribute of giving some measure of the importance of each factor.

## 12.2 POSTWAR GROWTH IN THE EAST MIDLANDS

The East Midlands occupies a unique position in the history of postwar regional growth in Britain. It is one of the country's prosperous regions, with a growth rate (over the period studied) which was 40 per cent higher than the national average. Yet this was achieved with one of the poorest industrial structures of any region. At national rates of growth in each industry its mix of industries in the early postwar years would have led to an aggregate growth rate of only three-quarters of that in the UK. Moreover this was achieved without any net in-movement of employment from other areas, and without any assistance from government regional policy. There is clearly an example here for Britain's Assisted Areas, which also tend to have an unfavourable industrial composition, but do not overcome the handicap without external assistance. The possibility of learning from the example makes it important to see how the East Midland's growth was achieved. Although this was dealt with in chapter four the main points can be profitably drawn together here.

As suggested in the last section net change is merely the balance between the larger changes brought about by new openings, growth and decline, closure and movement. In the East Midlands, half of the establishments in production in 1947 had closed by 1967 and been replaced by a similar number of new plants, most of which were operated by new firms. Most of these openings and closures were small but nevertheless a quarter of the employment in 1947 was lost in establishments (mainly whole firms rather than branches)

297

which subsequently closed. New employment, amounting
to almost a quarter of a million jobs in a region in
which employment grew from 500,000 to 600,000, made
good this loss and in addition created a net increase
of 100,000 jobs.

Nearly all of this employment was generated by
locally-based firms or by local entrepreneurs. A
small but significant number of jobs was also brought
in by establishments of companies based outside the
region. Although this input constituted a third of
the net increase in employment, it was matched by a
similar number of jobs in branches set up in other
regions by East Midlands companies. Taking the East
Midlands counties individually, 70 per cent of the
additional employment generated by local firms and
individuals was created by the net addition of jobs to
existing firms, although about one fifth of this ended
up in other areas. Some went to other counties within
the region especially in the early postwar years, but
most went to the Development Areas.

The major surprise of this study was that 28 per
cent of the new employment was contributed by completely new firms. Some of these were subsidiary
companies but most began life as small independent
concerns. Approximately 3,000 surviving firms were
involved and together these were responsible for two-
thirds of the region's net increase in employment.
Without these new firms, the region's growth rate
would have been less than half that of the country as
a whole. It is possible that these new firms merely
replaced closures among the new firms in the previous
period, thereby changing the names but not the number
of jobs. This is not the case, however, since a
number of old established firms are continually closing, and the new firms do provide real additions to
total employment. Many go on to become the major
employers of the future. It is estimated that even
the short-lived establishments which opened and closed
within the twenty year period of this study provided
up to 20,000 jobs at any one time. Although

individually small, the sheer weight of numbers makes
for significant employment totals.  Many new firms
entered old established trades but others entered
newer, expanding industries and contributed to the
important change in the industrial structure away from
textiles, clothing and footwear.  In some cases, they
were instrumental in the development of new trades as
in the plastics industry in Leicester.  By 1971, there
were over sixty plastics firms employing over 3,000
people and producing a wide variety of products.  In
addition, specialist engineering companies making
injection moulds and tools had begun to appear at the
end of the period.


12.3  PERSPECTIVES ON REGIONAL GROWTH

The details of how growth was composed in one region
is interesting and potentially valuable but does not
in itself explain why that region performed better or
worse than other regions.  There is an obvious need to
construct similar sets of employment accounts for
other regions in order to pinpoint these causes.
Comparative sets of accounts are likely to emerge over
the next few years, but until they do appear we are
left in the position of having to speculate on the
basis of what is known already.

   If we continue to confine attention to differences
in long-term rates of indigenous growth, then this
study suggests only a limited number of contenders to
explain regional growth differences. Labour supply
can be ruled out as a cause of poor performance since
poorly performing regions generally have a labour
surplus.  This leaves industrial structure, size
structure, occupation structure and remoteness from
the centre of gravity of the UK market as the major
factors from among the list in 12.1.  It can be
observed that most of Britain's Assisted Areas have
unfavourable characteristics in respect of some or all
of these factors.  Scotland is the most remote of the
British regions, although its industrial and size

structure are more advantageous than those of some other Assisted Areas. The Northern Region and Wales are less remote but have generally unfavourable industrial structure and are heavily dominated by large plants which, it was suggested, are unfavourable for growth on several counts. These regions also have the lowest proportions of higher status white-collar workers in manufacturing.

The Non-Assisted Areas in contrast are not remote and tend to have favourable industrial structures and a higher proportion of small plants. They also have higher proportions of white-collar workers in manufacturing. The balance of these four factors may explain much of the regional variation of indigenous growth with labour supply acting as the major mechanism (other than government policy measures) to redistribute employment from leading to lagging regions.

As with most complex socio-economic problems the causes of employment growth differences are probably multiple and variable, and it is this which makes their solution so elusive. In the case of employment growth it is difficult to say much about the importance of the various factors at this stage. The East Midland's investigation suggests that the factors influencing birth-rates (primarily size-structure and occupation structure) are unlikely to raise or depress net growth by more than 2 or 3 percentage points over a twenty year period. This suggests that the remaining influences, on the efficiency and survival of existing plants, account for the majority of the regional contrasts. Further progress on differentiating the importance of remoteness, industrial structure, and size structure, as influences must await the comparison of similar studies in other regions.

Before leaving this subject it may be worthwhile to take an even longer term perspective on growth to suggest that variations in birth-rates of new firms may underlie almost all of the factors including, paradoxically, that of remoteness. A high birth-rate leads in a fairly obvious way to a size-structure dominated by small firms and plants. This in turn will influence future rates of entry and also future closure rates. The importance of small firms is likely to lead to a more varied industrial structure and greater flexibility for change. Each of these in their turn will lead to an industrial structure more in tune with changes in demand and competition. Also the industrial structure can be adaptable to remoteness from major markets as in the Scandinavian countries. The opposite case of low adaptability to conditions of relative remoteness is likely to occur when birth-rates are low, and also when control over investment becomes located outside the area in question. The Northern Region, Wales, and Northern Ireland are perhaps the most disadvantaged of UK regions in this last respect, although the degree of remoteness is relatively low except in the last case.

It may be mere coincidence that the 'core' regions of the South-East and Midlands possess a favourable industrial structure, while the peripheral regions do not. A more appealing suggestion is that industrial birth-rates are higher in the core regions and this means that their industrial structures will almost constantly be the most favourable. A final step to complete the explanation would account for higher birth-rates in the core regions. This takes us too far from what can be deduced from the evidence in this study, but potential causes might be a history of greater commercial intensity and of greater economic security. In the peripheral areas greater dependence on primary activities and primary processing was historically less secure, and perhaps as a result co-operative and communal activities were more important. These might include trade unionism, building societies, the Co-operative Society and religion. These thoughts suggest a final, wider generalisation which might be termed a 'colonial economy effect'.

In areas where industry is introduced from outside by 'colonising' firms or individuals the result is usually an economy dominated by large plants which may have branch status or undertake assembly work. These generate relatively few new firms, and the large plant dominance may remain over long periods aided by two additional factors. It is likely that large branch assembly plants have less need than others for local industrial wholesalers or for small unspecialised subcontractors. If so, then both factors will further reduce the flow of new firms. In the long run, the process will continue with a slowly changing industrial structure. The local economy will prosper as long as the major employers do so, but will be vulnerable to serious contractions. Several towns within the East Midlands may have undergone a version of this process. These include Derby, Loughborough and Newark, although neighbouring Peterborough might be added to the list. All are on railway routes out of London and each attracted immigrant firms in the last century which subsequently grew to become dominant employers. Although the evidence is somewhat indirect except in the case of Loughborough, each of these towns appears to have a low entry rate. This type of economy is not a serious handicap when towns are located within prosperous regions, when the dominant employers are successful, or when government policy ensures a continuous supply of new firms and establighments. The example of Derby with its dependence on Rolls Royce and the British Rail workshops does, however, illustrate the vulnerability of such towns .

Another variant on the same theme may affect those peripheral areas which built flourishing economies on primary processing or low transport cost goods (including ships), often for world markets in which there was no disadvantage vis à vis domestic competitors. Areas like Clydeside, Merseyside and Tyneside all fall in this category. In Clydeside, the nineteenth century saw a succession of industrial problems, all of which were successfully surmounted often by local industrialists who switched capital between trades. These areas have, for some reason, not managed to overcome the problems thrown up in this century. The decline of important markets is obviously one factor but one which had been tackled before. A number of other factors have probably militated against continuing success. The development of lighter industries brought a different type of entrepreneurship which these areas with their large-plant industries may not have been well equipped to provide. Increasing technical complexity may have prevented the easy switching from one industry to another, although the progressive loss of locally-based control over local companies could have been more important. In addition, the loss of world markets has increased the need to compete in domestic markets and more recently in European markets. The higher distribution costs may have slowed growth in the long term for firms serving these markets since higher costs lead to lower profits or higher prices. If high distribution costs are significant, then a future inside the EEC may hold bleak prospects for remote regions.

## 12.4  REGIONAL POLICY IMPLICATIONS

Further research is needed on all aspects dealt with in the preceding chapters, but it may be useful to speculate on those policy options which might be available to counteract the apparent causes of the problems. If high distribution costs prove to be a factor of general importance, then some policy may be called for to aid those industries and areas affected. The only general regional subsidy on operating costs within the UK has been the Regional Employment Premium, but this contravened EEC regulations and has now been withdrawn. A subsidy specifically to counter high transport costs, perhaps on 'basing point' principle, may however prove politically acceptable.

The underlying problem is probably a lack of local control over the industrial distribution of investment

in peripheral regions, which obstructs an accomodation
with remoteness. The latter has occurred in Sweden
where high 'value added' industries complement those
based upon local raw materials. In recent years,
there is evidence of a trend in Sweden towards
industries which are intensive of human capital, and
such changes are more likely with both a high turnover
of companies and a high degree of local control,
neither of which appear to be characteristic of
peripheral regions in the UK. Policies which
stimulate the birth-rate of new firms will increase
the long-term responsiveness of businesses to local
conditions, but more immediate remedies are difficult
to envisage. The increasing concentration of ownership, and the branch plant economies which form the
consequence of regional policies both tend towards
the absence of local control over the form and amount
of investment. The Northern Regional Strategy Team
have suggested inducements to entice companies into
locating top management in remote branch plants and
subsidiaries. A significant improvement would
however necessitate considerable reorganisation of the
ways in which companies are run, and the scope for
change is probably not large given the nature of
inducements and controls which can currently be
envisaged.

Regional differences in the birth-rates of new
firms, or of growth in the early years of new firms,
might be countered in a number of ways. The two
main possibilities involve inducing entrepreneurs to
move, and measures to stimulate higher entry rates
in situ. Most new firms are tightly bound to the
home area of the founder by his (or her) network of
business contacts, and financial incentives to move
will not necessarily lessen this dependence. A
minority are, however, more mobile and fortunately
these are also most likely to include the firms with
the highest growth potential. Some stay in their home
area merely because there is no reason to move, as
with one new technology-based firm in Bournemouth
described by Little (1977). If such firms could be
identified when they are still at the stage of

producing in garden sheds or on kitchen tables, financial incentives might well induce them to move, especially if these included travel allownces to visit contacts in the home area, and perhaps also a rehousing allowance.

Efforts to stimulate those already resident in problem areas to establish new firms might have more success than attempts to move entrepreneurs, providing that there is a pool of potential founders who merely need encouragement. Training courses would help in this direction but only so long as they were non-academic and based on examples of successful entrepreneurs starting from similar conditions. A 'job swap' scheme to enable applicants to gain experience working alongside recent founders in new firms might achieve the same result, especially if those working in industries with high barriers to entry could be introduced to different trades. An active 'small firms agency' might co-ordinate these activities and might also encourage established local firms to direct their subcontract work towards new firms in the same region, perhaps with some government subsidy. Such an agency would have to win the confidence of strongly independent individuals often suspicious of bureaucracy, but this could be done if the approach bore this in mind and made due allowance. Comprehensive financial backing might be best left to the established institutions in the light of this suspicion, and also because existing institutions may be best equipped to assess financial risks. Nevertheless a 'launching' grant not to be repaid may be a different matter, as long as this is viewed as similar to grants for education or retraining and a high failure rate is accepted.

Policies like the above, would involve a relatively low exchequer cost although the benefits would be very long-term compared with most public expenditure, and the failure rates would be high. It is, however, easy to argue that a new direction in policy is required after thirty years of building control,

investment·incentives, and other aid. These policies
have achieved a great deal but in the last resort
have not solved the problem, and have now reached a
low ebb in which the donor regions for industrial
movement are beginning to suffer and in which areas
of very high unemployment are no longer restricted to
the traditional problem regions. A long-term policy
adopted soon after the war alongside the conventional
regional measures might by now have been paying
dividends. A further advantage is that the stimulation of enterprise might prove a net benefit to the
nation rather than merely moving investment between
regions. With general high unemployment, this becomes
an important factor.

The present policy measures are generally both low
key and passive, although the trend is for both
Central and Local Government to become increasingly
involved in the promotion of new firms. Direct
interest in new firms is nevertheless a very recent
phenomenon. The Small Firms Division of the Department of Industry for example was established within
the last seven years on the recommendation of the
Bolton Committee. Its task is to direct callers,
including potential entrepreneurs, towards appropriate
sources of advice. A more interventionist outgrowth
of this is the largely experimental Small Firms
Counselling Service in the South West region. This
scheme begun in late 1976 provides part-time fee-
earning consultants to give a low-cost diagnosis of
business problems for small companies.

Local authorities, especially those in problem
regions, are taking a more active line. The most
ambitious scheme is Northern Ireland's Local Enterprise Development Unit. This was founded in 1971 and
is currently creating about 1,000 new jobs a year in
small and new companies in manufacturing. Since 1971
LEDU has promoted over 6,000 jobs in almost 500
companies (Guardian 29 April 1977). This is done at
the relatively low cost of £2,000 per job, mainly by
providing loans, grants advice, and premises for

promising entrepreneurs.

A somewhat similar suggestion has also been advanced
for the Northern Region in the recent Northern
Regional Strategy Team Plan. This has yet to be
adopted although within the same region a Small
Companies Finance Board is currently being set up by
Tyne and Wear Council in conjunction with the High
Street banks. Tyne and Wear, like several other
councils, builds nursery factories and gives some
grants and loans to promote new firms. Most such
schemes are on a small scale and their long-term
success has yet to be established. Whatever their
nature and success, however, each of these schemes
will provide valuable experience in a field which is
likely to assume considerably increased importance in
coming years.


## 12.5 NATIONAL IMPLICATIONS

The focus of this study has been at the regional and
sub-regional scales rather than at the national, but
an investigation of growth in a prosperous region
inevitably raises issues which are relevant to the
nation as a whole. The principal issues in this
category are the question of the rate of establishment
of new firms and the rate of industrial turnover as a
whole. The evidence which is available strongly
suggests that the turnover of companies in Britain is
low by international standards. A small number of new
firms are opened and a relatively low number are
closed. The birth-rate, survival and vitality of new
firms all affect the importance of the small firms
sector. A recent study by Bannock (1976) suggests
that small business is much less important in Britain
than in Germany, and he and others have suggested that
this is true of many other industrial nations. Indeed,
it is said that the only country in which small firms
are actually increasing their overall share of
business is Japan!

There appears to be something of a loose correlation between industrial success and the importance of small firms. It is quite possible that the connection may be entirely spurious, but there are sound reasons for thinking this may not be so. New firms have a number of beneficial effects in economic growth. They may bring new products and processes, although a number of studies suggest that this is rare. Certainly, the number of new firms based on what can be called new-technology was found to be minute by Little (1977) for both Britain and Germany. In the USA, however, several important companies in electronics and other new technology fields have been started since 1945 from small beginnings, and this function of new firms appears to be more important in that country. The more important functions are probably in the gradual transference from slow growing to rapidly growing industries. Although birth-rates of new firms reflect ease of entry more than growth, it is easier for new firms to survive in growing industries, and in countries with a high turnover of firms, there will be more new firms to exploit expanding demand. Much expansion occurs in markets where no innovation is required, and in the economic competition between nations the share of these is important as well as share of markets for new products. If firms in one country can penetrate such markets in others, then this will expand the economy of the former relative to the latter. If this can be done in new fields like electronic calculators, then all well and good, but in the British market, American and German firms compete in selling a wide range of more prosaic products. If new firms in some countries exploit the opportunity to capture expanding markets of whatever sort, then the rate at which such firms are formed becomes a factor of importance in economic growth.

In the longer term, many new firms which start from tiny beginnings grow to become substantial and important companies in the national economy. The list of major East Midlands companies begun in the inter-war period is an impressive one. There are several

308

very large national ones with origins in the same
period, and the crop of early postwar companies is by
now beginning to make its presence felt. The position
is somewhat disguised at the national level, however,
because many growing young companies are acquired by
larger and older-established concerns. They still
make a considerable impact on total growth but much
of this is hidden in the increasing ownership of
industry by the very largest companies. The replacement. of existing companies with new ones, large or
small, has the important influence of bringing changes
in management. A rapid turnover of companies should
have the effect of weeding out inefficient or unsuccessful managements at a more rapid rate than would
otherwise occur. If a high birth-rate of new firms
puts a general pressure on resources of labour and
capital, then this may increase the number of
closures, in a range of industries outside those in
which the new firms are formed. As long as the slack
created by closures is rapidly taken up, then the
vigorous process of turnover and replacement will
continue.

If it is true that Britain has a low birth-rate of
new firms, to what is this due? An interesting comment on this question is provided by noting the
entrepreneurial importance of individuals who are
outside what might be called the secure and accepted
'establishment'. The importance of the Jewish and
Quaker communities in setting up businesses in Britain
is well known. Foreign entrepreneurs are also prominent in company histories, but the main group of
individuals in this category are the manual workers
from industry. Extrapolating from the experience of
the East Midlands, there are probably 3,000 - 4,000
new manufacturing firms established in Britain every
year, mostly by foremen and others who previously
worked in manufacturing industry. The occupational
structure in Britain is such that manual workers
rarely reach the professional or managerial levels and
some of those with ambition use the opportunity to
start a new firm as an opportunity to break out of the

barriers which prevent people lacking the necessary education or social background from joining the middle-class establishment.

It seems very likely that the attitudes of the establishment professions and occupations is markedly less well disposed to business and commerce in Britain than in other western industrial nations. Granwick (1962) notes that entrepreneurship holds a high status in Germany, to the extent that persons in upper management start their own small firms in addition to their main employment as a means of enhancing their prestige. In France, the most prestigious institutions in higher education are oriented strongly towards engineering and business. The less specialised universities on the British model are accorded lower prestige. The contrast between Britain and the USA in attitudes to business is probably greater than between Britain and its continental neighbours. The importance of these differences is that in Britain entrepreneurial activity may be left to non-establishment groups to a greater extent than elsewhere. The supply of individuals willing to open new firms is consequently diminished, and with it a degree of industrial diversity and vitality.

The reasons for the low prestige accorded to business in Britain have been widely discussed, although not usually in the particular context of starting new firms. The roots of the problem (assuming that economic uncompetitiveness is a problem) probably lie in the mid and late nineteenth century when the business community might have expected to replace the established upper classes as the dominant force in forging public opinion and attitudes. The distractions of glory, wealth and power derived from a period of unprecedented imperial extension seem to have prevented this. An unfortunate coincidence in timing was that the modern mass education system was born in the same period, with an emphasis in curricula on arts subjects and particularly those of colonial rather than commercial relevance including geography and history.

   The great inertia which is built into cultural
attitudes and systems of education makes it impossible
to suggest any easy measures that might change
matters.  Alterations to the education system would
have to be extremely radical with a massive shift in
resources from traditional subjects and those intended
to enhance leisure rather than production to those of
commercial importance.  Such a move would be painful
and would be resisted from many quarters.  Alterations
in the relative structure of pay and rewards towards
industry would similarly be difficult, and yet only
measures of this sort are likely to change the
prevailing attitude.  Whether the effort is worthwhile
depends on how effective the measures are and the
value placed on the end result.  However, even a small
increase in Britain's economic growth record since the
war from 3 to 4 per cent would have made the country
a third as rich again in real terms, and would have
allowed greatly increased spending on health,
education and other public services.

# Appendix 1

The major source of data in this study has been the
set of records covering every establishment within the
East Midlands.  This was obtained originally from the
registers of the Factory Inspectorate (now the Health
and Safety Executive), but has been considerably
augmented by an extensive process of checking in
street, trade and business directories and of cross-
checking through different time periods.

CONSTRUCTION OF THE DATA SET

The original records included details of name, address,
industry code and numbers employed by both operatives
and office staff (operatives only, before 1965).
Factories are inspected a statutory minimum of once in
four years, and the employment figures obtained in any
one cross-section are thus staggered across a four
year period.  They are not precise records of numbers
employed, and are only useful for gauging changes over
fairly lengthy periods of time.  Records were collected in 1970 for over 7,000 establishments in the East
Midlands.  For Leicestershire alone, previous cross-
sections were available for periods centred on 1947
and 1955, and there was a continuous record of change
between 1947 and 1955.

The establishments in Leicestershire were classified
as 'new', 'permanent' or 'closures' by noting the
dates of first and last appearance in the records.
New establishments were defined as those appearing
after 1947 and permanent establishments as those in
production throughout the period.  From questionnaire
survey evidence and the work of Rake (1972) it has
been possible to ascertain that only a handful of
openings or closures can have been misclassified
cases of transfers to or from other regions.  The

312

historical records also enabled local moves to be
detected. There were large numbers of these but the
great majority were within or around Leicester itself.
Establishments were further classified as independent
firms or subsidiaries, and as single plant firms,
parent plants or branch plants. This was done by
cross-checking names with the data set, and by
exhaustive checks through such directories as Kelly's
National Directory of Manufacturers, Who Owns Whom,
Kompass and Rylands.


CHECKING PROCEDURES

It has not been possible to rigorously assess the
completeness of the data set, since the Factory
Inspectorate records were the most comprehensive
available source. Although a few omissions were
detected, the degree of completeness appeared to be
satisfactory. One method of checking involved a
comparison between employment totals obtained from
the records and those from Department of Employment
E.R. II returns. The employment from the establishment records included 92 per cent of that from the
latter source and the proportion was similar in each
separate employment exchange area. The difference
must have partly reflected the lack of precision and
spread of timing of the establishment records, but
part of the difference may also have reflected the
Factory Inspectorate's lack of concern with those
employed off factory premises. These would include
salesmen, installation engineers, drivers, some
warehousemen, and perhaps a number of tempory workers
and outworkers.

The classification of establishments into categories
such as 'new' or 'permanent' was potentially fallible
due to delays in recording openings or closures, and
changes of name. The former possibility was checked
using a 10 per cent sample (questionnaire survey),
and the misclasifications were found to be both
infrequent and of marginal importance. A further

complete check for Leicester using annual street
directories reached the same conclusion. The detected
errors were corrected and it is doubtful whether any
significant numbers of misclassification remain.
Checks for name changes were undertaken by tracing
establishments through successive street directories,
to find those which were preceded by another firm in
the same trade. Pairs of this sort were traced
further to see whether both had been simultaneously in
existence at different addresses. This procedure
identified 4 per cent of establishments as having
potentially changed name. About thirty cases of name
changes were positively identified from a range of
sources, others were included as separate openings and
closures. Changes of name coincidental with a change
of address and/or product were not checked. However,
the distinction between major organisational changes,
and closures followed by a new opening is a fine one.

The industry coding of establishments is not fully
accurate and other researchers have found that up to
one in five cases are misclassified. A preliminary
check among the East Midlands establishments showed
that most misclassifications involved small establishments and similar minimum list headings industries.
Among many small jobbing engineering firms there is
probably a genuine difficulty in assigning a consistent classification. No general correcting procedure
was adopted. An important influence on this decision
was the fact that the codes (and miscodes) came
originally from the Department of Employment, and it
was felt important to maintain comparability between
the two sources of data even if this involved a degree
of inaccuracy.

# Appendix 2

At an early stage in the research project it was
decided that a large-scale sample survey of establishments was necessary to obtain information on those
aspects of industrial activity which could not be
gathered from published sources or from the establishment records.  The multi-purpose aims meant that a
large number of responses were necessary, and
consequently a postal questionnaire approach was
adopted, to be backed up by interviews on topics of
critical importance.  The questionnaire form and a
full description of the sampling methods are described
in appendix II of Gudgin (1974), and only a summary is
given below.

The questionnaire form included twenty-two questions
on two sides of a single sheet of paper.  After a
trial survey of fifty establishments in Leicestershire, forms were sent to 1,200 establishments in the
East Midlands, and a reminder was sent to non-
respondents a fortnight later.  The response rate of
fully usable replies was 63 per cent with the highest
response rates from rural areas, and the lowest from
the largest city.

The sample of establishments was selected on a
random basis using a three-way stratification by size,
industry and county.  The sampling fractions were
increased for rural counties, since these contained
relatively low total numbers of establishments.  It
was anticipated that the variability in responses to
many questions would increase with the size of
establishment, as would the importance of the
responses.  Hence, sampling fractions were increased
through five size strata from 7 per cent to 75 per
cent.  This emphasis was further accentuated by the
response rates which increased from 56 per cent among
the smallest establishments up to 75 per cent from

those employing 300 or more. Finally, the sample was stratified by eight industry groups using a uniform sampling fraction. The response rates varied from a low of 52 per cent for wood products up to 84 per cent for chemicals. The size structure of the industries probably accounts for much of the variation.

All names were checked in telephone directories before sending out the forms, but 2.5 per cent were returned presumed closed. This figure is a little below the closure rate of 4 per cent p.a. observed from establishment records in Leicestershire. The wide range of information required from a brief and simple questionnaire meant that several months had to be spent in attempting to reduce ambiguity in questions, and to achieve an efficient layout with concise wording. In the event most of the questions proved adequate for the required purposes, although not all ambiguity was avoided principally through a lack of a full understanding at the time of the intricacies of organisation within large companies. In the most important cases follow-up interviews showed that simple questions had elicited the intended responses.

# Appendix 3

| Minimum list heading | Industry |
|---|---|
| III | Food, drink and tobacco |
| 211 | Grain milling |
| 212 | Bread, cakes etc. |
| 213 | Biscuits |
| 214 | Bacon, meat and fish products |
| 215 | Milk products |
| 216 | Sugar |
| 217 | Cocoa, chocolate, sweets |
| 218 | Fruit and vegetable products |
| 219 | Animal foods |
| 229 | Other food industries |
| 231 | Brewing and malting |
| 239 | Other drink industries |
| 240 | Tobacco |
| IV | Chemicals and allied industries |
| 261 | Coke ovens |
| 262 | Mineral oil refining |
| 263 | Lubricating oils, greases |
| 271 | Chemicals and dyes |
| 272 | Pharmaceuticals |
| 273 | Explosive fireworks |
| 274 | Paint and ink |
| 275 | Vegetable and animal oils, fats, soap and detergents |
| 276 | Synthetic resins and plastics materials |
| 277 | Polishes, adhesives |
| V | Metal manufacture |
| 311 | Iron and steel (general) |
| 312 | Steel tubes |
| 313 | Iron castings etc. |
| 321 | Light metals |
| 322 | Copper, base metals |

| | |
|---|---|
| VI | Engineering and electrical goods |
| 331 | Agricultural machinery |
| 332 | Metal-working machine tools |
| 333 | Engineers' tools and gauges |
| 334 | Industrial engines |
| 335 | Textile machinery |
| 336 | Contractors' plant |
| 337 | Mechanical handling |
| 338 | Office machinery |
| 339 | Other machinery |
| 341 | Industrial plant |
| 342 | Ordnance and small arms |
| 349 | Other mechanical engineering |
| 351 | Scientific, surgical and photographic instruments etc. |
| 352 | Watches and clocks |
| 361 | Electrical machinery |
| 362 | Insulated wires and cables |
| 363 | Telephone apparatus |
| 364 | Electronic apparatus |
| 365 | Domestic electric appliances |
| 369 | Other electrical goods |
| VII | Shipbuilding and marine engineering |
| 370.1 | Shipbuilding |
| 370.2 | Marine engineering |
| VIII | Vehicles |
| 381 | Motor vehicle manufacturing |
| 382 | Motor and pedal cycles |
| 383 | Aircraft manufacturing |
| 384 | Locomotives |
| 385 | Railway carriages and wagons |
| 389 | Perambulators, hand-trucks |
| IX | Metal goods not elsewhere specified |
| 391 | Tools and implements |
| 392 | Cutlery |
| 393 | Bolts, nuts, screws etc. |
| 394 | Wire and wire manufacturers |
| 395 | Cans and metal boxes |
| 396 | Jewellery and precious metals |
| 399 | Other metal industries |

| X | Textiles |
|---|---|
| 411 | Man-made fibres (production) |
| 412 | Spinning of cotton, flax and man-made fibres |
| 413 | Weaving of cotton, linen and man-made fibres |
| 414 | Woollen and worsted |
| 415 | Jute |
| 416 | Rope, twine and net |
| 417 | Hosiery, knitted goods |
| 418 | Lace |
| 419 | Carpets |
| 421 | Narrow fabrics |
| 422 | Made-up textiles |
| 423 | Textile finishing |
| 429 | Other textile industries |
| XI | Leather, leather goods and fur |
| 431 | Leather (tanning and dressing) |
| 432 | Leather goods |
| 433 | Fur |
| XII | Clothing and footwear |
| 441 | Weatherproof outerwear |
| 442 | Men's tailored outerwear |
| 443 | Women's tailored outerwear |
| 444 | Overalls, shirts, underwear |
| 445 | Dresses, lingerie, infants' wear, etc. |
| 446 | Hats, caps and millinery |
| 449 | Other dress industries |
| 450 | Footwear |
| XIII | Bricks, pottery, glass, cement, etc. |
| 461 | Bricks, etc. |
| 462 | Pottery |
| 463 | Glass |
| 464 | Cement |
| 469 | Abrasives etc. |
| XIV | Timber, furniture, etc. |
| 471 | Timber |
| 472 | Furniture and upholstery |
| 473 | Bedding, etc. |
| 474 | Shop and office fitting |
| 475 | Wooden containers |

# Appendix 4

It was possible to construct employment accounts for Leicestershire using the establishment records, but for the remainder of the region this source was not available and a number of estimation procedures were used. These procedures were applied to the whole region in order to be able to use the Leicestershire estimates as a check on the reliability of the methods.

Three sources of data were available for the whole region; these were Factory Inspectorate records for 1967 only, Department of Employment ER II returns giving employment disaggregated by industries MLH for 1948 and 1967 and finally figures from the Department of Industry on industrial movement. The latter were available for four sub-regions and hence these provided the finest areal sub-division for which it was possible to construct a set of accounts. The three primary sources were supplemented by the results of the questionnaire survey (described as appendix II) which received responses from over 700 establishments, or approximately 10 per cent of all establishments in the region, and was carried out in 1970.

Total employment change for each of the four sub-regions was obtained from the Department of Employment figures. The proportions of 'new' and 'permanent' establishments were obtained from the questionnaire estimates, and these proportions were then applied to the 1967 population of establishments. The new establishments were further subdivided from question-naire estimates into new firms, new branches of local firms (i.e. those with the parent company in the same sub-region), and new branch plants of companies based in other areas. Branch plants could in some cases have been set up as independent firms and subsequently acquired. The questionnaire form asked respondents whether their establishment had been set up by its

present owners or acquired. Three-quarters of branch
plants had been set up by their present owners. Some
of the remainder will have been set up as branches by
other firms, but a small number may have been originally established as independent firms and if so the
birth-rate of new firms may have been underestimated,
although the effect can only be slight. Some of the
new firms were subsidiary companies, but almost 90 per
cent of these were revealed to have been acquired by
their present owners. The number of branches of non-
local companies was estimated from the questionnaire,
but the estimate could be compared with the Department
of Industry figures. The latter related to the period
1945-65 with employment recorded for 1966. The
Department of Industry figures include transfers as
well as branch plants, and have been used in some
cases to give a complete record of industrial movement.

The employment in new firms was estimated by
calculating the average size of new firms in five
size-bands, and multiplying these average sizes by the
estimated number of new firms in each size-band for
each sub-region. The bands were those used in
stratifying the questionnaire survey sample i.e. 1-8
employees, 9-29 employees, 30-99 employees, 100-299
employees and 300+ employees. A similar procedure was
used for estimating employment in branch plants,
except that average sizes in size-bands were calculated individually for each county. The relatively
smaller numbers involved meant that estimates were
less precise than for new firms. The employment in
permanent establishments was initially estimated as
above through multiplying average sizes by estimated
numbers of permanent plants.

This procedure is potentially inaccurate if a few
very large establishments happen to be missing from
the sample responses. In two counties it seems
probable (as outlined below) that this procedure led
to significant underestimates of employment in
permanent establishments. This view was formed by
summing the employment estimates for all four

322

components and comparing with Department of Employment
statistics. Any discrepancy between the two figures
was judged to have derived from the omission of large
permanent establishments, and the difference was thus
added to the employment of the permanent establishment
component.

There was no direct information on the employment in
establishments which had been in production in 1948
but had closed by 1967. In order to gain some notion
of how large this employment might have been, a very
approximate estimating procedure was used. It was
assumed that permanent firms based on each sub-region
grew in employment terms by identical amounts (omitting acquisitions or disposals). The growth of firms
was obtained by summing three quantities. The first
was the weighted growth of employment in permanent
establishments within the East Midlands as obtained
from the questionnaire survey (331 applicable
responses). The second was the estimated employment
in branch plants set up by East Midlands firms within
the region. Again this was estimated from the
questionnaire survey as described above. Finally, the
employment in branch plants set up outside the region
by East Midlands firms was taken as that given in the
Department of Industry figures for employment in 1966
within moves 1945-65. The sum of these three
quantities was then divided by a similarly constructed
estimate of employment in permanent firms in 1967,
omitting their subsidiaries either located outside the
region or established since 1948. This procedure
provides only an approximate guide to the growth in
permanent firms (omitting growth by acquisition).
Aside from technical questions of sample estimation,
a number of complications are present. Firstly, some
of the permanent plants in the East Midlands are
branches of companies located outside the region, but
have been included anyway. Secondly, some growth of
companies may have occurred in their branch plants
which were established outside the region before 1945.
Also, some pre-1948 branch plants could have closed in
the period under review here. Finally, a small

number of establishments in the Department of Employment figures were transfers and not branch plants, but it is unlikely that the employment involved was large.

These various omissions mean that only general magnitudes are indicated, although the importance of the omissions may not vary much between counties. The estimate is used to obtain a measure of aggregate employment growth 1948-67 in permanent establishments in each county. This is done by using the assumption that the growth-rate for companies is uniform and subtracting the variable (but known) proportion of growth which has been channelled into branch plant formation for each county. This allows an estimate of employment growth 1948-67 in permanent establishments to be constructed for each sub-region, and by working backwards from 1967 also allows an estimate to be made of employment in 1948 in permanent establishments. Subtracting this from the 1948 employment recorded by the Department of Employment gives the 1948 employment of plants which subsequently closed. It must be emphasised that this procedure provides only a rough guide. Despite its many deficiencies, however, it should still be capable of detecting any wide differences between sub-regions.

CHECKS ON THE RELIABILITY OF ESTIMATES

In the case of Leicestershire it was possible to compare estimates constructed by the procedures described above with figures compiled directly from establishment records. The later figures refer to a period centred on 1967, and for the purposes of assessing reliability of questionnaire employment estimates for 1970 they have been deflated by 1.5 per cent to take account of the downturn in the business cycle between 1967 and 1970. The employment from establishment records is also multiplied by 100/92 to take account of the difference (outlined in appendix I) between these records and the Department of

Employment figures.

With these modifications the two sets of employment estimates (referring to 1970) were as follows.

|  | Establishment records | Questionnaire-based procedure |
|---|---|---|
| Permanent establishments | 137,300 | 132,300 |
| New firms | 21,300 | 23,400 |
| New local branches of Leicestershire firms | 9,900 | 6,000 |
| Industrial movement into Leicestershire | 9,400 | 10,700 |

In addition, the figure for the last category obtained from the Department of Industry records is 11,000. The estimates are generally satisfactory for the purposes of this study, although the deficiencies of a 10 per cent sample become most evident when small numbers are involved, as seen above with the local branches of Leicestershire firms. The estimate of employment in closures was 38,000 and this can be compared with a figure of 32,500 operatives obtained from the establishment records. The ratio of operatives to non-operatives was 17.3 for UK manufacturing industry in 1948 and multiplying 32,500 by this factor gives a figure of 38,200. The closeness of the two figures must owe much to coincidence, but it nevertheless gives confidence that the procedures used are not too misleading.

For all other counties it is possible to check the accuracy of the estimation procedure in two respects. Firstly, the estimated total employment in each sub-region can be compared with Department of Employment figures. Secondly, the employment in establishments moving into each county (branches and transfers) can be compared with the Department of Industry figures. The comparison is described below.

| | Estimate | Dept of Employment | Dept of Industry |
|---|---|---|---|
| Nottinghamshire and Derbyshire (excluding Chesterfield and East Notts) Total 1967 | 203,500 | 267,700 | |
| Industrial in-movement | 12,500 | | 11,000 |
| Northamptonshire (excluding steelworks) | | | |
| Total employment 1967 | 68,600 | 77,700 | |
| Industrial in-movement | 6,900 | | 11,000 |
| Lincolnshire (including East Nottinghamshire | | | |
| Total employment 1967 | 52,600 | 51,900 | |
| Industrial in-movement | 6,300 | | 3,000 |

The figures reveal considerable discrepancies especially for total employment. The importance of a few very large employers in Nottinghamshire/Derbyshire, some of which were not included in the sample, has led to a serious underestimate. The high probability that the omissions were largely 'permanent' establishments resulted in a decision to add the shortfall in each sub-region to the permanent component. The errors in estimating employment within in-moving establishments stems from a variety of causes. Firstly, there is the possibility of sampling error with relatively small numbers. Secondly, some branches of non-local firms in 1970 had probably been originally set up by local firms and only subsequently acquired by their present owners. This has contributed to the overestimates in Nottinghamshire/Derbyshire and in Lincolnshire, since in both cases the removal of 'branches bought (rather than set up) by their current owners' reduces the estimate towards the official figure. In Northamptonshire a relatively high proportion of industrial movement consisted of transfers (from the South East) rather than branches. The smaller sampling fractions and lower response rates among small companies means that employment in transfers, many of which are small, is inaccurately measured.

In general, two problems are present in the estimates. One is in the estimation of employment in large establishments where a few omissions in a sample may cause serious underestimates. The correction procedure outlined above, probably does much to make allowance for such omissions. The second problem is in reliably estimating numbers of very small establishments, and this affects estimation of numbers of new firms. Even so the estimated proportion of new firms in Leicestershire, for instance, was 40 per cent with a standard error of only 4 per cent. Moreover, the employment in new firms is probably estimated to a reasonably high degree of accuracy.

Of all the estimates most confidence can be placed in those of new firms. However, official sources can be used to estimate employment within in-moving establishments. This leaves three components less accurately measured i.e. employment in permanent establishments, new branches of local firms and closures. In the first two cases, both components are part of the growth of permanent firms and failure to make a precise distinction is less important than in other cases.

# Bibliography

Aaronovitch, S. and Sawyer, M.C., Mergers, Growth and Concentration, Oxford Economic Papers, March 1975

Aitchison, J. and Brown, J.A.C., The Lognormal Distribution, with Special Reference to its Use in Economics, Cambridge University Dept of Applied Economics, Monograph no. 5., 1963

Atkins, D.H.W., 'Employment change in branch and parent manufacturing plants in the United Kingdom 1966-71', Trade and Industry, 30 August 1973

Bannock, G., Smaller Business in Britain and Germany. Wilton House, 1976

Bayliss, B.T. and Edwards, S.L., Industrial Demand for Transport, HMSO, 1970

Beesley, M., 'The birth and death of industrial establishments: the experience of the west Midlands conurbation', Journal of Industrial Economics, 4, 1965

Blalock, H.M., Social Statistics, McGraw-Hill, 1960

Bolton, J., Committee of Inquiry on Small Firms, HMSO, 1972

Boneau, C.A., 'The effects of violations of assumptions underlying the "t" test', Psychological Bulletin, 57, 1960

Box, G.E.P., 'Some theorems on quadratic forms applied in the study of analysis of variance problems. I. Effect of inequality of variance in the one-way classification', Annals of Mathematics Statistics, 25, 1954

Branton, N., Economic Organisation of Modern Britain, English Universities Press, 1966

Brough, R., 'Business Failure in England and Wales'. Business Ratios, 2, 1967

Brown, A.J., 'Surveys of applied economics I', Economic Journal, 79, 1969

Brown, A.J., The Framework of Regional Economics in the United Kingdom, National Institute of Economic and Social Research, Social and Economic Studies, CUP 1972

Cameron, G.C., Intra-Urban Location and the New Plant, University of Glasgow Urban and Regional Discussion Papers no. 5, 1972

Cameron, G.C. and Clark, B.D., Industrial Movement and the Regional Problem, University of Glasgow, Social and Economic Studies Occasional Papers no. 5, Oliver and Boyd, 1966

CBI, Problems and Small Firms, Evidence to the Bolton Committee of Inquiry on Small Firms, HMSO, 1970

Census of Production, Department of Trade and Industry, 1968

Census of Production, Summary Tables Business Monitor PA 1002, Dept of Industry, 1971

Child, J., Managerial and Organisational Factors Associated with Company Performance, University of Aston Management Centre Working Paper no. 4, 1973

Chisholm, M., Geography and Economics, Bell 1966

Chisholm, M., 'Freight transport costs, industrial location and regional development' in M. Chisholm and G. Manners (eds), Spatial Policy Problems of the British Economy, CUP, 1971

Churchill, B.C., 'Survival patterns of the postwar business population', Survey of Current Business, December, 1952

Churchill, B.C., 'Age and life expectancy of business firms'. Survey of Current Business, December, 1955

Churchill, B.C., 'Rise in the business population', Survey of Current Business, May, 1959

Cleland, S., The Influence of Plant Size on Industrial Relations, Research Report Series no. 89, Princeton University, 1955

Coates, B.E. and Rawstron, E.M., Regional Variation in Britain, Batsford, 1971

Collins, L., Industrial Migration in Ontario, Statistics Canada, Ottawa, 1972

Collins, N.R. and Preston, L.E., Concentration and Price - Cost Margins, University of California Press, 1961

Cook, W.R., 'Transport decisions of Black Country firms' Journal of Transport Economics and Policy', I (3)

Crum, R. and Gudgin, G., Non-Production Activities in UK Manufacturing Industry, Report to Dept of Industry and the EEC Commission, 1976

Dahmen, E., Entrepreneurial Activity and the Development of Swedish Industry, Irwin, 1970

Davies, J.R. and Kelly, M., Small Firms in the Manufacturing Sector, Research Report no. 3, Committee of Inquiry on Small Firms, HMSO, 1972

Dept of Employment and Productivity Gazette, 'Effect of regional employment structures on average earnings', 1969

Downie, J., The Competitive Process, Blackwell, 1958

Dunlop Co., Dunlop at Work 1974, published by the company

Economic Advisory Group, Financial Facilities for Small Firms, Research Report no. 4 to the Report of the Committee od Inquiry on Small Firms, HMSO, 1972

Edwards, R.S. and Townsend, H., Studies in Business Organisation, MacMillan, 1964

Edwards, S.L., 'Regional variation in freight costs', Journal of Transport Economics and Policy, 9(2) 1975

Expenditure Committee, Regional Development Incentives, Minutes of Evidence, HMSO, 1973

Fisher, G., 'Further calculations on regional differences in profitability and growth', Scottish Journal of Political Economy, 9, 1962

Gibrat, R., 'On economic inequalities', International Economic Papers no. 7, 1957

Granick, D., The European Executive, Doubleday, 1962

Granick, D., 'Use of Corporate and Divisional Head-quarters', MSU Business Topics, 22(4), Michigan State University Graduate Business School, 1974

Gudgin, G., 'Industrial Location Processes, The East Midlands in the postwar period', unpublished PhD thesis, University of Leicester, 1974

Hart, P.E. and MacBean, A., 'Regional differences in productivity, profitability and growth', Scottish Journal of Political Economy, 8, 1961

Hart, P.E. and Mellors, J., 'Managerial youth and company growth: a correlation', Managerial Decision, Spring, 1970

Holl, P., 'The effect of control type on the performance of the firm in the UK', Journal of Industrial Economics, 23, 1975

Howard, R.S., The Movement of Manufacturing Industry in the United Kingdom 1945-65, HMSO, 1968

Hymer, S. and Pashigian, B.P., 'Firm size and rate of growth', Journal of Political Economy, 70 (6), 1962

Ijiri, Y. and Simon, H.A., 'Business firm growth and size', American Economic Review, 54, 1964

Ingham, K., 'Foreign ownership and the regional problem', Oxford Economic Papers, 28 (1), 1976

ILAG, Expenditure Committee (Trade and Industry Sub-Committee) Minutes of Evidence. Inquiry in Location Attitudes Group. HMSO for the Dept of Trade and Industry, 1973

Jones, R. and Marriot, O., Anatomy of a Merger, Cape, 1970

Kalecki, M., 'On the Gibrat distribution', Econometrica, 13, 1945

Kaplan, A.D.H., Small Business: Its Place and Problems, McGraw-Hill, 1948

Kapteyn, J.C., Skew Frequency Curves in Biology and Statistics, Astronomical Laboratory, Groningen, Nordhoff, 1903

Keeble, D.E., Industrial Location and Planning in the UK, Methuen, 1976

Kinnard, W.N. and Malinowski, Z., The Turnover and Mortality of Manufacturing Firms in the Hartford Connecticut Economic Area, 1953-58, Small Business Administration, Washington DC, 1960

Knowles, K.C. and Hill, T.P., 'The structure of engineers earnings', Bulletin of the Oxford Institute of Statistics, vol. 16, 1954

Knowles, K.C. and Hill, T.P., 'The variability of engineers earnings', Bulletin of the Oxford Institute of Statistics, vol. 18, 1956

Knowles, K.C. and Verry, M., 'Earnings in the boot and shoe industry', Bulletin of the Oxford Institute of Statistics, vol. 16, 1954

Law, D,. 'Industrial movement and locational advantage', Manchester School of Economic and Social Studies, 32, 1964

Lee, N. and Jones, R.M., 'Industrial and market structure' in Devine et al.(ed), An Introduction to Industrial Economics? Allen and Unwin, 1974

Lepeltier, C., 'A simplified statistical treatment of geochemical data by graphical representation', Economic Geology, 64, 1969

Leser, C.E.V., 'Output per head in different parts of the United Kingdom', Journal of the Royal Statistical Society, Series A, vol. 113, 1950

Little, A.D., Ltd, New Technology-Based Firms in the UK and the Federal Republic of West Germany, Anglo-German Foundation, 1977

Losch, A., The Economics of Location, Yale University Press, 1954

Luttrell, W.F., Factory Location and Industrial Movement, vol 1, National Institute of Economic and Social Research, CUP, 1962

Lydall, H.F., 'The growth of manufacturing firms', Bulletin of the Oxford Institute of Statistics, 21 1959

Manners, G., 'The British energy market' in M. Chisholm and G. Manners (eds), Spatial Problems of the British Economy, CUP, 1971

Mansfield, E., 'Entry, innovation and the growth of firms', American Economic Review, 52, 1962

Marcus, M., 'Firms' exit rates and their determinants', Journal of Industrial Economics, 16, 1967

Marris, R., The Economic Theory of Managerial Capitalism, MacMillan, 1964

Merrett Cyriax Assocs, Dynamics of Small Firms, Research Report no. 12, Committee of Inquiry on Small Firms, HMSO, 1972

Ministry of Labour Gazette, 'Labour costs in Britain in 1964', December 1966

Moore, B. and Rhodes, J., 'Evaluating the effects of British regional economic policy', Economic Journal, 1973

Moore, B. and Rhodes, J., 'Regional policy and the Scottish economy', Scottish Journal of Political Economy, 21 (3), 1974

Moore, B. and Rhodes, J., Regional Policy and the Economy of Wales, Welsh Office, 1975

Moore, B. and Rhodes, J., 'A quantitive analysis of the effects of REP and other policy instruments' in A. Whiting (ed), The Economics of Industrial Subsidies, HMSO, 1976

Muir, A., The History of Baker Perkins, Heffer, 1968

National Building Agency, Land Costs and Housing Development, London, 1968

National Economic Dev. Committee for Mechanical Engineering, Company Financial Results 1966/67 - 1970/71, HMSO, 1972

NEDO, A Study of Profitability in the Hosiery and Knitwear Industry, HMSO, 1971

New Earnings Survey, Dept of Employment, HMSO, 1972

Nicholson, R.J., 'The regional location of industry: an empirical study based on the regional tables of the 1948 Census of Production', Economic Journal, 66, 1956

Oxenfeldt, A.R., New Firms and Free Enterprise, American Council of Public Affairs, Washington DC, 1943

Penrose, E., The Theory of the Growth of the Firm, Blackwell, 1959

PEP, The Location of Industry, London, 1939

Preston, L., 'Giant Firms, Large Mergers and Concentration', Industrial Organisation Review, 1 (1), 1973

Radice, H.K., 'Control Type, Profitability and Growth in Large Firms', Economic Journal, 81, 1971

Rake, D., 'The Economic Geography of the Multi-Locational Industrial Firm with Special Reference to the East Midlands', PhD Thesis, University of Nottingham, 1972

Rayner, A.C. and Little, I.M.D., Higgledy Piggledy Growth Again, OUP, 1966

Revans, R.W., 'Industrial morale and size of unit', Political Quarterly, 27 (3), 1956

Singer, H.W. and Leser, C., 'Industrial productivity in England and Scotland', Journal of the Royal Statistical Society, Series A, vol. III, 1948

Singh, A. and Whittington, G., 'Growth, Profitability and Valuation: A Study of UK Quoted Companies', OUP, 1968

Smith, D.M., Industrial Location, Wiley, 1971

Smith, N.R., The Entrepreneur and his Firm, Bureau of Business and Economic Research, University of Michigan, 1967

Smyth, R.L., 'A note on regional differences in productivity, profitability and growth', Scottish Journal of Political Economy, 8, 1961

Steele, G.R., 'The migration of industrial firms from Sheffield in the postwar period', East Midlands Geographer, December, 1972

Stone, P.A., Urban Development in Britain: Standard Costs and Resources 1964-2004. Vol. 1 Population Trends and Housing, National Institute of Economic and Social Research, CUP, 1968

Strategic Plan for South-East, Volume One, HMSO, 1976

Tamari, M., A Postal Questionnaire Survey of Small Firms. Bolton Report on Small Firms, Research Report no. 16, HMSO, 1968

Taylor, M.J., 'Location decisions of small firms', Area, 2, 1970

Taylor, M.J. and Wood, P.A., 'Industrial linkage and local agglomeration in the West Midlands metal industries', Transactions of the Institute of British Geographers, 59, 1973

Taylor, P., 'Distance transformation and distance decay functions', Geographical Analysis, 3, 1971

Temporary National Economic Commission, Problems of Small Business, Monograph no. 17 Washington DC, 1941

Tornqvist, G., Transport Costs as a Location Factor for Manufacturing Industry, Lund, 1964

Watts, D., 'The location of the sugar beet industry in England and Wales 1912-36', Transactions of the Institute of British Geographers, 53, 1971

Wedervang, F., Development of a Population of Firms, Universitetsforlag, Oslo, 1965

West Central Scotland Plan Supplementary Report No. 1, Glasgow, 1974

Woodruff, A.M. and Alexander, T.O., Success and Failure in Small Manufacturing. University of Pittsburg, 1955

# Place name index

# Subject index

English Electric Co. 84, 103, 124

Entrepreneurs: and closures 174; and employment 61; and growth 149; and location 97-101, 105-8, 121-3; and new firms 98-102; attitudes to 203; capital 106; craftsman 97 ff; definition 141; history of 131; home area of 105, 129; inventor 104; local 60, 81, 197; opportunities 97 ff, 108; potential 134, 212, 218, 260; previous experience 100-1, 104-5, 113-17, 211-12, 226; Scottish 290-1; small 63; social class 98-100, 129; typology of founders 97

Entry rate (see birth rate)

Environmental factors 53

European Economic Community 303

Exit rates (see closures)

Expenditure Committee 20

Export of employment 5, 51, 61, 70, 72, 83, 160, 163, 235, 262

Extra Manufacturing Co. 104

Factory Inspectorate 312, 321

Female participation rates 3, 254

Ferranti Ltd. 178

Food industry 25: frozen foods 33; growth 152; processing 72

Footwear industry: branches 255; closures 182, 274;

growth 168; in Leicestershire 217, 223, 269, 299; new firms 97, 101; plastic heels 124; production areas 65, 70, 115

Foremen 212

Foreign films 60, 309

Forvac Ltd. 124

Founder (see entrepreneur)

Fuel and power costs 32

Full employment threshold 72

Furniture industry 107

Gas Turbine Research Station 84

General Electric Co. 30, 103

Geographical scale 4

Gloster Aircraft Co. 102

Golden Wonder Crisps 225

Growth of establishments: and employment 143; and size 155-65, 260; branches 251; definition 55, 160, 248; exported growth 154; following acquisition 284; industry variations 152, 165-9, 263; within East Midlands 247-55; within Leicestershire 255-62

Growth of firms: age of managers 148; and branches 165; and competition 151; and industry 151-3; and profitability 146; and size 149-51, 163; company organisation 148; influence of founder 149; internally

340

generated 151, 163;
theory 143-6;
variability 165;
variation within UK
242-4
G.T.C. Engineering Co.
126-7

Hawker Siddeley Ltd. 103,
127, 225
Herbert, Alfred Ltd. 178
Herbert-Ingersoll Ltd.
124
Hosiery industry 34-8,
217, 223, 227, 255, 274
Housing shortages 3

Independent firms 58, 60
Indigenous: change 280,
299; employment 5 ff;
industry 53, 209
Industrial areas 15, 83,
76, 231
Industrial Development
Certificates 61, 72,
247, 258
Industrial establishments
61, 62
Industrial estate 123
Industrial movement: as a
component 48, 51, 54, 91;
build-up of employment 7;
employment 86, 215;
influence on growth 4;
intra-regional 61; national
6; statistics 57, 60;
within East Midlands 249-
51
Industrial premises 106-7,
123, 126-7, 129, 165, 222,
248, 262
Industrial structure: and
closures 193, 276; and

plant size 206-7; and
policy 10; and wages
31; effect on growth
11, 53, 85, 153, 292,
295-6, 299, 301; new
firms 223, 295-6
Inflation 241
Inner city problem 273
Innovation 101-2
In situ change 48
Integration of acquired
firms 284-5
Interest rates 33, 42
Intermediate Areas 270-
3, 280
International Caravans
Ltd. 105
Investment 8, 9, 242,
286-7
Ironfounding industry
24, 38-9
Ironworks 78, 260

Jewish businesses 309
Job satisfaction 107,
213

Knobil H. 131

Labour: availability 25,
41, 47, 61, 129, 251;
catchment areas 274;
competition 83; cost
25-31, 34-5, 41, 235-
6, 244-6; female 254;
markets 213; problems
173, 283; productivity
38, 43, 266; shortage
61, 72, 81, 85, 130,
214, 255, 260, 263;
skilled 31, 107-8, 130,
194; supply 52-3, 87-8,
214, 293

rate of formation (see
birth rate); size 92-7,
214, 217
New establishments  50, 81,
312
Non-Assisted Areas  5, 8-9,
204, 207, 270-3, 280, 300
Northern Region Strategy
Team  304, 306
Nursery factories  307

Oil refining  17, 33
Operatives  74, 264
Overtrading  172, 176
Own design products  117, 119
Ownership  201, 282, 288-9,
304

Parent plants  85, 270-3,
288, 294
Participation rate (see
female participation rate)
Pedigree Petfoods Ltd.  85,
260
Permanent establishments: as
a component 54 ff; data 58;
definition 51, 58, 256, 312,
334; employment 62, 78, 84-5,
215, 256-62; growth 54, 214,
334 ff: importance 58, 62,
65, 74
Planning restrictions  41, 52
Plastics industry  124, 137,
269, 299
Poisson model  218
Ports  15
Power Jets Ltd.  125
Printing industry  97, 131,
227, 269: new firms 97, 227;
Leicestershire 269; local
competition 131
Production costs  11, 13
Productivity  202

Profitability and
closure 172, 174;
and size 151;
distribution of 37,
40; influences on
145-9; hosiery 37;
mechanical engineer-
ing 39; regional
variation 235-42;
stability over time
146-7
Profit: capital ratio
239 ff
Profit: sales ratio
236 ff

Quaker businesses  309
Questionnaire method
108, 121, 315-16

Radio and Allied Ltd.
30
Rationalisation of
production  173-4
Raw materials  15, 20,
72, 108, 294
Refugees  124
Regional Employment
Premium  8, 29, 241,
246, 303
Regional policy  4, 5,
6-8, 20, 29, 62, 70,
273, 280, 288, 303ff
Relocation (see
industrial movement)
Rolls Royce Ltd. 103,
126-7, 176, 232, 302
Rowley, G. Ltd.  128
Rubber industry  137
Rural areas  76, 78-9,
84-86, 116, 219, 222,
228-9, 255, 258, 261-
2, 274, 277

343